*Accountancy
Comes of Age*

Paul J. Miranti, Jr.

Accountancy Comes of Age

The Development of an American Profession, 1886–1940

The University of North Carolina Press

Chapel Hill and London

© 1990 The University of North Carolina Press

Library of Congress Cataloging-in-Publication Data
Miranti, Paul J.
    Accountancy comes of age : the development of an
American profession, 1886–1940 / by Paul J. Miranti, Jr.
        p. cm.
    Includes bibliographical references.
    ISBN 0-8078-1893-3 (alk. paper)
    1. Accounting—United States—History.   I. Title.
HF5616.U5M54   1990
657'.0973'09034—dc20   89-27925
                                                              CIP

The paper in this book meets the guidelines for permanence
and durability of the Committee on Production Guidelines
for Book Longevity of the Council on Library Resources.

Design by April Leidig-Higgins

Manufactured in the United States of America

94 93 92 91 90   5 4 3 2 1

To Louis Galambos,
with gratitude and affection

Contents

Preface   ix

1   The Professions in America: A Historical Model   1

Part 1   The Dawn of Professional Accountancy, 1880–1900   23

2   Prelude to Professionalization, 1886–1892   29

3   The Emergence of the CPA Movement, 1892–1906   48

Part 2   Accountants in an Age of Progress, 1900–1916   69

4   Defining a Professional Image   73

5   In Search of Professional Roles   86

Part 3   Mobilization, Prosperity, and Autonomous
Associationalism, 1917–1929   101

6   The Crisis in Professional Governance   105

7   Technical Challenges and Professionalization   128

Part 4   Economic Crisis and Countervailing
Associationalism, 1929–1940   143

8   A New Structure of Financial Market
Governance, 1929–1934   146

9   A New Structure of Professional
Governance, 1935–1940   160

10   Conclusion   178

Notes   193

Bibliography   223

Index   257

Preface

The focus of research is often conditioned by a scholar's personal experience. This was first impressed upon me when I was a student in Alfred Chandler's recent American history course at Johns Hopkins University during the 1960s. He explained how the vast and complex naval operations in which he participated during World War II crystallized his appreciation of the importance of organization and management in comprehending the past. It was this fortunate epiphany that later inspired his masterpieces in American historiography.

My testimony has also been indirectly influenced by personal experience. Although less dramatic than the navy's actions in the Pacific, the activities of professional groups are certainly as important in understanding contemporary American society. Specifically, I write about public accountants, a profession I have been associated with as a practitioner, associational executive, or educator for nearly two decades.

Initially, I planned to concentrate narrowly on the question of how organization helped to promote function. I believed the key to understanding lay in analyzing the connections that developed between professional associations and important external groups. This partly involved assessing how associations succeeded in persuading prospective clients, particularly in business, of the value of the accountants' trinity of services: auditing financial statements, tax planning and compliance, and developing reporting systems. A second dimension was how these groups not only won special recognition from government of their members' competency but also secured a permanent place in economic regulation.

Although these lines of analysis proved fruitful, they did not completely explain the role that representative organizations played in "professionalizing" accountancy. To understand more fully the complex developments that shaped the strategies and structures formulated by these groups to advance their interests, it was also necessary to prospect in the rich streams of social and political history. This shift was conditioned by the quasi-political nature of these institutions.

They were not as tightly controlled as were bureaucracies in business or government. Instead, they depended upon the voluntary support of members who were often deeply divided by differences in social background and nature of practice. Thus, the success of these groups also hinged on the ability of their leaders to resolve the corollary problems of building consensus and maintaining cohesion within a practitioner community populated by many particularistic elements. This was vital in bolstering the profession's image of authority in the eyes of clients and the general public; it was also vital in building the political power necessary to mediate successfully with government.

Many have helped me in the course of this study. I am especially grateful for the encouragement and patience of my loving wife, Adrienne, throughout this time.

I am also indebted to many at Johns Hopkins University for having instructed me in the historian's craft. Foremost on this list is Louis Galambos, who directed my work when I began this study as a doctoral dissertation. Professor Galambos gave unstintingly of his time and his invaluable advice. He served as a model to me and others of what is best in American scholarship. I will always be thankful for the interest he took in my work. Guidelines for the study of history were also provided by Alfred D. Chandler, Jack P. Greene, David Spring, and the late Frederic C. Lane.

I also appreciate the support that has made my current academic home, Rutgers University, an ideal location for scholarly endeavor. The progress of this study was facilitated by the financial support and release time that my dean, Arthur P. Kraft, and my chairman, Bikki Jaggi, thoughtfully helped to arrange. The Rutgers University Research Council was also generous. Others contributed their ideas about professionalization or provided useful criticisms of portions of the study. For this I wish to thank Andrew Abbott, Peter Gray, Leonard Goodman, Gerry Grob, Yaw Mensah, Louis Orzack, Phil Pauley, Hugh Rockoff, Michael Seidman, and Eugene White.

I also want to acknowledge the many useful suggestions I received from William Becker, James Don Edwards, Gerry Kamber, Ed Perkins, and Gary Previts as well as four anonymous reviewers for articles derived from this study for the *Business History Review* and the *Social Science Quarterly*.

Finally, this work could not have been completed without the able support of dedicated librarians and archivists. Five were especially helpful. I want to thank Karen H. Nelloms of the American Institute of

Certified Public Accountants, Bernard Kristol of Columbia University, Kathy Kohler of the University of Michigan, and Masha Zipper and Dennis Dilno of Price Waterhouse and Company in New York for all they have done on my behalf.

The Professions
in America:
A Historical Model

An Apocalypse for a Profession

Robert H. Montgomery, twenty-fifth president of the American Institute of Accountants (AIA), sat on the dais in the Grand Ballroom of the Waldorf Astoria. It was October 19, 1937, the institute's fiftieth anniversary. He must have been exasperated at the violent storms lashing the Northeast and have wondered if they were an omen. Two days earlier, torrents had disrupted the garden party at his Fairfield, Connecticut, estate for the hundred-odd dignitaries participating in the AIA's golden jubilee. Forcing his guests indoors, the rains had prevented him from leading them on a tour of his arboretum and its prized conifers. Today the rains were causing the keynote speaker, Raymond Moley, editor of *Newsweek*, former assistant secretary of state, and fellow faculty member at Columbia University, to be absent with chills and fever. His paper on world peace would be read by an obscure Columbia instructor in banking.[1]

These frustrations must have been particularly galling to Montgomery, coming as they did during the closing days of what had been an exceptionally successful term as president. Two years earlier at the Boston convention, after running on a platform to merge the AIA with its chief rival, the American Society of Certified Public Accountants (ASCPA), he had been elected by a three-to-one majority. The merger of the associations left the AIA as the surviving entity and materially strengthened its claim to be the legitimate national representative of the entire public accounting profession.[2]

The merger in effect united two rival factions who had competed for leadership of the profession since its earliest years. One was the original AIA, founded in 1887 in New York by emigrant English and Scottish chartered accountants in concert with American accountants who admired and wished to emulate the former's professional traditions.

Their leaders were, by the 1930s, primarily senior partners of the elite national firms serving the nation's largest and most prestigious businesses. The leaders of the ASCPA, on the other hand, were primarily from the small, local firms and reflected their members' diverse regional, national, and ethnic backgrounds. Their association had been founded in 1921 to represent practitioners holding state-issued certified public accounting licenses, a uniquely American credential that had competed for preeminence since the 1890s with charters granted British public accountants as the symbol of professional competence.

It was fitting that Montgomery should preside at this landmark in the life of the accounting profession. Few leaders had the charisma that had helped Montgomery to unite a badly divided community of practitioners. In spite of the many successes of his fifty-year professional career, he still remained one of them. Born in Mahoneytown, Pennsylvania, in 1872, the son of a poor and sickly Methodist circuit preacher, Montgomery quit school and began work at the age of thirteen. After a variety of jobs, he was hired as an office boy by John Heins, a Philadelphia public accountant.

Although never formally enrolled in a degree program, Montgomery, like many practitioners of his generation, was nevertheless able to qualify as a certified public accountant (CPA). He was also able, through diligent independent study, to pass the bar examination in Pennsylvania. He then formed a partnership with other accountants from John Heins's office. Probably because of feelings of insecurity about his lack of formal education, and also to supplement his income, Montgomery, in his early twenties, became an adjunct professor of accounting. He first taught in the night program at the Wharton School of Finance and Economy. After relocating to New York, he taught at the newly organized School of Commerce, Finance, and Accounts at New York University and then at what would eventually become Columbia University's Graduate School of Business Administration, where he eventually achieved the rank of full professor. His professional prestige was enhanced when he wrote the first American text on auditing, the standard reference for more than a generation. In addition, he helped to build Lybrand, Ross Brothers, and Montgomery into one of the nation's largest and most successful public accounting practices. Throughout his career he was a leader in professional accounting associations, serving twice as the president of the AIA and once in the same office of the New York State Society of Certified Public Accountants (NYSSCPA), the largest of the state professional organizations.[3]

Yet the aspect of his career most exciting to fellow practitioners was his service as a soldier. The image of a modern-day knight, with its overtones of adventure and physical courage, must surely have appealed to many practitioners confined for years to the counting room. In 1899, during the Spanish-American War, the young Montgomery volunteered for service as a private in the Philadelphia Light Artillery, commanded by John Wanamaker's socialite son-in-law, Barclay Warburton. Montgomery's unit took part in the Puerto Rican invasion. During World War I he volunteered again and was commissioned a lieutenant colonel, serving first under Hugh L. Johnson as chief of the property appraisal section of the General Staff and later under Bernard Baruch as the army representative to the War Industries Board (WIB). Although the "colonel" had won major military distinctions not as a result of combat but rather as a result of his expertise as an accountant, he had served with honor in the two great military events of his generation. His image as a red-blooded patriot, always ready to fight for his country or his profession, was an element of his charisma.[4]

Montgomery was preceded on the agenda by John Lansing Carey, the young executive secretary of the AIA. He spent nearly a half hour reading the many congratulatory letters and telegrams received from professional accounting associations and leading practitioners in the United States, Europe, Canada, and Australia. Carey wrapped up his performance by reading the telegram from Emil S. Fischer, the sole AIA member in practice in Tientsin, China. The telegram from a forlorn missionary of public accountancy operating in a remote Asian city caused at first some snickering and finally outright laughter and applause. On this note Carey turned over the podium to Montgomery for the president's annual address.[5]

After reviewing the organization's accomplishments during his presidency, Montgomery delivered an address filled not with jubilation but with metaphors of fighting and conflict. He apprehensively described a world experiencing a war of ideas inevitably influencing America. He recounted, not very sympathetically, the rise of popular notions about the government's role in assuring social justice through increased taxation and business regulation.

He was particularly concerned about changes in the public image of public accountants, changes that had dire implications for their future. While he did not dwell on the newly promulgated securities acts (which had markedly increased public accountants' responsibilities) or the Securities and Exchange Commission (SEC) (which was organized to enforce the acts' sanctions), these subjects were clearly on his mind. He mentioned the new agency by name only once and then only in faint praise. In other contexts, however, he used code words such as "dictatorship."

It has been suggested that private corporations do not always furnish to the public all the information to which the public is entitled and the professional accountants are not consistent enough on such disclosures.

Any law which imposes dictatorial mandates of irresponsible officials is tyranny—nothing else. It may be Communism, Nazism or Fascism. Mussolini says the state is absolute. We do not agree.

As without vision a people would perish, so without courage the profession of public accountancy would perish. The profession of accountancy can not survive or flourish under a dictatorship. For its growth, its strength, its maintenance it requires free air, free thought, free speech.[6]

Although he was concerned about the New Deal, Montgomery conceded that some aspects of the new corporate-disclosure requirements mandated in the securities acts were beneficial. He was under some pressure to make concessions: the revelations of the Pecora Commission and the publications of William Z. Ripley, Adolf A. Berle, Gardiner C. Means, and a host of less prominent business writers evidenced the need for new rules requiring more complete disclosure to protect shareholder interests. The new acts would weed out corrupt or incompetent practitioners. Moreover, the sanctions would enable honest practitioners to restrain clients who wished to defraud the public by issuing false or misleading financial statements.[7]

Yet, in spite of the many tangible benefits, the colonel felt uneasy about this legislation. The SEC seemed designed to supplant the profession as the focus of authority in financial accounting matters, for, among other things, it was empowered to enforce standards in accounting and auditing, to determine who was qualified to audit public companies, and to judge the competency of practitioners' services. This unprecedented extension of governmental power called into question the profession's claim to autonomy and threatened to undermine the status, income, and wealth that the practitioners had enjoyed.[8] The New Deal seemed intent on destroying what had taken a lifetime to build. Montgomery counseled his fellow accountants to preserve their autonomy and independence.

I do not ask for standardization of accounting practice or procedure. That would mean the substitution of fixed rules for opinion and discretion. In fifty years we have learned much. If we had been standardized and unionized at any time during those fifty years, I am sure we would have lost one of our choicest possessions—independence to express our convictions in each particular case submitted to us, and most cases differ from every other case.

In the coming years shall the accounting profession keep what it gained in fifty years, fall behind or make further progress? It may surprise you to hear that I shall be satisfied if we can keep what we had gained.[9]

Montgomery stressed practitioner unity to preserve the gains the profession had made. As most in his audience understood, competition between rival organizations had weakened the profession and made it vulnerable to outside encroachment. Moreover, disunity helped to undermine its autonomy by confusing the public as to the proper source of sound opinion in accounting matters. Now, however, as a result of the consensus-building efforts of recent years—efforts in which Montgomery had played a prominent role—unity had been achieved, and the profession could speak with one voice on national matters. The political leverage provided would allow the profession to deal with external threats and to promote policies to advance its interests.

We have been members of different groups and organizations; we have held different ideas regarding administration and procedure. Accountants are bound to differ in matters of this kind. We always have and always will. But we have decided that we shall have only one national organization and that we will not divide our strength and our influence.

In all matters affecting principles and standards we will present a united front. I propose that we celebrate this occasion which marks the fiftieth anniversary of the bringing together of the public accountants of the United States by dedicating ourselves to a stern fight to protect our profession against all that may be detrimental to its high aims. Let us determine to maintain and increase the confidence in which we are held by the business public.[10]

By noon the colonel completed his speech and stepped down as leader of the unified AIA. Soon the rains abated, and the glow of fair weather was visible over the Palisades. The profession's storm also came to an end. The colonel had revealed the line of defense: a viable structure for professionalism in a society dominated by political pressures and by large economic and political organizations. Unified, the profession was strengthened by New Deal measures. Montgomery and his associates built an effective organization to promote the status, income, power, autonomy, and perquisites of public accountants, a legacy that was to serve the profession for years to come.

Professions in America: Quo Vadis?

Like Colonel Montgomery and his colleagues at the AIA's fiftieth anniversary celebration, historians have grappled with the problem of explaining the significance of the new professions and the nature of the society in which they flourished.[11] Although a proliferation of professions distinguished the new society from what had existed earlier, the literature on this development lacks central patterns of analysis or dominant explanatory themes. What does the increasing specialization and professionalization of the work force tell us about the new society? How did it fit into the mosaic of an industrial economy, the formation of large-scale, bureaucratic organizations, and a great flood of new immigrants from southern and eastern Europe? What was the nature of its soul? Opinions vary widely. Given the many different interpretations, one would hardly think that they were analyzing the same society and historical epoch. Had America found the New Jerusalem, or was it merely waiting tensely in Gethsemane for a signal of impending doom?

Although controversy among scholars is normal, such disparities suggest both a problem and an opportunity. The problem, a double one, is that ambivalence about the past may undermine the future. What lessons can we learn from this disagreement? More disturbing is that these discordant views may be not merely the result of different focuses on different aspects of the American experience. Instead, they may herald a new and deep division in outlook with implications for a polarization of opinion within American society.

The opportunity is a vital one for future historical research. The study of public accountants offers important advantages. Their history is a window through which scholars may view the interactions of important groups within the new society. Because their status, like that of attorneys, physicians, and, to a lesser degree, engineers, depended upon state licensure, their experience provides insights into the changing pattern of relationships between government and expert groups. Furthermore, their specialized skills, useful in assuring probity in the governance of the new society's most important economic institutions, provide the basis for analyzing the developing connections among business, government, and investors. The accountants' success depended on their ability to satisfy these different interests.

The American Institute of Accountants, the predecessor of the 200,000-member American Institute of Certified Public Accountants (AICPA), had been since 1937 the national representative organization for the public accounting profession in America. Moreover, it aided these specialists in finding a niche in the new society. Through this association, practitioners sought to obtain wealth, income, status, and authority. In addition, the AIA ordered activities within the profession itself. It promulgated and enforced ethical rules and established standards for auditing, accounting and review services, tax practice, and management advisory services. Until 1973, one of its committees served as the authoritative body for defining "generally accepted" principles for financial accounting. It prepared and graded the uniform certified public accountants' examination (used today by all of the nation's state licensing agencies). The organization also helped to shape accreditation standards in accounting education and to define the basic requirements for state professional licensing.[12]

Patterns of Interpretation in Professional History

Historians have proposed different explanations of professions in America. They may be classified into five categories: (1) progressive, (2) corporate-liberal, (3) organizational, (4) paradigmatic, and (5) international-comparative. Their conclusions demonstrate the dangers in formulating broad historical generalizations. Although a rich literature for individual professions has emerged, few have tried to reconcile their differences to create synthesis. Instead, they either portray these groups as corollary to broader patterns of social development or focus on selected facets.

The progressive historians, the earliest school, saw professionalization as an adjunct to their primary focus, political and social reform. For them the central dynamic was competition between liberal and conservative ideals. Professional leaders were frequently presented as the natural allies of liberal reformers. Together, these groups successfully promoted new governmental powers to protect American society from the ravishments of "corrupt" business and political interests. For the progressives, the developments that gave this period its unique character culminated in the New Deal and an activist, liberal state.[13]

Corporate-liberal scholars study the connections among business and professional organizations and other political and social groups. Unlike the progressives, these scholars do not regard the exercise of power over the political process as a triumph of enlightened liberalism. They argue that liberal reform movements are captured by conservatives who modify them to serve their own ends.[14] Some analysts show how professional organizations obtain market power for their members;[15] others analyze how power strengthens elites and excludes or contains the marginal, incompetent, or merely competitive;[16] still others address the struggle of practitioners to adhere to values in conflict with employing institutions.[17]

Organizational historians, on the other hand, concentrate on the social implications of the new functions and organizations brought about by industrialization and urbanization. Optimistic about profession building, these scholars portray these groups as new social categories competing with the traditional local, ethnonational, and religious patterns of an older, agrarian America. Their acceptance ultimately resulted from the efficiency and social uplift achieved by applying their special knowledge. The emphasis shifts from the impassioned advocacy of liberal ideologues to the cool analysis of technocrats.[18]

The paradigmatic school traces the advance of professional skill. These scholars identify paradigms providing new insights and ways of thinking about particular bodies of knowledge,[19] a technique first applied by historians of the social and natural sciences.[20] Although these studies emphasize changing patterns of thought, few make more general statements about the nature of the society in which these new perspectives flourished.

Finally, international-comparative studies make differing national experiences more understandable, and even points of difference help us comprehend how professional developments are often influenced by external economic, social, and political events. The heroes not only recognized their profession's special knowledge but also addressed more general societal concerns, emphasizing the interconnectedness of professional and social factors.[21]

The Historical Matrix for Professional Development

During the last quarter of the nineteenth century, extensive economic change created conditions favorable to the rise of the professions.[22] The closing of the western frontier provided strong incentives for conservation and efficiency in the use of the nation's dwindling supply of natural resources. This encouraged a more intensive exploitation of scientific knowledge leading to the discovery of the new products, processes, and sources of energy vital to an industrial economy. New managerial techniques and forms of organization also facilitated economic takeoff. Besides transforming communications, transportation, and manufacturing, these two causative factors also contributed to the rise of great urban centers.

A more complex and interdependent society emerged that created opportunities for achieving status, wealth, and income through careers in new fields of expertise. The pathway of opportunity turned inward toward discovering new frontiers of the mind. The farmer and the frontiersman—longtime symbols of traditional America—gradually gave way to the sociologist, the statistician, the chemical engineer, the biochemist, the public accountant, and other specialists.[23]

These changing economic patterns also transformed the American university. The humanities and theology steadily gave way to new disciplines that were more secular and emphasized objective facts. Natural philosophy gradually diversified into biology, chemistry, and physics; moral philosophy was soon displaced by history, economics, sociology, psychology, and political science.[24]

Besides teaching, the modern American university also advanced research. Through both public and private largess, an increasing portion of society's economic surplus was dedicated to these ends. Graduate education programs designed to train scholars quickly developed at such universities as Johns Hopkins, Columbia, Harvard, Chicago, Pennsylvania, Michigan, and Wisconsin. However, universities in America, unlike those in Europe, did not limit their activities to academic fields. They also provided professional training in such fields as medicine, law, engineering, and business.[25]

But these developments also had negative aspects that seemed to threaten the cherished ideals of the older agrarian society. The interdependence of the new mass society cast doubt on the frontier self-sufficiency; the concentration of power seemed to threaten democratic institutions; the influx of new immigrants from eastern and southern Europe, with their alien languages, customs, and religions, seemed to threaten what were thought to be uniquely American moral qualities. This pluralism portended either a wondrous or a depraved national future within which many professionals began to form organizations to order their specialized activities as well as to define a social contract between their members and the community.[26] The modification of this Rousseauean notion, first proposed by Robert H. Wiebe, emphasizes the moral bases of these new relationships. The contractual metaphor of an exchange of status for service reflects their character. The new age needed more precise definitions of professional roles and responsibilities. Although Tocqueville's perception of a people unencumbered by formal social constraints may have been true for the frontier, it was no longer true for the new commonwealth based on function and organization.[27]

Representative associations sought two objectives in the strategies and structures they developed to promote their professions. First, they socialized their members' expertise, especially by winning acceptance from established elites and government. Second, they promoted consensus, critical in a society dependent on large, cohesive organizations. They were continually engaged on two fronts, and the requirements of one shaped the options available on the other.

Successful socialization was critical because it justified a profession's special claims to status, income, and autonomy. A function of the representative organizations was to develop pathways for the socialization of their members' specialized activities. Society was made aware of the individual practitioner's special knowledge by direct service to specified clients, while the association promoted recognition by broader social groups. The goals of the socialization process (from the standpoint of the representative organization) included the definition of acceptable roles and specific responsibilities to which the community of competent practitioners should adhere.[28]

Successful socialization, however, also depended upon these expert groups maintaining among their members a consensus about professional life. Professionals needed to agree about the allocation of authority, status, rights, and income. They were concerned also with the legitimacy of the institutions with the authority to adjudicate conflicts, inevitable in the competition for scarce resources. Although consensus does not imply complete accord, it does involve general agreement about how conflicts should be resolved. For emerging professional organizations, three elements were essential: (1) general agreement on the validity of laws, rules, and norms; (2) recognition of the authority in professional institutions to establish and enforce these laws and norms; and (3) a strong sense of identity between the practitioner and his profession, its institutions, and its particular values.[29]

Once achieved, consensus diminished conflicts, resolved disagreements, and encouraged mutual accommodation. Consensus helped to establish the profession's authority in the eyes of other elites whose support it needed for acceptance of its special professional skills. Competition and discord would have confused the general public, who was unable to evaluate the issues dividing professionals. Confusion among laymen was dangerous. Discord invited encroachment by outside groups, including governmental authorities, where the profession's special functions were critical to the public welfare.[30]

Important as they were to associations, socialization and consensus were not easy to achieve. This was particularly evident in the experience of the professions that sought special jurisdiction over specific societal problems through state-mandated licensing. The following sections present a model explaining how these groups achieved consensus and acceptance during a critical transitional period in America's history.[31]

First Epoch: The Federated State and the Incipiency of Professional Associationalism, 1880–1900

Initially, the building of licensed professions took place at the state and county levels. This pattern was conditioned by several factors. First, power to regulate these activities had traditionally belonged to the states. Insofar as the federal government remained limited, few opportunities emerged for advancing professionalism at the national level. Furthermore, the markets for professional services were usually local; only a few practitioners operated across state boundaries. Moreover, profession building was narrowly limited to a few regions. Most of these developments first occurred in the northeastern and north central states—the epicenters of other major changes transforming American society.[32]

A second question arose concerning the demarcation of the spheres of authority between representative associations and government agencies in controlling professionalism. Some wanted these activities governed by autonomous professional organizations. This model, patterned after British professional groups, seemed more consistent with American individualism. Autonomous associations could insulate professionals from the pressures of politics. However, others, favorably impressed by Continental nations, believed the state should play the key role. Those who favored statist solutions also felt that individual liberties could best be preserved if these institutions were more sensitive to political influences. In this latter view, government was perceived as a potential counter against excessive private power.[33]

Early professional organizations also experienced difficulty in promoting consensus because of their differences over the meaning of professionalism: dissimilarities in the type of practice as well as in the backgrounds of practitioners. Members of the new professions had to resolve four key questions: how to define the limits of the community of competent practitioners; how to coordinate and control the activities of the profession's members; how to promote the status, income, and power of a profession's membership; and finally, how to maintain contact with and control over factors in the external environment.

Two broad patterns emerged. On the one hand were the elite whose status stemmed from specialized practice and the sophistication of their skills. Since they operated at the frontiers of knowledge, they were usually innovative. Examples included attorneys responsible for developing new legal entities such as pools, trusts, and holding companies to help their larger business clients accommodate to the provisions of the antitrust laws; accountants who advised the managers of these innovative enterprises about the best ways to present their financial positions; and early physicians who pioneered medical specialization. Virtuosity excited the admiration of professional colleagues, and research-based practice attracted elite clients. This augmented their status and assured their leadership in associational affairs.[34]

On the other hand were the less distinguished professionals with routine and less complex practices—generalists rather than specialists. In medicine, for example, general practitioners were frequently called upon to treat a wide range of medical ailments as well as to provide counseling services not strictly medical in character. Furthermore, they served more ordinary patients and did not have large and profitable practices. In medicine, general practitioners feared the emergent specialty practice brought about through research; in accountancy, on the other hand, ordinary practitioners thought research less important than practice promotion.[35]

A second issue was professional training. In law, medicine, accounting, and engineering, new university-based programs first began to challenge an older apprenticeship. Although university training ultimately prevailed because it was more efficient, partisans of apprenticeship differed in their attitudes about professional life beyond educational issues. Monte Calvert has pointed out that shop training in engineering encouraged a more entrepreneurial than professional outlook. Among the academics, the dispute raged over which disciplines were appropriate to a university. Those trained in the older liberal arts viewed with skepticism and sometimes alarm the rise of professional studies in engineering and business.[36]

Social and regional backgrounds were another polarizing issue. Elite status was usually associated with white, Anglo-Saxon, middle-class origins in the Northeast. This helped to assure acceptance among other elites who shared the same heritage. It also implied greater access to educational opportunities to develop the skills for professional life. Although professions emphasized system, function, and organization, ascriptive concerns—characteristic of the waning traditional society—remained strong.

Immigrants seemed to threaten the "uniquely" American values seen as essential elements to professional life. One notable exception was British chartered accountants, who played a leading role in promoting public accountancy. But the acceptance of foreigners depended on their being of a nationality with which American elites could identify. Practitioners were, secondly, divided by regional differences because of "character deficiencies" of those inhabiting a particular region. The South, for instance, was seen as a place of self-indulgence and social inequity, while the agricultural Middle West was seen as a vast untutored "boobocracy," to use Mencken's word. Consequently, there were strong concerns about the quality of practice there and its effect on the profession's overall image of competency.[37]

Although contacts with state governments were most critical during this period, the size of the practitioner community seemed to be the most important factor in determining the scope of their representative organizations. In the older and larger professions whose members practiced independently, county and state organizations seemed to have been the primary forms. National organizations for some of these fields, such as the American Medical Association (AMA) and the American Bar Association (ABA), initially remained small and not broadly reflective of the professions they purportedly represented. In accounting and engineering, national representative organizations were, in reality, regional bodies. The New York–based American Association of Public Accountants (AAPA), the American Society of Civil Engineers, and the American Society of Mechanical Engineers were drawn predominantly from the Northeast, failing to form nationally representative organizations.[38]

Whether national or local, representative associations employed similar techniques in ordering professional life. First, they built cohesion and coordinated professional activities through periodic meetings, special member committees, and professional periodicals and books. Second, they lobbied their states for laws legitimizing a formal framework of professional governance. These laws established practice prerequisites, standards for accrediting educational institutions and formal qualifying examinations. Third, they increased public awareness by encouraging leading practitioners to volunteer for governmental advisory bodies. Finally, they encouraged organizing in other states where their professions had not yet been established.[39]

Toward the end of this period, however, the focus of profession building shifted from the state to the national level. The political and administrative structures established during the eighteenth and nineteenth centuries were no longer appropriate in light of the changes transforming American society.

Second Epoch: Pioneering the National Executive State and the Rise of Federative Associationalism, 1900–1916

The extension of federal executive power during the first sixteen years of the current century provided an incentive for professional groups to form broad-based national federations. Federal structures, previously effective in ordering the nation's political affairs, were now applied to the professions. A pattern of horizontal integration was widely followed by groups that, with varying degrees of success, sought to maximize their political power. In law, medicine, and accountancy, the drive for federal structures concentrated on unifying county, state, and national representative bodies. The activities of these federations were usually coordinated by a national executive board, which confronted the national government on matters affecting their profession. The group's subsidiary bodies contributed to the formulation of its national policies and provided political support by lobbying their congressional representatives.[40]

Federations helped to standardize professional life nationwide. National organizations encouraged legislatures to ratify model uniform licensing laws. Increasingly, they supported the newly organized university-based training programs. They also sought to extend their models to new states—particularly in the less advanced South and West. To assure effective coordination, the national organization encouraged the state or regional auxiliaries to adopt uniform associational bylaws and to promote model professional licensing legislation.[41]

Federation offered more efficient ordering of operations. Professional publishing activities, for instance, were transferred from state bodies to a national association. In addition, special committees of the national associations more efficiently resolved matters of mutual concern. The deliberations of these central groups eliminated the need for duplicative efforts on the part of the component organizations.

Federal structures aided consensus formation. Decentralization provided maximum member involvement in associational affairs. Furthermore, because federations diffused power among their constituent bodies, national leaders encouraged accord and compromise. Successful policy formulation thus required a broad coalition of subsidiary organizations.[42]

A national organization advising the government also enhanced the prestige of its members. Besides recognition, expert testifying in government made the public aware of the usefulness of their profession. This was often coordinated through umbrella reform organizations such as the National Civic Federation and the National Municipal League. Accountants, engineers, attorneys, economists, political scientists, and physicians were prominent in the league's efforts to improve municipal services and to assure "good government." Professional associations also volunteered their services as advisors to the new agencies of the growing national executive state. Accountants, for instance, advised on financial reporting systems for the new bureaucratic agencies of Theodore Roosevelt's administration; physicians also aided by combating medical nostrums and promoting federal food inspection legislation; and engineers helped national conservation efforts. The achievements of professional elites in these ventures reflected favorably on their colleagues' efforts to promote their profession nationwide.[43]

Yet federations often proved inadequate to resolve the concerns of all professional factions—especially the elite. The cultivation of state governmental bodies, for instance, was not as successful as many professional leaders had hoped, most notably lawyers and accountants who were dissatisfied with the type of professional governance that had emerged. The states had not embraced the autonomous associationalism favored by these elites. Instead, they granted professional associations only limited authority and relied on their own regulatory agencies. In addition, for some professions, such as accountancy, state licensing merely certified competency but did not limit entry to practice. Even the medical profession, which had convinced state authorities to close medical schools deemed substandard, was unable to curtail the growth of competing professions such as osteopathy, homeopathy, chiropractic, and eclectic medicine. The ease of entry into these professions undermined the economic viability of practice. Substantial differences in preparation still existed for virtually all professional groups in various states. The challenge of qualifying examinations, the insulation of the licensing process from political favoritism, the qualifications of those serving on professional regulatory boards, and interstate licensing reciprocity remained to be accomplished.

The federations also experienced difficulty in reconciling the differences that divided internal factions. The elites, often displeased with their limited control of associational affairs, eventually perceived federalism as restricting. Furthermore, new men of differing backgrounds and practice were beginning to dominate many state and regional associations, thus diluting the power of the elite. Coalitions of these elements, for instance, often defeated efforts to strengthen the national leadership by expanding the codes of professional ethics.

Nor did the elite, already successful in practice, promote basic services among prospective clients. Instead, they wanted greater emphasis on market stability and research activities that could both enhance and differentiate the specialized services they provided. These new circumstances threatened to place the control of affairs in the hands of groups who espoused a form of professionalism they did not favor.[44]

The less distinguished feared the elite's market power. Nor did they agree that associational resources should be redirected toward research rather than promotional ends. In medicine, general practitioners saw their services become the province of rising classes of specialists. Engineers feared that an elite closely allied with "big business" might frustrate associational involvements in social reform.[45]

Yet the disappointment of the elite about the direction of professional development did not last long. The subsequent military mobilization brought about new conditions that seemingly vindicated the type of associationalism they favored.

Third Epoch: National Mobilization and the Ascendancy
of Autonomous Associationalism, 1917–1929

The preparedness movement on the eve of America's entry into World War I represented a major turning point in the socialization of the new professions. Volunteerism, prevalent in earlier attempts to build professional recognition, found an outlet in mobilization. The executive branch did not yet have bureaus large enough or knowledgeable enough to marshal the nation's industries for war. Instead, the federal government relied heavily on the elite leadership of business and professional associations. The prestige of engineers, chemists, bacteriologists, statisticians, accountants, physicians, psychologists, historians, attorneys, and political scientists was enhanced by their contributions to this country's military and diplomatic efforts. Key agencies, such as the War Industries Board and the Shipping Board, could not have functioned without the support of a host of civilian experts. War was fulfillment for the elite leaders of many expert groups.[46]

But the preparedness crystallized among federal bureaucracies, business and professional groups, and Congress a tripartite form of government that had been in gradual formation since the late nineteenth century—what Louis Galambos termed "triocracy." Henceforth, each component would play a role in shaping public policy. This interactions became more intense with the proliferation of specialized federal agencies to order various aspects of America's changing social scene.[47]

In economic affairs, for example, federal executive power was extended through the Interstate Commerce Commission (ICC) in 1886, the Department of Commerce in 1902, the Federal Reserve Board (FRB) in 1913, and the Federal Trade Commission (FTC) in 1914. Private groups eager to advance their special interests—sometimes cooperatively, at other times competitively—confronted these agencies. In any case, Congress, highly sensitive to public opinion, remained the ultimate arbiter of competing policy alternatives.[48]

The success of professional groups during the war justified their peacetime demands for greater autonomy. After all, had they not been contributors to victory and unprecedented peacetime prosperity? Was not America's rapid victory a proof of the inherent superiority of the volunteerism of a free people over the stultifying statism of the exhausted European belligerents? To congressional leaders, there was little merit in extending the power of federal agencies over activities managed so well by private groups. The laissez-faire attitudes of the postwar decade were conditioned more by a growing deference to these elites than by ill-defined notions about returning to "normalcy." Compared to previous circumstances, what emerged during the 1920s was anything but normal.[49]

Associationalism also appealed to political leaders because it seemed consistent with American democratic traditions. The regimentation and curtailment of individual freedom during the war disturbed many Americans. Associationalism emphasizing individual participation seemed an attractive alternative for ordering a mass society and more consistent with the personal liberty that had long been thought of as the American condition.[50]

The deference shown to professional elites because of their war service encouraged their control of associational activities. Their motives were partly aimed at stabilizing the market for professional services and reducing competition, especially in law, medicine, and accountancy. It often barred advertising and other "unprofessional" forms of practice promotion. Competition was further reduced by the barriers to entry into the profession: by implementing standardized, rigorous certifying examinations that supplanted state tests of uneven quality, by increasing educational prerequisites, and by closing down professional schools deemed marginal. Practitioners reduced competition still further by promoting more restrictive legislation limiting practice to license holders. Challenging, lucrative specializations, such as surgery and ophthalmology, also became the exclusive domain of small cadres of practitioners who had benefited from postgraduate residency programs.[51]

Associations redirected their resources to extend their knowledge base by subsidizing fellowships, research libraries, bibliographic services, and more technical publications.[52]

Professional elites continued to reduce the influence of those thought to be marginal in background because of the nature of their practice or because of their social outlooks and who, since the end of the war, dominated many state organizations. The elite became disenchanted with federations as a means of ordering the professions, for they were much too sensitive to the pressures of the less distinguished practitioners. In accountancy, for instance, federation was abandoned completely, and a more centrally controlled national organization was established. In law this blunted the earlier drive to unify the various county and state bar associations under the ABA banner.[53] In medicine, an acceleration in the formation of new practice specializations reinforced these trends. Although the federated AMA maintained its leadership, its authority was chipped away by a growing number of specialist boards and colleges.[54] In engineering, the patterns were somewhat different. There the elite fought against social reform. The focus of these activities was the American Engineering Council, an umbrella organization representing civil, electrical, mechanical, and mining engineering. The social activists ultimately failed because of their inability to muster the needed majorities specified in the bylaws to receive the council's support.[55]

This reordering of associational activity, however, had negative consequences for group cohesiveness. The efforts of the elite to control professional life alienated those outside their circle. Some organized oppositions that led in accountancy to rival associations competing for national leadership. More often, it took the form of unseemly debates, which confused the public about what was authoritative. Factionalism invited challenges from external groups that wished to appropriate to themselves the prerogatives of a divided profession. The crisis of the Great Depression revealed how dangerous these internal fissures were.[56]

Fourth Epoch: The Maturation of the National Executive State and the Emergence of Countervailing Professionalism, 1930–1940

The economic and social dislocations resulting from the Great Depression brought about a new balance in the triocracy. Unlike the First World War, the depression undermined the prestige of professional groups, especially those closely associated with business and finance, and led to a call for a renegotiation of the social contract. The crisis that private groups seemed impotent to control encouraged those who favored the extension of governmental regulation.

During Franklin D. Roosevelt's first administration, federal agencies were created to restore price stability in the agricultural, financial, and industrial markets. During his second administration, the federal executive authority attempted to assure social welfare and to achieve a more equitable distribution of income. The encroachment on professional prerogatives was widespread and difficult to resist.[57]

Accountants, for instance, felt threatened by federal regulation of the financial markets; medical doctors resisted plans for more comprehensive national health insurance; engineers opposed rural electrification and other efforts to promote national economic planning. The factionalism that had divided practitioner groups for over a decade increased their vulnerability to this intervention. A revival of statism threatened associationalism.[58]

This calamity encouraged reformulation of professional strategies and structures. By the mid-1930s, many associations restored practitioner unity to counter the expanded power of federal agencies and increase their political leverage. The curtailment of open factionalism also reduced the public's confusion about authority in professional matters and rendered more credible practitioner claims for greater autonomy.[59]

Prejudice was not relevant to professional life and could be dangerous. To promote unity, the elite and their less distinguished colleagues compromised on priorities for professional development. Programs promoted organization and function. Closer relationships between state and national organizations were developed. Coalitions were formed with allied professions to achieve common political objectives. These patterns were especially apparent in the licensed professions of law, medicine, and accountancy.[60]

Although the major elements of the triocracy were in place by the 1920s, the depression years changed people's attitudes toward the government. The crash and the subsequent economic and social dislocations revealed a blind side of associationalism. An earlier implication, that what was good for the professions was also good for America, seemed now too facile. Private groups could not restore order in the nation's depressed economy. Public demands for relief from this crisis forced government leaders to extend state power to restore social welfare.

The broadening of federal power, however, did not ultimately supplant associationalism. The objective was to restore the vitality of institutions that had earlier been contributors to the nation's well-being. Consequently, government tried to expand regulatory authority through existing associational structures. The displacement of professional associations was too costly and difficult, besides which it might generate political opposition to the government's reform programs. New regulations that made these groups more responsive to public policy but that did not stultify individual initiative were needed. In this sense the New Deal was conservative but not reactionary.[61]

The New Deal strengthened government's role in the triocracy and made this system protective of the public interest. Like the classical notion of *concordia discors*, accord was achieved by balancing the interests of conflicting groups. Society was best served by an adversarial relationship between public and private groups seeking to regulate the professions. Criticism, no longer limited to technical matters among practitioners, widened its scope and became institutionalized within the administrative state. Practitioners would defend and justify their collective performance in protecting society's interests.[62]

The professional triocracy was consistent with traditional representative government in two ways. First, professional associations were voluntary but needed consensus in order to function in a national political arena. The triocracy provided an efficient forum for these groups and government to address their mutual concerns. Second, the New Deal rendered professionals more sensitive to public opinion. Although the public was often passive, it could in times of crisis become sharply focused and dramatically affect the interests of expert groups. This was clearly demonstrated by the expansion of state power in response to public demands for relief from the worst consequences of the crash. Public opinion could tip the regulatory balance in favor of either public or private groups.

Finally, the triocracy provides insight into the national character, into certain predominant values to which Americans broadly subscribed. They did not select fascism, with its racialist emphasis on the mystic connections of the blood. Nor did they choose communism, with its dialectic of inevitable class conflict. Their concern was a restoration of economic and social stability. Americans were not responsive to a political rhetoric either as passionate or as heroic as that emanating from overseas.

Mindful of the vulnerability of their diverse and complex society to internal turmoil, Americans preferred persuasive, subtle, and understated dialogue. The new society's emphasis on organization, function, efficiency, and conservation helped to achieve coalescence among its particularistic elements. So too did the rediscovery of the traditional American virtues of tolerance and compromise as professional groups worked out their political problems during this crisis.

Part 1

The Dawn of
Professional Accountancy,
1880–1900

The last quarter of the nineteenth century in America marked the beginning of a period of substantial economic change providing an environment conducive to the establishment of the new profession of public accountancy. During these years the exploitation of new sources of energy and the development of new modes of transportation and communication accelerated the nation's transition from an agricultural to an industrial economy. These broad economic changes prompted a steady exodus of Americans from rural and small town settings to the new, rapidly growing urban centers. There, the increasing scale of activities was reflected in the emergence of giant, bureaucratic organizations to provide order first in business and later in other important functions of the new society. The growing complexity of these basic functions created new demands for the services of a wide range of knowledge specialists.[1]

One of the earliest groups of specialists to benefit from these developments was the new profession of public accountancy. Though accountancy as a business function dated back to antiquity, the organization of a substantial service industry to provide counsel about these matters was one of the many new outgrowths of the nation's industrialization. Initially organized in Britain more than a generation earlier, the profession of public accountancy first flourished in America during the 1880s as a result of the growing need among businessmen and investors for objective economic data. In an increasingly complex industrial society, it was no longer feasible to rely on local authorities for guidance on the many bewildering economic questions confronting Americans. The scope, scale, and dispersion of business activities had become too great for persons to cope with in the traditional manner. No longer could local luminaries be relied upon to provide the answers to all of the pressing questions about business. New and more objective sources of information were needed.

This need to reorder the communication of vital economic information provided the basis for practitioners of the new profession of public accountancy for income, wealth, status, and authority. Business managers perforce turned to these new experts to develop reporting systems to provide comprehensive data summarizing the activities and conditions in large organizations. Public accountants also provided useful services to investors in the form of the audits they performed of the financial statements of companies whose securities were traded by the public. Finally, public accountants found profitable new applications for their special knowledge in later years in the form of tax compliance and planning services they provided to their clients.[2]

Although a demand for these specialized services expanded during these early years, leaders of this new profession experienced frustrations in their efforts to organize their calling on a national basis. Two different problems impeded the progress of professionalization. The first was external: to obtain an important role in the emerging national structure of economic regulation. The second problem was internal: to build consensus for a common program of professionalization. Both objectives remained elusive during this period.

With respect to national economic regulation, some practitioners wished to emulate the example of the older profession of chartered accountancy, which had steadily won greater acceptance from British governmental authorities for its certification during the latter half of the nineteenth century. A primary focus of these activities was a new association, the American Association of Public Accountants. The AAPA, the direct predecessor to the AIA, was organized in 1886 by a few elite American practitioners in alliance with British accountants with client interests in this country. Although these practitioners were successful in promoting their services among some businesses and even local governments, they made little progress in finding outlets among national governmental bodies.

The accountants' lack of progress in these affairs was due to several factors. First, public accountancy was not a well-known profession to many governmental leaders; many of them, instead, preferred alternative models of economic regulation that depended on the operation of strong bureaucratic agencies rather than independent professional groups such as accountants. Secondly, few federal agencies existed during this early period to regulate the major economic developments transforming American society. The major exception to this general pattern was the ICC, which in 1886 introduced a new mandatory system of accounting as a key tool for regulating the railroads. But the effectiveness of this early federal effort was soon vitiated by the ICC's limited resources, conceptual flaws in its uniform accounting system, and successful challenges to its authority in the courts. Finally, the interests of important client groups also acted to curtail the AAPA's advocacy in these matters. During this early period, many practitioners served local shippers and merchants who were strong supporters of broader governmental regulation of the railroads. Few of these practitioners had succeeded in developing any substantial clientele within this industry at the time these accounting reforms were first implemented.

The ability of this small and relatively obscure profession to achieve its national regulatory objectives was further undermined by the fact that its practitioners were divided and unable to form a consensus about professional matters. A rival professional association, the New York State Society of Certified Public Accountants (NYSSCPA), emerged during this period and competed with the AAPA for leadership of the early profession in its first important center, New York. These two professional groups had different concepts of the profession and its role in society. They disagreed over such matters as whether accountancy was essentially an art or a science, whether professional governance should be organized primarily on state or national levels, whether responsibility for certifying practitioner competency should be vested in an agency of the state or in a practitioner association, and whether the individual firms or the new universities and colleges should serve as the primary means of training prospective candidates for entry into the profession.

Besides professional differences, the two groups recruited members of different cultural and social backgrounds. The British chartered accountant leaders of the AAPA, for instance, found themselves drawn into conflict by some American public accountants who resented what they viewed as the foreign practitioners' intrusion into a domestic profession. Regional differences also divided practitioners. Finally, concerns about the great influx of new immigrants from southern and eastern Europe also moved some practitioners to restrict entry into the profession to those from "safe" and "acceptable" social origins. This too generated tensions.

In spite of the desire of some practitioners for national solutions, the earliest efforts at establishing a comprehensive structure for ordering professional affairs were on the state level. This movement first centered in New York during the 1890s. This pioneering experience was significant because it established a prototype for professional governance eventually imitated in its broadest contours by virtually every state in the Union. In New York rival practitioner groups disagreed and offered competitive plans to control professional certification. The result was the establishment of the state as the primary agency responsible for examining and certifying public accountants.

Although the establishment of this new model of state regulation represented an important step in achieving recognition for public accountancy, it was not sufficient for addressing all the problems the profession confronted in a rapidly changing social and economic milieu. Major differences in outlook about the technical details of practice as well as deeply felt concerns associated with differences in social backgrounds of members of this profession remained unresolved. Furthermore, an accelerating trend toward economic concentration and the concomitant growth of giant business enterprises serving national markets made controlling professional affairs more complex. Accountants who were compelled to practice across state lines to serve these new business institutions had to adjust to regulation by a proliferation of state accountancy boards. Moreover, the extension of the federal government's power to regulate the economy after the turn of the century weakened accountants' ability to order these affairs.

Prelude to Professionalization, 1886–1892

The American Association of Accountants: Origins and Expectations

The American Association of Public Accountants was launched by a small group of pioneering accountants on December 22, 1886, in Philadelphia at the offices of Colonel Montgomery's old mentor, John Heins. Most of the twenty-four American and British accountants in attendance were practicing in New York. They had traveled to Philadelphia in hopes of inducing Heins and other leading practitioners of that city to join what they envisioned as the first national association organized exclusively for the upper level of public accountants. In this sense their motives were similar to those of the organizers of the American Society of Mechanical Engineers. Moreover, by emphasizing a common function—the practice of public accountancy—the new association differentiated itself from other contemporary accounting societies formed in such business centers as New York, Philadelphia, St. Louis, Chicago, and Cincinnati. Although these other groups primarily attracted low-status bookkeepers, they were usually led by elite practitioners, educators, and businessmen with a general interest in accounting.[1]

Many of the AAPA's members also wished to emulate British chartered accountants who earlier had succeeded in obtaining a prominent place in society for their special expertise. This British model seemed relevant because it was part of the professional experience of several of the organization's founders; furthermore, the British accountants earlier had used their professional organization with great success as a vehicle for promoting their status, authority, income, and wealth. Local institutes of chartered accountancy formed first in London and Liverpool in 1870, in Manchester in 1873, and in Sheffield in 1877. These were eventually united through the formation of the

Institute of Chartered Accountants in England and Wales, which received a royal charter in 1881. Substantial progress in professionalization had been achieved also in Scotland, where royal charters had
been granted to accountancy associations in Edinburgh in 1854, in
Glasgow in 1855, and in Aberdeen in 1866.[2]

But prior to industrialization, public accountancy in Britain had
been considered a marginal occupation not ranking in status with
medicine, law, or theology. This was understandable, given the work
most accountants did. They provided rudimentary accounting services such as posting and adjusting ledgers, and prepared the occasional financial statements for the many small and local proprietor-
ships and partnerships which were the characteristic forms of business organization. Many also provided a miscellany of other services,
including writing letters, painting or lettering signs, and acting as
auctioneers, factors, stockjobbers, financial advisors, appraisers, general agents, and insurance brokers.[3]

With industrialization the demand for accounting services grew,
aided by the special provisions of new legislation for ordering affairs
in industry and finance. The Bankruptcy Act (1831) allowed the courts
to appoint independent accountants as "official assignees" or liquida-
tors of insolvent estates. Later, a series of companies acts extending
business regulation facilitated the formation of joint stock companies.
The most important from the perspective of public accountancy were
those of 1856 and 1862, which allowed commercial and industrial
companies to sell their shares to the public. They encouraged the
employment of independent public accountants to audit the financial
statements required to be provided to shareholders. An additional
requirement—that dividends be paid only from earnings and not from
an enterprise's capital—also motivated many boards of directors to
engage public accountants to help in this important determination. By
the end of the century, it was common to find audited financial statements included as part of the prospectuses for new securities offered
on the London Stock Exchange. Finally, the Companies Act of 1900
mandated that audited financial statements for all regulated companies be filed annually with the registrar of companies in the Board of
Trade.[4]

The expansion of British industry and commerce provided other
opportunities for chartered accountants to distinguish themselves.
Leading practitioners developed both financial and cost accounting
systems as well as innovative modes of accounting expression for the
managerial and technological innovations some of their most important clients were using to transform the British economy. The experi-

ence gained in pioneering these developments for a host of new types of business organizations—railroads, gas and electric utilities, and technologically complex manufacturing operations—greatly strengthened the technical skills of the leading British practitioners. These unique engagements represented the emergence of a new research-based practice that depended upon the ability of leading accountants to satisfy the changing information requirements of a dynamic industrial economy. By the end of the century, because of successes achieved in meeting these challenges, an elite of public accounting firms had emerged in Britain.[5]

The success of the early chartered accountants also stemmed, in part, from their ability to build confidence among other important social groups. Accountants had to convince them that their new concept of professionalism was a valid substitute for older sources of authority, which were breaking down because of the changes brought about by industrialization. Opportunities for investing savings, for instance, were no longer limited to local real estate, mortgages, and bills of exchange—investments in which decisions could be guided by informal communication with local authority figures such as bankers, leading merchants, and attorneys. Instead, financial statements became increasingly important in efficiently conveying vital economic information to a far-flung class of anonymous investors in the stocks and bonds issued by large-scale businesses. The older, local sources of authority lacked access to relevant economic information about these companies. The wealthy classes in British society needed new technical experts to certify the truthfulness of the information that influenced key investment decisions; they needed experts who possessed the same high degree of personal integrity and honor expected from the older, local sources of authority.[6]

Accountants needed to achieve social acceptance from elite groups if they were to play that role, and a primary focus of their efforts was the professional association. The organization's tenets assured that only "reliable" men would be admitted to practice. Through professional associations, chartered accountants built confidence that their members were both technically competent and morally fit. To this end, candidates for admission were required to serve a five-year apprenticeship under the direct guidance of a chartered accountant and successfully complete at the end of this term a rigorous four-part examination administered by the Institute of Chartered Accountants. The danger of admitting entrants lacking the requisite degree of integrity and honor was thought to be minimized by structuring the long and arduous apprenticeship so that only candidates from reliable middle-class backgrounds could qualify. Those of more dubious social origins were excluded by requiring apprentices to serve without compensation and also by allowing masters to charge substantial fees for providing training. Thus society could be reasonably assured that only gentlemen of respectable backgrounds would be admitted.[7]

The profession in America at the end of the 1880s was not nearly so secure as that in Britain. Although the process of industrialization was beginning to provide opportunities to American practitioners, they were neither well organized nor well positioned enough to promote the benefits of their services in a skeptical business community. For instance, although demand for the development of financial reporting systems was generally strong during this period, much of this work was performed not by public accountants but by members of the more numerous and better-established engineering professions.

Nor were American practitioners as successful as their British counterparts in finding outlets for their expertise in national economic regulation. Neither government nor other interested bodies, such as stock exchanges, encouraged these services.

In fact, the organization of the ICC heralded the advent of a new mode of state regulation more akin to the practice followed in Continental nations. Its key architects were Judge Thomas M. Cooley, first chairman of the commission, and his former student and protégé, the chief statistician Henry Carter Adams, recipient of the first doctorate granted by the recently organized Johns Hopkins University. They wanted to develop a new mode of administrative regulation based on financial information provided through a new uniform system of accounts for the railroads. In this effort he was guided by his experience in the 1870s as a student in a seminar held at the University of Berlin and directed by Ernst Engel, head of the Prussian State Statistical Bureau.[8]

The innovative ICC system was seen as a more efficient and effective alternative for assuring social equity in operating the nation's railroads than that of regulation through the courts. Cooley and Adams believed their new system would be effective in resolving the complaints of shippers about the fairness of rates. They also believed that it would make the allocation of financial resources more efficient by providing investors with timely and accurate financial information relating to railroad operations. Their plan, however, did not involve the use of independent accountants but relied instead on federal bureaucrats. The AAPA's leaders viewed these actions with misgivings; they were reluctant to see government preempt their ambition to play key roles in ordering accounting for this important industry.[9]

The AAPA's ability to advocate British forms of associationalist governance over economic activities was also constrained by the interests of important client groups. Few practitioners had railroad clients. The most important clients of the majority were local manufacturers and merchants eager to see stronger governmental regulation of railroad tariffs. This affinity with shipper interests was reflected in the selection of James Thurber, one of New York's great wholesale grocers, and Lucius M. Stanton, a successful importer of silk novelties and sundries, as honorary trustees of the AAPA. The choice of Thurber was particularly significant because of his leading role in the New York Cheap Transportation Association, which earlier had lobbied for the passage of the Interstate Commerce Act.[10]

In spite of these difficulties, the AAPA continued to promote a more positive image of the profession and also to assist British practitioners with client interests in this country. Foremost among these early British chartered accountants was Edwin Guthrie of Manchester, who encouraged the founders of the AAPA and was with them at their organizing meeting in Philadelphia in 1886. Guthrie and practitioners like him wished to maintain contact with reputable and competent local practitioners who could serve as correspondents and thereby reduce the expensive, dangerous, and time-consuming travel needed to serve clients with North American interests. Frustrated by the lack of any organized body of public accountants, Guthrie had in 1884 tried unsuccessfully to induce the United States consul in Manchester, Albert D. Shaw, to have the State Department encourage the development of a domestic profession to aid foreign practitioners. Even the establishment in 1886 of a New York branch did not entirely solve Guthrie's problems because his clients' interests were scattered about the nation.[11]

A national association was needed to draw together resident practitioners familiar with British accounting and business practices and to identify representatives in all the major business centers; this sort of organization would be of inestimable value to British practitioners whose clients were steadily increasing their investments in America. Total European investment in the United States was estimated to have grown from $1.3 billion in 1870 to $3.3 billion by 1900. Much of this derived from British sources. These trends, which drew Guthrie first to New York and later, in 1891, to Chicago, soon exerted a similar influence on other leading British firms. Price Waterhouse and Company opened offices in New York in 1890 and in Chicago in 1891; Deloitte, Dever, Griffiths, and Company established a New York office in 1895; and Broads, Patterson opened a Chicago office in 1894.[12]

The importance of the AAPA to the chartered accountants grew as these early British firms expanded their practices in this country. The prestige of the AAPA and its image as an elite association increased because of the successes of some leading members. Key investment banking firms, such as J. P. Morgan and Company, J. and W. Seligman, and Kuhn Loeb and Company, typically selected the chartered accounting firms prominent in the AAPA to audit the financial statements included in the prospectuses for security issues floated through the London market. The certificate of a well-known accounting firm was thought to improve the marketability of American securities among European investors. In addition, the chartered accountants' long years of experience in preparing financial statements and presentations from the perspective of creditors (as a consequence of the bankruptcy reporting requirements of the companies acts in Britain) made them excellent technical advisors to American bankers.[13]

The AAPA also grew because it was able to attract many American practitioners who had developed strong connections with British business interests. Richard F. Stevens, for instance, was a member of the family that had established the Stevens Institute of Technology in Hoboken, New Jersey; he served clients in Newark, New Jersey (in the rope-making industry), with strong connections to British jute and hemp importers. Frank Allen, who served as private secretary to Mayor Seth Low, had worked closely with British businessmen through his involvement with the Silk Importers Association and the Fire Insurance Association. Richard M. Chapman and Frank Broaker served as correspondents for several small British chartered firms based primarily in midland cities.[14]

The AAPA's emulation of British professional traditions also seems to have appealed to American practitioners and business leaders, particularly those living in northeastern cities, because of the imagined threats posed to traditional values by the influx of new immigrants from southern and eastern Europe. In a period of great technological and economic transformation, the problems of maintaining order in society were complicated by the great wave of new immigrants who did not share a common cultural heritage with the native population. Although the immigrants certainly did not threaten the living standards of the AAPA practitioners, their incomprehensible languages and alien religions and ideologies were perceived by some as threatening to existing social values.

The AAPA's program was also appealing because it provided, in effect, an additional comforting "proof" of the hypothesis that Anglo-Saxon culture was inherently superior. Those who identified with this tradition were, I think, searching for evidence to reinforce the belief in their cultural superiority and perhaps to justify actions taken to suppress the influence of the new immigrants. A successful new profession pioneered by Anglo-Saxons was thus readily accepted as a positive and reassuring force in American urban society.[15]

But British professional ideals did not satisfy all who were concerned about ordering affairs in American accounting. The AAPA organizers somewhat naively underestimated the importance of those who looked to other values and to rival associations. The differences created fissures along which the profession fragmented during crises. Disagreements over four primary issues proved difficult to resolve: the nature of accounting knowledge; the best methods for training novices; conflicting national and social identities; and agencies and symbols of professional authority. The AAPA failed to reconcile all these concerns, and this resulted in substantial conflict within the profession. Differences in outlook with respect to the role of educational institutions and the nature of accountancy knowledge, for instance, were pervasive during these years. The competition to control the new profession was intense, as we shall see, and it forced the AAPA and its rivals to sort out the internal inconsistencies in their thinking and to crystallize more comprehensive positions on professional matters. Differences with respect to national and social identities, on the other hand, provided clear and lasting demarcations separating the practitioners of the AAPA from others in the early accounting community. Although these attitudes actually had little to do with professional issues, they were major sources of polarization. Finally, competition over the validity of professional agencies and symbols of competency became the outward manifestation of the complex and often contradictory impulses that influenced the early profession. Unable to resolve these issues independently, some practitioners ultimately turned to the state.[16]

The New York Institute of Accounts
and the Science of Accountancy

One of the early associations to compete successfully against the AAPA was the New York Institute of Accounts (NYIA), whose membership broadly accepted the notion that accountancy was a form of knowledge akin to the physical sciences. The rivalry that emerged during the 1890s between these two groups was thus influenced in part by differences in opinion over the basic nature of accounting knowledge. The practitioner leaders of the NYIA and their rivals at the AAPA, particularly the British chartered accountants, had different opinions as to whether accountancy was in fact a science or an art.[17]

Foremost among the NYIA's leaders was Charles Waldo Haskins, whose outlook had been partly shaped by his early training in engineering. Son of a successful stockbroker who had migrated from Boston in the 1840s and settled his family in comfortable middle-class circumstances, Haskins could trace his ancestry back to the *Mayflower*. This nephew of Ralph Waldo Emerson had been trained in civil engineering at the Brooklyn Polytechnic Institute, from which he was graduated in 1867. Choosing to enter business instead of engineering, the young Haskins began his career as an accountant in the dry-goods firm of Butterfield and Company in Manhattan. During 1875–76 he interrupted his working career to spend two years traveling and studying in Europe. Returning to America, he entered the brokerage business, working for his father's firm until 1886. In that year, at the age of thirty-four, he first established his own office as an "expert accountant."[18]

Haskins's prospects for success in public accountancy received a strong boost from his marriage to Henrietta Havemeyer, the daughter of the wealthy businessman Albert Havemeyer and niece of William F. Havemeyer, the former Democratic mayor of New York who lead the drive to oust the Tweed Ring a decade earlier. Through the Havemeyers, whose fortune was based largely on their control of the American Sugar Refining Company, Haskins obtained a series of choice business and political assignments. During these years he developed the accounting system for the Manhattan Trust Company and also served as that firm's secretary; he was the controller of the Central Georgia Railroad Company, the Ocean Steamship Company, and the Chesapeake and Western Railroad Company.[19]

In politics Haskins served as an expert advisor to various organizations. In 1893 he was appointed, along with his future partner, Elijah Watt Sells, to a bipartisan congressional commission chaired by Congressman Alexander M. Dockery (Democrat, Missouri) to make recommendations for increasing the efficiency of the executive departments of the federal government. Acting on this commission's recommendations, the Cleveland administration eliminated from the federal payrolls hundreds of sinecures that had been filled by persons largely appointed under previous Republican regimes.[20]

Haskins also figured prominently in local governmental affairs. He served for many years on a special committee organized by the National Municipal League to design standardized accounting and finan-

cial reporting systems to enhance the efficiency of municipal governments. In addition, he was a special advisor to a commission established in New York by the reformist Strong administration to study the
financial feasibility of merging Manhattan and Brooklyn into a Greater
City of New York. His firm also pioneered the development of auditing techniques for large municipal governments.[21]

Besides these accomplishments and his excellent connections, Haskins was temperamentally well suited to serve as a leader. Tall and
heavy, with a large, balding pate and a stout bull neck, the Big Chief,
as he was nicknamed, was clearly a vigorous man of great physical
drive. He could project, when the occasion demanded, an image of
cultivation and (for modern tastes, at least) a somewhat ostentatious
erudition. Yet for all these qualities, he never lost the common touch.
In spite of his distinguished background, Haskins could be "one of the
boys" and revel uninhibitedly with great and small alike during
NYIA's "hoot club" dinners.

With regard to the nature of accountancy, Haskins had strong opinions. He was an early and articulate apostle of the notion that this new
"science" could help to perfect society by promoting efficiency and
honesty. This notion seems to have been shaped in part by his uncle's
writings about statistics and the insights it provided into what was
believed to be an ordered universe. Emerson had been favorably
impressed by the conclusions reached by certain European positivists,
particularly Lambert-Adolphe-Jacques Quetelet, who held that statistics had the potential for discovering the underlying harmony between the physical and social worlds. Through the knowledge deriv-
able from statistical analysis, it was possible for man to control what
was previously believed to be ungovernable.

Because of his early training as an engineer, these ideas about the
favorable potentials for statistics and its subset, accountancy, greatly
attracted Haskins. He felt that accountancy should be studied in such
a way as to discover the underlying and fixed principles that would be
vital in both business and governmental affairs. In an age experiencing great changes in values and the structure of social organization,
the potential of a new "science" of accountancy held great appeal.
Accounting allowed the quantification of experience; this prompted
Haskins to believe that business affairs must conform to natural and
immutable laws, as was thought to be the case in engineering and
science. He was eloquent and even lyrical in describing the science of
accounts.

Scientific accountancy is the hub of the universe of commerce, trade and finance; the pivot as it were of the wheel of fortune; the point, if truly centered, about which the business world revolves with the velocity and ease and restful silence of a spinning top.

. . . Accountancy—the higher accountancy if we must distinguish it—is a science and not as some have seemed to suppose, a mere collection of approximate rules. The true accountant thinks out with mathematical accuracy the condition of affairs in any business enterprise. Accountancy is therefore none the less a science whether it works with the knotted strings of the old Peruvians, or with the jackknife and tally-stick of the European baker [sic] or the checkered cloth and counters of the Norman English Exchequer, or with the logismography of the Italian Government. Accountancy—I still say the higher accountancy—records its employer's affairs so that a proprietor, whether a nation, a municipality, a company, a body of voters, or an individual, may know how financial matters stand. Out of this science of accountancy has risen in the development of modern business, our young and sturdy profession.[22]

Other NYIA leaders shared Haskins's view of the essentially scientific nature of accountancy and the useful role it could play in addressing contemporary social problems. Charles E. Sprague, for instance, president of the Union Dime Savings Bank and a close friend of Haskins, described accountancy as a scientific and precise body of knowledge in his classic contributions, "The Algebra of Accounts" and *The Philosophy of Accounts*. Sprague had been a member of Phi Beta Kappa at Union College; his interest in accountancy (like that of his friend Haskins) reflected a broad concern with the perfection of new types of knowledge helpful in ordering modern life. The impulse that sparked Sprague's interest in the theory of accountancy was the same one that caused him to play a prominent role in movements designed to simplify spelling, to promote the use of a world language, "Volapük," and to devote time to the development of bookkeeping and office machinery.[23]

Another NYIA leader, Silas S. Packard, popularized similar notions through the training programs he provided at his highly successful school. The elderly Packard had amassed a fortune through the operation of a successful bookkeeping academy in Manhattan. A generation of bookkeepers in New York had received their training through attendance at Packard's school and the use of his classic work, *The Manual of Theoretical Training in the Science of Accounts*. This educational entrepreneur was highly active in the affairs of the NYIA, partly because its membership was dominated by his former pupils and partly because it provided a vital point of contact with important employers of his school's graduates.[24]

In fact, increasing criticism of the training provided in his academy during the 1890s motivated Packard to keep abreast of new ideas being propounded by leading practitioners like Haskins and prominent businessmen like Sprague. Packard graduates, though capable in routine bookkeeping functions, were thought to be poorly trained for solving the many new and bewildering accounting problems brought about by rapid industrialization. Through contact with these practitioner theorists at the NYIA, Packard hoped to be able to refocus his school's curriculum so that his graduates would be better able to perform their duties successfully.

The last of the early quartet of NYIA leaders was Anson O. Kittredge. Though a practicing public accountant during the 1890s, Kittredge had started his career as editor of a number of metal industry journals, including *Iron Age*, and journals for lawyers and credit managers. In 1901 Kittredge, building on his previous experience in journalism and his current involvement in public accountancy, established a new journal entitled *Commerce, Accounts, and Finance*. This journal and *Accountics*, the official magazine of the NYIA, popularized the new ideas about the science of accounts among both professional accountants and laymen.[25]

Unlike the NYIA, the AAPA did not have a consensus among its leaders as to whether accountancy was "scientific" or not. While they did not articulate their views vehemently (probably to help maintain unity and accord), it is apparent that many of the leading chartered accountants did not view practice as a science. They were influenced by the writings of British statistician Francis Y. Edgeworth of Oxford University, who stressed the inherent limitations of statistical data in providing precise knowledge about conditions in either the physical or the social worlds. To these practitioners, the implications of Edgeworth's writings did not support Haskins's view. Accounting, like statistics, was to them, in essence, "a series of useful approximations" helpful to the master practitioner in depicting economic realities. From this perspective accounting seemed more an art than a science, and its utility seemed dependent upon the virtue, experience, and steady judgment of the seasoned accountant. Although they agreed with their NYIA rivals that accountancy offered great potential for social uplift, they disagreed that it was a precise science connecting business activities to the fundamental ordering of the cosmos.

Many of the American members of the AAPA, however, had absorbed notions about the nature of scientific knowledge during their college training and agreed with Haskins's view. Included in this group were members such as Richard F. Stevens, who had been graduated in engineering from Columbia University; David P. Fackler, who had been trained as a statistician at the City College of New York; William Trenholm, who had been graduated from the University of the South; George H. Church, who had attended Yale University; and Frank Broaker, who had gone to City College. Partly through the influence of these members' ideas, the AAPA was strongly motivated (as we shall see later) to organize an educational institution providing instruction in scientific accountancy.[26]

Changing Patterns of Preparatory Training

Determining the proper focus for training those who wished to enter the profession was a major concern during these years. Discussion of the inadequacies of bookkeeping academies for entry-level practitioners began to emerge during the 1890s. In the view of many public accountants, the training provided in these schools was insufficient to prepare experts. Their programs were criticized for overemphasizing basic bookkeeping procedures and for underemphasizing the theory of accountancy. Appropriate for low-level clerks who could be expected only to perform routine functions requiring little technical judgment, this training did little to prepare graduates for top-level practice.[27]

Sensitivity to the inadequacies of the proprietary academies made many leaders of the AAPA and NYIA highly receptive to the new ideas of such pioneer business educators as Edmund J. James, dean of the new Wharton School of Finance and Economy at the University of Pennsylvania. James, who had received his doctorate in economics from the University of Halle, led a successful movement, first at Wharton and later at the University of Illinois, to establish formal business education programs in the curricula of American colleges and universities. Following models perfected in Germany earlier in the nineteenth century, the Jamesian curricula provided pragmatic training in such basic business functions as accountancy, finance, insurance, marketing, and transportation.

The new school's emphasis on research and the building of comprehensive theoretical frameworks for each of the business specializations were other important departures from the educational directions followed previously in America. Though training was still provided in the basic procedures in narrow specializations such as accountancy, the academic business colleges gave prospective practitioners a sound theoretical grounding. Trained in basic principles, neophytes were thought to be better prepared to apply their special knowledge in an increasingly complex business setting.[28]

Some of the AAPA's leaders wanted to emulate this new school's success in New York. Later, John Heins and John Francis, another prominent Philadelphia practitioner, provided personnel from their firms (including Robert H. Montgomery and Joseph E. Sterrett, both future presidents of the AAPA) to teach evening accounting classes at Wharton beginning in 1904. Impressed by the Wharton curriculum and the central place accorded to accountancy, college-educated American members such as Stevens, Broaker, Church, and Trenholm were soon developing plans to establish an AAPA-sponsored college of accounts in New York. Besides providing practical training like that offered at Wharton, the proposed college was envisioned by its founders as a mechanism for controlling entry into the profession.[29]

Though many chartered accountants who had been apprentices viewed these developments skeptically, a substantial number of British members who had not received a charter strongly supported the college proposal. These practitioners constituted 82 of the 206 members accepted into the association between 1886 and 1905. Indeed, only 20 of the British practitioners admitted during this first period appear to have been chartered accountants. The willingness of the nonchartered practitioners to embrace these new ideas was probably conditioned by the frustrations experienced in their own careers.[30]

Although in Britain the chartered accountants were recognized as an elite class of practitioner, they had not been able to exclude other accountants. In fact, rival associations, the most prominent of which was the Society of Incorporated Accountants and Auditors (SIAA), organized in 1885, arose to provide a formal basis for certifying public accountants from families unable to finance a five-year apprenticeship. While detailed records on the careers of the early British-born members of the AAPA are limited, existing evidence suggests that those who were not chartered shared much the same background and outlook as the SIAA practitioners. Only a few had ever worked in a chartered accountant's office. The majority—including such leaders as H. R. M. Cook, William H. Veysey, and James Yalden—had received their training working in industry or banking or for nonchartered public accountants. Few had become members of the SIAA, apparently because they had emigrated before this association had become well established. Apprenticeship was not a practice these members wished to see adopted in America. Instead, educational institutions accessible to all who had ability were more appealing to those whose advancement in the old world had been retarded because of humble origins.[31]

Neither the academic business colleges nor the (increasingly discredited) proprietary academies had much appeal to those chartered accountants in the AAPA who felt the proper focus for training should be the individual firm. To that generation of experts, the firm was the only place a man could develop judgment and creativity in the solution of accounting problems. There, too, character could be tested and shaped. The chartered accountants believed that by placing the responsibility for screening candidates in the firm, they could prevent entry into the profession of those lacking the gentlemanly qualities of honesty and integrity. Experts called upon to certify the fairness of financial statements and allowed access to their clients' most confidential financial information had to be trusted.[32]

Others, however, thought formal education necessary, and key NYIA leaders would later seek to establish a formal college of accountancy in the context of an existing university. Unlike those in the AAPA, these practitioners did little to implement these ideas through their professional association. Instead, the elite acted independently of their association and tried to interest the trustees of leading universities in New York in establishing a college of business like the one at the University of Pennsylvania. Rebuffed initially by Columbia University, Charles Haskins tried to induce President John H. Mac-Cracken of New York University to organize a new school of "commerce, accounts and finance." Supported by his brother-in-law, James F. Havemeyer, on the four-man board of trustees, Haskins succeeded in 1899 in convincing the cautious MacCracken to support his plan; but, it was rumored, Haskins first had to guarantee personally to reimburse New York University for any loss it might incur in operating the school.[33]

The ideas popularized by James influenced the thinking of the leaders of the new School of Commerce, Accounts, and Finance. Selected as the school's first dean, Haskins hired as instructors his old friends Sprague and Kittredge, who had been instrumental in promoting scientific accountancy. The new educational ideas were further reinforced when Haskins (in 1901) hired Joseph French Johnson, James's colleague at Wharton and fellow graduate student at Halle, to teach and to refine the school's curriculum. In 1903, after Haskins's untimely death, Johnson became the new dean. A leading exponent of Jamesian educational ideas was therefore in a key administrative post in this highly successful school.[34]

Problems of National and Social Identity

Besides their differences over the nature of accounting knowledge and the appropriate training for new entrants, the NYIA and the AAPA practitioners also disagreed about national values. Like the elite practitioners of the AAPA, the top men of the NYIA were sensitive to the threat to traditional values posed by the influx of new immigrants. Unlike the AAPA practitioners, however, the NYIA leaders reacted by asserting what they thought were uniquely American values. They did this in their individual careers and through their involvement with nonprofessional associations.

In the experience of Charles Haskins, certainly an important leader in the NYIA, we can see how the changes caused by massive immigration, industrialization, and urbanization heightened concerns about preserving distinctly American values. During the 1890s Haskins became deeply involved in several elite, ultrapatriotic associations, including America's Founders and Defenders, the Sons of Colonial Wars, and the Sons of the American Revolution (SAR). In the last-named organization he eventually became national treasurer and a member of the governing board. The patriotic ideals espoused by these organizations represented the reaction of the older nativist elites to perceived threats to the country's traditional social structure and values.[35]

Although the changes America was experiencing promised material abundance, they also seemed to men of Haskins's background to threaten the basic values on which it had been established. The new opportunities for building wealth created greater opportunities for venality, corruption, and the decline of both civic and personal virtue. Massive immigration from countries with cultural traditions and values quite dissimilar to those in America made the crisis more acute.

Typical of the responses of the more liberal and optimistic nativists were the "Americanization" programs promoted by the SAR. This national association (1889) was led by elite eastern businessmen and politicians, including such notables as Chauncey M. Depew, president of the New York Central Railroad and Republican senator from New York, and Whitelaw Reid, editor of the *New York Tribune*.

A primary concern of the SAR was how best to assimilate the immigrant hordes flooding into the nation's cities, particularly those in the

Northeast. Their answer was through a vigorous educational program aimed at propagating American values among the new arrivals. The SAR printed literature in many languages for recent immigrants. The programs and pamphlets would help the immigrant, it was thought, to adjust successfully to a new society that allowed greater freedom but also demanded greater individual initiative than was typical in Europe. Through its literature the SAR tried to draw the immigrant away from the dark and dangerous political doctrines of socialism, anarchism, or autocracy and to substitute a love for American democratic and liberal traditions.[36]

This preservation of distinctly American traditions may also have pulled Haskins away from the AAPA, which identified closely with British traditions. Although he could trace his own ancestry back to the founders of the Bay Colony, he did not identify strongly with British traditions. Although Haskins had been a charter member of the AAPA, he soon lost interest and resigned in 1889. There was, perhaps, some "push" as well as "pull," since the leading chartered accountants were cool toward Haskins's notions about the "science of accountancy."[37]

Haskins's connection with the Havemeyers, a link so important in helping to advance his career, probably influenced his attitude about an organization as strongly Anglophilic as the AAPA. As leaders of the German community in New York, the Havemeyers must have been sensitive to the tensions generated by the increasing competition between British and German business interests in world markets. Henry O. Havemeyer, the organizer of the Sugar Trust, had experienced extreme competition from the Scotch-Irish Arbuckle Brothers Company (based in Pittsburgh). As leaders in the liberal, reform wing of the Democratic party, the Havemeyers championed the rights of man and vehemently opposed imperialism. From their perspective, Britain represented one of the worst examples of a nation practicing imperialistic policies in world affairs.[38]

Another nationalist strain affecting the NYIA leadership derived from the experiences of those who had fought in the Civil War. Charles Sprague for instance, had volunteered as a private and had distinguished himself in combat at the Little Round Top during the second day of fighting at Gettysburg. Invalided out because of wounds received in this engagement, Sprague still remained active in the New York state militia (in which he eventually rose to the rank of colonel); after the war he served for a period as an instructor in military science at the United States Military Academy at West Point and at the Peekskill Military Academy.[39] Selden R. Hopkins was another

NYIA leader who had served in the Union army. A consciousness of having been involved in the great struggle to preserve the legacy of the Founding Fathers was a central emotional constellation in both their characters.

From the perspective of men with such experiences, an organization such as the AAPA was too closely associated with British professional traditions. Though they might trace their ancestry back to Britain, it was difficult for them not to feel suspicion toward a nation that had abetted the Confederacy in its effort to withdraw from the Union. This may help to explain why Sprague had declined an offer of membership in the AAPA when it was originally organized in 1886.

There were also diplomatic tensions between the United States and Great Britain during the 1890s in Latin America and the Pacific. American nationalists were shocked by the British challenge to the Monroe Doctrine in Nicaragua in 1895. Relations worsened further when portions of the American press stoked the flames of war hysteria over the conflict that had arisen between these two countries about the resolution of the Venezuelan–British Guianan boundary dispute. The events leading to the eventual annexation of the Hawaiian islands also created well-publicized friction between these two nations. Understandably, the old soldiers at the NYIA thought the worst about British diplomatic intentions.[40]

There were, in addition, many practitioners of Irish descent in the NYIA. Leaders such as John E. Hourigan of Albany and E. L. Fitzgerald, Henry Harney, and James M. Kelly of New York City were members of a generation to which the great famine of 1842 and the suppression of the revolutionary Fenian Brotherhood were relatively recent events. For them, the American republic represented an ideal society that had achieved self-determination and democracy, goals long frustrated in Ireland by British rule. Consequently, it was not difficult for them to feel antagonistic toward any association promoting British traditions in their new homeland.[41]

Competition over Professional Designations

These deep-seated differences in outlook surfaced in the form of an open competition over designations of professional competency. Criticism of the legitimacy of particular symbols of competence was a major factor contributing to the intraprofessional conflicts prior to enactment of licensing legislation in 1896. The NYIA members felt, with some justification, that the chartered accountants' success in attracting quality clientele resulted largely from the prestige associated with their special insignia of professional competence. The NYIA members attempted in two ways to counter the advantage that the special initials "C.A." provided chartered accountants. First, the NYIA members invented their own unique designations. Institute practitioners began to place the letters "F.I.A.," for "Fellow of the Institute of Accounts," after their names. Later, the NYIA developed and administered a four-part examination certifying the competency of successful candidates. Anyone who passed the test was given a certificate designating him or her as a "certified accountant" (CA).[42]

The NYIA's issuance of these certificates induced the AAPA's leaders to initiate legal action barring the rival association from granting degrees. They were infuriated by what they regarded as the NYIA's fraudulent misrepresentation. American practitioners such as Frank Broaker and Richard Chapman were so incensed that in 1895 they lodged formal protests with Melvil Dewey, secretary to the New York State Board of Regents. They successfully asserted that by granting "degrees," which the regents regulated in New York, the NYIA had, in effect, exceeded the authority granted in its charter of incorporation. This action soon ended the NYIA's brief experiment.[43]

A second response of some NYIA members was not so constructive as the effort to create a mechanism for validating competency. This competition took the form of some practitioners' disparagement of their rivals' claims to authority. Mutual defamation took place, for instance, through advertisements and later through scorching letters to the editor of the *New York Tribune*, messages written by Farquhar MacRae, a fiery American accountant who had served as NYIA president. He was annoyed by William Waddell, a chartered accountant practicing in New York. In their advertisements for staff accountants, each pointedly implied that accountants certified by the association to which they did not belong were inferior. This pettiness gradually escalated to rancorous and vituperative letters in the editorial page. The exchange was finally extinguished by the newspaper's owners, who were reluctant to allow their journal to be transformed into a cockpit for two valued but eccentric advertisers.[44]

Problems and Prospects

The polarization in the public accountancy profession during this early period thus derived not only from fundamental differences in attitude about technical accounting matters but also from the differing values and outlooks about the major events affecting American society. The two groups had opposing outlooks about the directions that the process of professionalization should follow. Differing ideas about science, economic regulation, and education as well as concerns about nationality, ethnicity, and social status remained unresolved. Operating in a social milieu that provided few incentives for seeking accommodation and compromise, practitioners used these differing outlooks as rallying flags in their efforts to dominate the new profession for their particular coteries.

Practitioners first tried to resolve their differences during the 1890s, when they sought power from state governments to regulate their profession. This initial effort centered on the state rather than national level for several reasons. First, the scope of practice for most independent accountants was often confined to a single state, as was the case in the older professions of law and medicine. Second, under America's federal system, professional licensing had traditionally been a power of state governmental bodies. Furthermore, contemporary efforts to establish new national structures of economic regulation that might have influenced the development of accountancy were seriously impeded by legal actions for over a decade. The success of business groups in challenging in the courts the authority of agencies such as the ICC obviated the need for the type of associational governance that admirers of British forms of economic regulation advocated. Finally, many members were also reluctant to see the AAPA play a more active role in the emerging debate over national economic regulation for fear of alienating important client groups.

But the failure of these rival groups to reconcile their differences thwarted their efforts to obtain from the state special status for their unique skills. The hurtful competition between rival practitioner organizations in New York during the critical years from 1892 to 1896 confused the political leadership whose aid was sought in securing this desired special status. During these years it was impossible for potential political allies to determine with confidence where the proper focus of authority was centered in this new and poorly understood profession. As a consequence, political leaders were reluctant to provide strong regulatory powers for the governance of public accountancy. Instead, unlike for the better-established professions of law or medicine, for accounting they passed a weak bill that did not restrict practice to licensees. The New York law—which was to function as a model for virtually all of the states that later adopted similar legislation—merely provided legal protection to a special title of professional competency.

The Emergence of the CPA Movement, 1892–1906

The continued competition between the AAPA and the NYIA set in motion a complex series of events that eventually resulted in the establishment of a formal framework of professional governance at the state and national levels. This chapter analyzes these related developments. First, it traces the pioneering of New York accountants to gain legal recognition for their special skills. Ultimately, this drive led, as it did earlier in medicine and law, to the promulgation of licensing legislation. Second, it focuses on the subsequent formation of a new, federated organization to coordinate the profession-building activities of accountants nationwide.

In the first transition the AAPA tried independently to obtain special status for its members in New York by redefining the boundaries of the community of competent practitioners through specification of formal educational requirements. This failed largely because of the greater political acumen and influence of the NYIA among the leadership of the New York State Board of Regents, the agency regulating higher education. Later, the AAPA tried to achieve its goals by promoting legislation for qualifying licensing examinations. Though delayed by a falling-out among leaders of the Republican party, this effort finally succeeded after the rival associations suppressed their competition to lever the state's legislators more effectively. The resultant unity reassured a legislature called upon to mandate regulatory laws.

But the AAPA soon lost control over both the content of the new law and the board appointed to administer it. Its leaders underestimated the importance of getting the active support of bureaucrats in the state's educational civil service and the members of the independent board of regents.

The failure of the state licensing model to resolve the problem of assuring access to local markets for firms developing national practices catalyzed the second transition in professional ordering. To serve large-scale enterprises in manufacturing and transportation efficiently, leading firms established networks of offices in major cities. But the danger existed that they might be prevented from so doing by restrictive legislation promoted by local groups.

Like their major clients, the larger public accounting firms found it vital to practice in all states. The development of national practices had started on a limited basis during the early 1890s, when leading chartered accounting firms began opening branches in Chicago to serve clients in the Middle and Far West.[1] This trend accelerated during the merger boom of 1898–1904. Investors, particularly those in Europe, increasingly demanded the certification of the financial statements included in the prospectuses for securities issued to finance these consolidations.[2]

The growth of the national firms directly paralleled the organization of a host of state public accounting associations, whose members followed New York's example by lobbying for licensing legislation. By 1905 twenty-one state professional societies for public accountants (in, for instance, Illinois, Pennsylvania, Maryland, Massachusetts, and New Jersey) had been organized. Although membership remained modest in many, several associations became large enough to support successful efforts to establish state licensing laws in nine states by 1905.[3]

The proliferation of state laws induced many leaders of national firms to support the program of a new association organized in 1902, the Federation of State Societies of Public Accountants in the United States of America. Elite national practitioners founded the federation primarily in order to solve the problem of inconsistent state regulation and to thereby avoid having to pursue the alternative of federal legislation. They concentrated, as did contemporary medical practitioners, on developing model professional laws to assure uniform national regulation that did not discriminate against their interests.[4]

Confederation eventually succeeded because it proved effective in resolving two major problems critical to national professional governance. The first was that of structuring the institution so that professional development within particular states conformed to a common standard without threatening the jealously guarded autonomy of local professional societies. The second was that of inducing both the state societies and the older and more prestigious AAPA (which already viewed itself as the true national representative of the profession) to merge under the aegis of the Federation.

The First Effort: The College of Accounts, 1892–1895

In 1892, the AAPA began a drive to receive a charter from the New York State Board of Regents both to establish a college providing accounting instruction and to control entry into the profession. Not surprisingly, the plan was most strongly supported by British and American AAPA members—including Frank Broaker, Richard M. Chapman, Richard Stevens, and the British-born sea captain *cum* public accountant, H. R. M. Cook—who were not members of the prestigious Institute of Chartered Accountants.[5]

Besides soothing status anxiety, the college was also viewed as an effective mechanism for controlling entry into what was then a highly amorphous free market for accounting services. Under the AAPA's plan, prospective entrants to the profession were required to complete a one-thousand-hour course of studies over a two-year period. Like the pragmatic program being developed at the Wharton School in Philadelphia (involving some AAPA members), the program of the proposed College of Accounts sought to train experts in a narrow business specialization.[6] The curriculum included training in auditing, business law, accounting theory, and accounting practice. Unlike the Wharton School, however, the college was to operate independently of any established university, and its faculty was to be composed exclusively of practitioners with no apparent interest in promoting research or other scholarly endeavors. Successful candidates would receive a bachelor's degree. Graduates would also be required to complete a one-year apprenticeship before receiving a master's degree and becoming eligible to practice independently.[7] This plan foundered, however, because of the opposition of the NYIA and its allies in the state bureaucracy and because of the worsening of the long economic depression.

The NYIA's success in Albany was due to the influence of Sprague, Packard, and Haskins among the regents and their administrative staff. Charles Sprague was a close friend of the regents' secretary, Melvil Dewey (inventor of the Dewey decimal system for cataloging library materials).[8] The colonel had served as an officer in Dewey's Modern Language Association, which promoted, among other causes, "simplified spelling" of the English language and a world language known as "Volapük."[9] Sprague and Charles Haskins also advised Dewey on accountancy and finance instruction for the secretary's pioneering program in home economics at the state university in Albany. Silas Packard was also close to Dewey, for they had been drawn together by their mutual interest in vocational education.[10]

Additionally, Haskins enjoyed strong connections in the liberal wing of the Democratic party through his marriage into the politically influential Havemeyer family.[11] Dewey, originally appointed in Albany by a Democratic regime, soon began to cultivate Haskins's friendship. The NYIA also enjoyed influence with key regents because of Haskins's SAR involvement. Through this connection he became acquainted with three regents: Chancellor Whitelaw Reid (editor of the *New York Tribune*), Vice-Chancellor William Croswell Doane (national chaplain of the SAR), and board member and Republican senator Chauncey M. Depew (president of the SAR).

Like the NYIA leaders, Dewey was concerned about the implications of the new immigration, but, unlike Haskins, who shared his uncle Emerson's optimism about America's ability to assimilate new peoples, he was far more pessimistic. Indeed, anxieties about immigration and its effects warped the personality of this modern Renaissance man, who played a key role in the professionalizing of library science, home economics, and philology. This xenophobia manifested itself in flagrantly racialist feelings that later drove Dewey from public life.[12]

From Dewey's perspective, the threat to the political leadership of the old nativist elite was already apparent in his own Democratic party. Containing the power of the despised Irish Catholics (who dominated Tammany Hall and the state's urban machines) had long been a problem for the independent Cleveland Democrats. Maintaining control of the party became increasingly difficult because of the influx of new immigrants beginning in the 1890s.[13] Particularly feared were the representatives of the state's rapidly growing Jewish community. Led by an elite of successful bankers and merchants, this group was becoming more influential, to Dewey's dismay, in politics.[14]

The special pleading of the NYIA's leadership was appealing to Dewey. Besides providing a means for validating practitioner competency, their plan would place control in the hands of reliable men whom he may have mistakenly believed shared his profound pessimism about contemporary social trends. In New York the older elites' ability to order society through the electoral process was diminishing as the numbers of immigrant voters grew. State agencies such as the regents and their subsidiary licensing boards, however, remained bastions of the elite. These agencies, which could restrict the entry of those judged either incompetent or unfit, were ideal vehicles for preserving the economic and social positions of the nativist middle class.

Dewey was also reluctant to accept the AAPA's college plan because of the political opposition it was expected to engender. As the chief

administrative officer responsible for formulating the regents' legislative recommendations, he had to consider the attitude of the incumbent governor. David B. Hill, a Tammany Democrat, was unreceptive
to proposals for increasing the regents' influence. He was hostile
because this institution was largely staffed by independents, such as
Dewey, from the hated Cleveland wing of the Democratic party and
because its board was dominated by a mélange of independent Democrats and Republicans. Hill unsuccessfully sought to merge the regents into the New York Department of Public Instruction, which
regulated secondary and primary education.[15] Besides enabling him
to cast out political opponents, such a reorganization would have
provided Hill with great patronage opportunities. Frustrated by his
inability to generate support for this design, Hill adopted a policy of
obstructionism.[16]

Because of the positions of the governor and the NYIA's leadership,
the regents rejected the AAPA's plan and suggested that it be modified
in crucial ways. Though concerned about the college's potential monopoly power, they opposed most the curriculum, which seemed
insufficient to warrant the granting of a degree. Instead, the regents
recommended that the AAPA consider operating a school to train
novices. They also criticized the proposal's lack of a financial plan.[17]

Though the plan was recast to conform to the regents' requirements, the AAPA soon abandoned the strategy of using educational
institutions as mechanisms to define professional boundaries. When
organized, the School of Accounts lasted only one year. It failed because of competition from better-established proprietary academies
and the worsening of the economic depression. Moreover, many
members lost interest after it became apparent that the school would
not exercise any significant control over the profession.[18]

The Second Effort:
The Success of Licensing Legislation, 1895–1896

Although the College of Accounts did not succeed, the AAPA was
soon again drawn into competition with the NYIA over state licensing. The AAPA wanted licensing legislation to displace the NYIA's
practice of issuing certified accountant's degrees to members who
passed its qualifying examination. Individual AAPA members lodged
formal complaints with the regents. From the AAPA's perspective, this
certification violated both the powers granted the NYIA in its state
charter and the state regulations for educational degrees.[19]

In 1895, the AAPA sponsored a licensing bill to head off a similar effort that the NYIA was rumored to be planning. The AAPA's bill limited practice to those who passed a state-administered examination. In developing this design, its leadership was probably influenced both by the existing patterns for law and medicine in New York and also by the Institute of Chartered Accountants' unsuccessful 1891 bill in Parliament for the exclusive right to provide public accounting services in Britain.[20]

The AAPA submitted its bill to the New York State Senate through Senator Daniel Bradley on February 28, 1895. It restricted practice to those who passed the examination or to those in practice for at least five years at the time of the legislation's enactment. Emulating the chartered accountants, the AAPA also required a five-year apprenticeship before a candidate could sit for the examination.[21]

The NYIA submitted through Republican representative Payson Wilds a competing bill on March 6. It differed from the AAPA's in two important respects. First, it did not limit practice exclusively to licensees. Instead, it sought only to establish a state examination for certifying professional competency and to limit the use of the title "certified public accountant." Second, the NYIA bill allowed only American citizens to sit for the examination, a provision aimed at disqualifying the many British subjects in the AAPA.[22]

The presentation of the competing bill in the New York assembly caused the leadership of the AAPA to seek a compromise. They desired rapprochement for two reasons. First, the image of a united profession supporting legislation, especially for a relatively obscure one such as public accounting, would impress skeptical legislators. Second, unity would allow the AAPA to benefit from the NYIA's political influence.[23]

To form a consensus, the AAPA's leaders organized a public meeting in New York City on March 13, 1895. At this conclave the Committee of Fourteen was established, representing the AAPA, the NYIA, public accountants not affiliated with either professional association, and operators of the proprietary bookkeeping schools. Eventually, the committee agreed to back the NYIA bill after it was cleared of the section barring accountants who were not citizens. During April and May of 1895, the committee and its attorney, E. G. Whitaker, worked with Dewey to advance this legislation.[24]

Nevertheless, the accountants were unsuccessful in 1895 in part because of Senator Thomas C. Platt, leader of the regular Republican party organization in New York, and his disinterest in legislation thought to benefit elements close to the reform wings of both major parties. The effectiveness of Boss Platt's political machine depended upon its ability to preserve the loyalty of his upstate constituents through patronage. This need to distribute public largess to maintain political power, however, drew the Platt Republicans into conflict with urban reformers. The long-standing gulf between the regular Republicans and the reform leadership of both major parties widened because of Platt's efforts to increase his political power after his organization's great victory in the New York state elections of 1894 over a badly divided Democratic party.[25]

Encouraged by electoral success, Platt tried to strengthen his organization in the traditionally Democratic city of New York, thereby starting a conflict with some of the profession's staunchest political allies. He supported the Lexow bill to consolidate Manhattan and Brooklyn into a Greater City of New York and introduced bills to enable the state to regulate many municipal services.[26]

When professional leaders allied with reform politicians opposed Platt, he denied his support for the licensing legislation. Senator Bradley opposed Platt's proposals, as did New York's mayor, William L. Strong, whose fusion administration had engaged Charles Haskins as an advisor on the economic feasibility of a Greater City of New York.[27] The opposition to Platt's legislation also included Joseph H. Choate, who was identified with the public accountants.[28] Bitter feelings would shortly develop between Choate and Platt from their rivalry over a legislative appointment to a vacated United States senate seat for New York in 1897.[29] Boss Platt thus had ample cause to deny the support of his organization to the proposed licensing legislation.

Meanwhile, the newly elected Republican regime, anxious to increase the scope of its patronage opportunities, attacked Secretary Dewey's management of the state university and library. Platt sought to oust the independent Democrat Dewey and fill the many comfortable sinecures available in the state university. The attack took the form of a legislative investigation of Dewey's alleged graft and malfeasance in office. Although the investigation ultimately failed to substantiate any charges, Dewey's ability to function effectively as the regents' legislative liaison was greatly diminished.[30]

Because of these developments, Payson Wilds, sponsor of the NYIA bill, did little to advance the legislation in 1895. Impatient for results, however, the AAPA leaders, operating apparently on their own initiative, induced their spokesman, Daniel Bradley, to begin legislative action on the compromise bill in the senate. But lacking Platt's support, independent Democrat Bradley was unable even to get the bill reported out of committee.[31]

The denouement occurred in 1896, when the regular Republicans decided to cooperate with its reform wing in a presidential election year. Boss Platt was receptive to compromise to build support for New York governor Levi P. Morton's candidacy for the Republican nomination. Though Morton's bid failed, it was still important for Platt to accommodate the urban reform wing to assure the victory of the McKinley-Roosevelt ticket over Bryan. This cooperation was expressed by the regular Republican leadership accepting a broad range of issues—including a weak licensing bill for public accountancy—important to urban liberals.[32]

By that time, too, the investigative committee had failed to prove its charges against Dewey. Now free from political harassment, the regents' chief administrative officer was again able to function as an effective legislative liaison.

Although the political impediments to licensing were removed in 1896, the fragile coalition of practitioners soon disintegrated. The rival associations again acted independently to gain their own legislative objectives. The AAPA concentrated on working closely with legislators, whereas the NYIA worked through the regents' secretary.

The prime mover in shepherding the AAPA's bill in Albany was Frank Broaker, who worked closely with two reform Republican politicians from Brooklyn, Albert A. Wray and Henry Marshall. These two had been swept into office in the 1895 Republican landslide. Under their aegis the licensing bill moved swiftly through committee and ultimately through both chambers of the legislature.[33]

The NYIA, on the other hand, represented by Sprague, Packard, and Haskins, shaped the legislation through their connections with Melvil Dewey. In their dealings Sprague exploited the economic pressures Dewey was experiencing in trying to develop the Placid Club.[34] Dewey had undertaken an ambitious plan to expand the small resort into an important summer retreat for leading intellectuals and men of affairs. Though the new club ultimately succeeded outstandingly and attracted vacationers of the caliber of Nicholas Murray Butler, in 1896 Dewey was heavily in debt to finance the construction of enlarged facilities, and he was anxious to attract prospective renters or purchasers. To build goodwill, Colonel Sprague, the banker, and his family patronized the resort and also led his friend Dewey to believe that he wished eventually to become an investor.[35]

The relationship between Sprague and Dewey proved advantageous in helping the NYIA to achieve its objectives. Through his role as liaison, Dewey, during the course of negotiations with legislative committees, could significantly modify the proposed law to strengthen his friends' position. These conferences resulted in two favorable changes for the NYIA. First, the revision authorized the regents (and not the professional association) to appoint the three-man examining board, in effect assuring Dewey a key role in the selection process. Second, the revised bill limited certification to American citizens or those "intending to become American citizens." Though the Americanization clause did not discriminate against the foreign-born as blatantly as the original NYIA draft did, its ambiguity caused real concerns to British practitioners in the AAPA.[36]

After this law's enactment on April 17, 1896, the surprised AAPA leadership realized how extensive the NYIA's victory was. Traveling to New York City that month to negotiate with prospective purchasers for the Placid Club, Dewey met with Sprague to discuss appointments to the three-member examining board. In May he also consulted S. S. Packard.[37] Dewey, of course, chose two NYIA leaders—Charles Haskins, who would be chairman, and Colonel Sprague—to serve on the board. Haskins and Sprague and later their nominees continued to dominate the board until 1905.[38]

Dewey's desire to preserve what he perceived to be the threatened leadership of the nativist middle class strongly influenced his choices during these years. He believed the old social order was endangered. Dismayed by the inability of the electoral process to control alien elements, he tried to protect an older social order by creating a new regulatory structure. Forging alliances with "reliable" practitioners, Dewey—insulated from the electoral process by a board whose nativist members were appointed for life—exerted significant power over activities in a new profession that steadily became important in the emerging urban-industrial society. These structures promised to harness new forms of useful knowledge in support of the social objectives he desired.

Conflict over the New York State
Board of CPA Examiners

Although the AAPA's prestige had been temporarily enhanced because of its role in gaining enactment of the New York licensing law (1896), it soon entered a period of relative decline. Its leadership allowed themselves to be distracted by competition over local matters with rival professional groups. Though the AAPA claimed to be a national professional association, it had in fact been dominated for years by an elite largely limited to the New York metropolitan region.

While the association included individuals who would eventually build large national practices, the majority's perspective was local. This was reflected in the close relationships, noted above, that developed between this organization and such great local merchants as James Thurber and Lucius M. Stanton.[39]

Consequently, the AAPA leaders focused their main energies after 1896 on an unsuccessful attempt to control the New York State Board of Examiners for Certified Public Accountancy. It was soon apparent that the regents had relegated the AAPA to a minority position. Although the AAPA nominated Frank Broaker and W. Sanders Davies, an English chartered accountant, as examiners, the regents appointed only the former.[40]

The AAPA's position soon became even more tenuous. Haskins and Sprague tried to force Broaker's resignation in 1898 because of an alleged conflict of interest. Because he had published a book entitled *American Accountant's Manual*, which was designed to prepare candidates for the CPA examination, he was said to have undermined his ability to function as an independent and unbiased examiner. Though Broaker successfully defended his position with the assistance of his attorney, Clarence F. Birdseye, his prestige was badly tarnished, and the incident undermined his effectiveness as an examiner.[41]

Haskins and Sprague's capture of the examining board appeared ominous to the AAPA leadership. Although, in fact, most practitioners licensed through 1903 did so under waiver, the board's procedures were frequently lengthy and frustrating for applicants. Clarence Birdseye soon developed a thriving practice representing practitioners whose credentials the board had challenged. The expense and delay frequently experienced in certification reinforced the suspicions of many AAPA members about the motivations of a board dominated by their rivals.[42]

Concern over impartiality heightened in 1900, when the board decided not to grant licenses under waiver to four eminently qualified English chartered accountants. This decision was made by a reconstituted board, the majority of whose members were close to Haskins (who had recently resigned to become the dean of New York University's new School of Commerce, Accounts, and Finance). The English accountants were Arthur Lowes Dickinson, the partner in charge of Price Waterhouse's practice in America; his partner, Henry M. Wilmot; Rupert S. Hughes, operating on his own account; and George Wilkinson, most recently affiliated with Barrow, Wade, and Guthrie. They were denied licenses not because they lacked experience or qualifications but because they had not applied for citizenship in the requisite five years before the law's effective date. This decision was sustained on appeal to the regents in 1902. What was most ironic about this development was that in 1902 Dickinson directed the audit of the newly organized United States Steel Corporation, the largest industrial engagement hitherto performed in this country.[43]

Concerns about evenhandedness also may have extended to the board's administration of the semiannual examinations. The test was divided into four parts: commercial law, the theory of accounts, auditing, and accounting practice. Many established practitioners—particularly those not affiliated with the associations of the majority of the examiners—were reluctant to sit for the exam, and their reluctance may have stemmed from that fact that portions of the test consisted of oral interrogations by the board. Since only about one-third of the candidates passed during these years, there may very well have been misgivings about the equitableness of this process, particularly of the subjective oral portion. Later, the pass rates declined further, reaching an all-time low of 2 percent in New York in 1916. Interestingly, none of the four chartered accountants denied licenses by waiver tried to cure his problem by sitting for the examination.[44]

Dissatisfied with its role in professional governance, the AAPA, from 1898 to 1900, attempted to overturn the law it had earlier worked so hard to promote. In 1898, with the presidency of the disgruntled Broaker, the AAPA sponsored legislation transferring authority for appointing the board from the regents. But this measure did not pass.[45]

Because of its lack of success, the AAPA began to lose members to rival organizations. The primary beneficiary was the New York State Society of Certified Public Accountants (NYSSCPA), founded in 1897 by Charles Haskins and several of his close associates from the NYIA (including Colonel Sprague, Anson Kittredge, and Henry Harney). It was committed to promoting the CPA certificate as the sole badge of professional competence and to "the purpose of cultivating and promoting the science of public accounting." It was led by practitioners having influence on the examining board and potent political connections in Albany. It attracted those who wanted an organization dedicated exclusively to promoting the CPA. The AAPA's efforts to force the revision of the 1897 legislation contributed to the defection of some members who, like Francis Gottesberger, had worked hard to assure its initial enactment. Meanwhile, the success of such NYSSCPA leaders as Haskins and Sprague in establishing the new College of Commerce, Finance, and Accounts at New York University also helped to draw away AAPA practitioners. Besides, the NYSSCPA's membership fees were lower than the AAPA's.[46]

Several prominent AAPA members from New Jersey and Pennsylvania either withdrew or reduced markedly their commitment to its activities. Joseph E. Sterrett, for instance, resigned and concentrated on the Pennsylvania Institute of Public Accountants and its efforts to obtain professional licensing there. Three-time president Richard Stevens also followed a similar course at the New Jersey Society of Public Accountants.[47]

In response to these developments, the AAPA's leaders encouraged the organization of yet another association, the National Society of Certified Public Accountants (NSCPA), devoted to the promotion of CPA legislation. The NSCPA grew rapidly during its early years to about fifty members, but its impact on the profession was slight. Although it continued to exist until 1940, it did not meet the challenge of the NYSSCPA or the other state associations.[48]

Since rivalry among organizations was not working, the AAPA's leaders turned toward cooperation. In 1899, Leonard H. Conant, who was strongly committed to establishing amicable relations among New York's major professional associations, was elected to the first of two consecutive terms as AAPA president. Conant's initiatives were reciprocated by Charles Haskins, who had gradually come to realize that he had much in common with the elite practitioners of the AAPA. Although this rapprochement lacked grass-roots support (particularly among the NYSSCPA membership), the skillful diplomacy of like-minded leaders cooled tensions in the New York professional community through 1903.[49]

Conant and Haskins compromised on the examining board's membership. The regents unofficially agreed to appoint to the board one representative from each of the three leading New York professional associations. Though a formal request had been turned down, the regents implemented this policy after 1900, when Charles Haskins and Colonel Sprague resigned their posts to take up teaching duties at NYU's School of Commerce, Accounts, and Finance. The board included Conant as the representative of the AAPA, John Sparrow as the representative of the NYSSCPA, and John R. Loomis as the representative of the newly organized NSCPA.[50]

Haskins had personal reasons for cooperating with Conant and the AAPA. He was aware of how these connections could enhance his firm's reputation in the London financial market. Although his firm had built a strong reputation as accounting specialists and auditors serving railroads and municipalities in America, it was not well known in Britain. To remedy this, he first merged with the partnership of Conant and Grant, which maintained a London office. His decision to seek readmission to the Anglophile AAPA in 1901 was also consistent with his desire to gain acceptance and recognition in London, as was his trip there the following year to address the Institute of Chartered Accountants.[51]

Haskins and Conant helped to generate a new spirit of cooperation between the rival associations. The groups created joint legislative liaison committees. The AAPA also supported Dean Haskins's new School of Commerce, Accounts, and Finance at NYU, and Haskins and Sells personnel joined the AAPA. As early as October 1899, Conant succeeded in establishing a joint legislative liaison committee with the NYSSCPA. Although the associations still differed over the Bennett bill, an unsuccessful effort to extend the qualifying period for a license under the waiver provision, they cooperated on other legislative matters. In an important symbolic move, Conant induced the AAPA to establish a one-hundred-dollar scholarship at Haskins's School of Commerce, Accounts, and Finance.[52]

Still, tensions remained. Many American accountants resented the growing national practices of the British chartered accountants. The plight of the recently arrived chartered accountants who were denied licenses in New York, for instance, was virtually ignored during Conant's presidency as well as that of his successor and fellow examining board member, Ferdinand W. Lafrentz. Arthur Lowes Dickinson had asked the AAPA for help in his efforts to receive a CPA license in New York, but his appeal was "placed on the table." Conant apparently decided to avoid the danger of resurrecting interassociational factionalism by ignoring the Dickinson matter. While in the short run this choice solved a problem for Conant and Haskins, in the long run it gave rise to an effort to build yet another national professional organization.[53]

Moreover, the efforts of Conant and Haskins were incomplete because their plans concentrated exclusively on New York. Although this state had for many years the largest and fastest-growing community of public accountants, the profession was also growing in other parts of the nation. The leaders of the New York professional associations did little to guide the efforts of practitioners in other states. While the AAPA provided monetary support to some practitioners who sought to build state public accounting organizations (as in New Jersey), it really had no comprehensive plan for developing a national structure for the profession.[54]

The Illinois Licensing Law and Interstate Reciprocity

The movement to create a national structure was launched by British chartered accountants based in Chicago. They sought a uniform national system. They opposed legislation, such as that in New York, which militated against the interests of foreign practitioners, particularly those who had landed in this country immediately prior to the law enactment. At the center of this new movement was Arthur Lowes Dickinson of Price Waterhouse. Possibly sensing that professional jealousy lay at the heart of his rejection, Dickinson, the Cambridge master wrangler in mathematics, refused to submit to examination in New York (as had a few other chartered accountants who sought CPA licenses).[55]

Dickinson and other leading chartered accountants had shifted the primary focus of their professional activities to Chicago, where they sought to shape developments through the Illinois Society of Public Accountants (ISPA). Working through this society, Dickinson and his colleagues obtained favorable licensing legislation and, later, strove to start a national movement. Cleverly, Dickinson had members of his firm throughout the United States apply for membership in the Illinois society. By 1903, nearly one-third of the ISPA's fifty-four-man membership was from Price Waterhouse, thus assuring Dickinson's control.[56]

He and the ISPA pushed through a licensing law (1903) broadly similar to New York's in its practitioner training and experience requirements. The examining board was, in this case, a special department in the state university, and the Illinois legislation also introduced two additional innovations advantageous to the large local community of chartered accountants. First, through its reciprocity clause, the new law sought to protect national firm practitioners from exclusion in other states because of restrictive laws. Practitioners licensed in other jurisdictions and possessing qualifications equivalent to those required in Illinois were granted licenses provided that their home states extended this same privilege to Illinois practitioners. Second, a candidate's years of professional experience outside Illinois qualified when the candidate applied for a license under the waiver provision (provided his firm had maintained an office in Illinois for at least five years prior to the effective date of its law). This benefited many chartered accountants whose firms had operated in Chicago since the early 1890s. Not surprisingly, it did not favor the firm of Haskins and Sells, which had not established a Chicago office until 1899.[57]

The reciprocity clause put a premium on other states adopting a similar provision and encouraged the organization in 1902 of the Federation of State Societies of Public Accountants in the United States of America. This body promoted state CPA licensing throughout the country that was both uniform in content and did not discriminate against accountants practicing nationwide.

The Federation of State Societies of Public Accountants in the United States of America

George Wilkinson was the prime mover in launching the federation. His plan, similar to one adopted by the Chicago-based American Medical Association, was based on a decentralized administrative structure. He realized that in such a vast country as America a loose federation of state societies working in concert with a closely affiliated national organization would be more effective than the highly centralized structures appropriate for smaller nations like England.[58]

Wilkinson also recognized the need for the active participation of the larger and more prestigious associations such as the AAPA and the NYSSCPA. He experienced his first success during October 1902. While in Manchester, England, to celebrate his parents' golden wedding anniversary, he met with Charles Haskins to discuss the feasibility of his plan. Haskins, who was in Britain to heighten the recognition of his firm in the City of London, was favorably impressed by Wilkinson's plan. He immediately pledged the support of the NYSSCPA.[59]

Self-interest and professional interest were in harmony in Haskins's case. The proposed federation promised important benefits to him personally and to his firm's practice. It was vital that he participate in the activities of an association that sought to standardize professional licensing throughout the United States. His practice was rapidly growing national, with new offices in four cities outside New York State between 1899 and 1903. Like the managing partners of the larger chartered accounting firms, he did not want to be excluded from important state markets. This new basis for cooperation with British practitioners also promised to buttress his position in the City of London.[60]

The federation met at the New Willard Hotel in Washington, D.C., on October 21, 1902, attracting representatives of virtually all of the leading public accountancy associations. Delegates representing the AAPA, the NYSSCPA, the ISPA, and the state societies in Pennsylvania, Massachusetts, Maryland, and Michigan had been chosen in proportion to the sponsoring societies' total membership (one delegate for every ten members). Charles Haskins was elected president, Robert H. Montgomery, treasurer, and George Wilkinson, secretary.[61]

Though the federation expanded rapidly because of the admission of many new state societies, its initial operations depended heavily on the financial support of the elite national firms who contributed much of its initial capital. Price Waterhouse, Haskins and Sells, and Barrow, Wade, and Guthrie each donated one hundred dollars. Additional contributions of fifty dollars each were received from the growing Philadelphia firm of Lybrand, Ross Brothers, and Montgomery and the Chicago firms of Reckitt and Williams, and Walton and Joplin. Moreover, the national firms, whose personnel had multiple state society memberships, provided another indirect subsidy through the five-dollar-a-member annual assessment levied by the federation on each of its constituent organizations.[62]

Despite this impressive support, from the very beginning the federation experienced great difficulty in keeping the two largest societies, the AAPA and the NYSSCPA, in its program. Although Wilkinson's direct appeal to Haskins had assured the NYSSCPA's participation, it proved difficult to hold the AAPA in the federation's orbit. In fact, the AAPA decided not to join the federation in 1902, primarily because its leaders did not wish to relinquish its claim to being the profession's premier national organization. This reluctance may also have stemmed from the fact that about a quarter of the AAPA's membership was not certified and therefore was disenchanted with the federation, which was dedicated to promoting CPA legislation.[63]

Though an influential faction led by Conant and supported by Haskins and Dickinson was eager for the AAPA to join the federation, other leaders whose practices were essentially local opposed the move. The three-man committee sent by the AAPA to observe the October organizational meeting of the federation recommended against joining. Conant and his allies undertook a letter-writing campaign calling for a reversal of this proposal. Faced with this rebellion, the trustees called a special meeting of the membership on December 17, 1902, to vote on the matter. Those who favored affiliation were in a minority (twenty-eight were against and twenty were for joining), indicating that the national firms were at this juncture still in a minority in their own primary organization.[64]

The federation experienced an unexpected setback as a result of the sudden death of Charles Haskins on January 9, 1903. Although Dickinson, who hitherto had operated in the great man's shadow, emerged as the new leader of the federation, he had to consolidate his position in the AAPA. He was appointed in January 1903 to the trustee's seat vacated by Broaker, and he worked quietly with the other trustees to identify a basis of agreement for the merger of the AAPA and the federation. It would take two years, however, for these negotiations to bear fruit. In the long run he paved the way for the merger of the two groups, but in the short run his efforts contributed to the NYSSCPA's decision to withdraw from the national movement.[65]

The Federation Stalemated

After Haskins's death, none of his successors mollified the resentments felt by various factions in the NYSSCPA toward a national movement in which prominent chartered accountants played leading roles. Besides the strongly American nationalistic element, there was also a "Celtic" faction of Irish and Scottish accountants, who harbored sour feelings toward the English chartered accountants. The outstanding success of the English firms did not ease these feelings, and no firm epitomized that success better than Price Waterhouse, whose managing partner succeeded Haskins as leader of the federation.[66]

Meanwhile, Haskins's surviving partner, Elijah Watt Sells, shifted the focus of his business from London to New York. As his firm entered into open conflict with leading chartered firms, particularly Marwick, Mitchell, and Company and Price Waterhouse, Sells undermined the efforts to foster nationwide cooperation. The competition came to a head at the November 9, 1903, meeting of the NYSSCPA, when Sells introduced a motion to send an official notice to the firm of Jones and Caesar (the name under which the Price Waterhouse partnership initially operated in the United States) that it was committing a misdemeanor by advertising itself as a firm of CPAs since several of its senior partners resident in Britain were not, in fact, certified. At a special meeting of the NYSSCPA held on November 27, attorney Clarence Birdseye rendered a legal opinion essentially concurring with Sells's motion. Consequently, the NYSSCPA membership formed a special committee to monitor this matter and debated for over a year on whether or not to initiate action against Price Waterhouse.[67]

The NYSSCPA's leaders resented the way Dickinson had neutralized their influence in the federation. Although New York's was the largest single state association, Dickinson formed countervailing alliances between the ISPA and the other medium-sized societies from Pennsylvania, Maryland, Massachusetts, and New Jersey. He was also continuing his work for AAPA membership, further diluting the NYSSCPA's influence and perhaps its claim to leadership in New York.

The tension was heightened by Dickinson's 1904 proposal that the federation sponsor a world congress of accountants as part of the Louisiana Purchase exposition being organized in St. Louis by one of his firm's clients. The accountants' conclave was part of the broader International Congress of Arts and Sciences for a discussion of the progress achieved in a wide range of fields of scholarly and professional endeavor. As such, it helped to establish public accountancy's image as a learned calling. But to Sells this plan was particularly galling. Since the Paris exposition of 1900, it had been the special dream of Haskins and his associates to organize such a conclave to raise public awareness of accountancy. Instead, this idea was now being exploited by one of Sells's archrivals.[68]

The growing crisis came to a head at the regular meeting of the NYSSCPA on June 13, 1904, when the association learned that the AAPA had agreed in principle to join the federation. Sells's new partner, Charles S. Ludlam, then proposed that the NYSSCPA continue to participate only on the basis that one professional organization be allowed to represent the practitioners in each individual state. He wanted to be sure that the NYSSCPA, and not the AAPA, was the recognized representative of New York's practitioners. This brought the conflict between the two associations again to the surface. At this point Thomas P. Ryan introduced a resolution to withdraw from the federation, which carried twenty-eight to eighteen.[69]

Hopes of building professional unity seemed dead. The symbolic Congress of Accountants, which Dickinson hoped would unify practitioners, was conducted with the AAPA and the NYSSCPA representatives acting as observers rather than participants. Nationalist stirrings and practice rivalries again arose to divide accountants and inhibit their efforts to create a comprehensive structure for their profession. It would take the force of external events to induce the leadership of these competing factions to seek a new modus vivendi.

Political Change in New York and the
Emergence of a Federated AAPA

Within six months Dickinson enticed both the NYSSCPA and the AAPA back into the federation's fold. The reconciliation came about largely as a result of external events which changed the relationships between the leaders of the rival associations and their allies in business and government. One of the events was the reorganization of the New York State Board of Regents in 1904. The other, in 1905, was the Armstrong investigation of life insurance companies operating in the state.

In the case of the regents, a unification act passed in September 1904 was the first of several steps to undermine the power of the bureaucrats allied with the NYSSCPA since 1896. The new law authorized the merger of the regents with the state's Department of Public Instruction. The new act, designed to increase the efficiency of educational regulation through administrative reorganization, represented a compromise between the reform and regular wings of the Republican party. The regulars under Boss Platt, however, emerged as the real winners. This became clear with the appointment as state commissioner of public education of Andrew Sloan Draper, an old Conklingite Republican and former president of the University of Illinois.[70]

This restructuring reduced substantially the powers of some of the NYSSCPA's closest allies in Albany. Secretary Dewey and his successor and protégé in the examinations division, James Russell Parsons, Jr., lost their influence on professional licensing. Dewey tried to hang on in the state government, but Parsons was forced out entirely. A reduction in the size of the board of regents also led to the retirement of such strong NYSSCPA supporters as Senator Depew and Bishop Doane.[71]

Soon after his appointment, Commissioner Draper successfully challenged the authority of the board of CPA examiners. Henceforth this body would be primarily responsible to the new regime at the state education department and not to particular professional factions. Draper's unilateral action (in January 1905) in approving a license under the waiver provision for Perley Morse, the nephew of Boss Platt, crystallized the situation. Since his initial application in 1901, the examiners had denied Morse a license under this provision because of his inability to prove that he had the requisite number of years in practice before the enactment of the licensing legislation. John R. Loomis and John Sparrow, Haskins's personally selected successor, resigned in protest over Draper's action, leaving only Ferdinand Lafrentz, the AAPA representative, on the board. Though Draper continued to appoint replacements to the board from each of the major associations, the new members were carefully chosen by a commissioner out of sympathy with the NYSSCPA.[72]

The regular Republican leadership questioned Dewey's ability to control the petulant public accountants. Dewey seems to have recognized that his NYSSCPA allies were contributing to the deterioration in his position at Albany. The association considered but rejected a compromise allowing partnerships, the majority of whose members were certified, to designate themselves as CPAs. This would have eliminated the cause of action against Price Waterhouse and the need for politically distasteful appeals to the legislature, the regents, or the courts, but the NYSSCPA membership was not in the mood for a compromise.[73]

Dewey never got another chance to restore harmony because in 1905 a delegation of leading Jewish businessmen petitioned for his removal for promoting anti-Semitic policies at the Placid Club and for malfeasance in office. Though the charges were not sustained in the regents' 1905 inquiry, Dewey's effectiveness in Albany was now at an end. Soon he submitted his resignation, effective January 1, 1906, and retired to the Placid Club.[74]

Losing influence in Albany, the NYSSCPA's leaders were soon willing to accept a compromise. By February 20, 1905, the NYSSCPA and the AAPA had again formed a joint committee to develop a common policy, and during that same year the state investigation of the insurance companies boosted yet again the spirit of cooperation. A series of articles appearing in *Everybody's Magazine* had alleged improprieties in the investment policies of the state's leading companies. Charles Evans Hughes's skillful cross-examination unearthed evidence of corruption and mismanagement that besmirched irreparably the reputations of several senior executives and their political allies in Albany.[75]

The boards of directors of the companies engaged several well-known public accounting firms to audit their financial records. To rebuild confidence among both policyholders and investors in New York and London, the audits were performed by two public accounting firms, one American and one British. All three of the major companies were audited by Haskins and Sells. The Equitable Life Assurance Society chose Price Waterhouse as its British auditor; New York Life Insurance Company and the Mutual Insurance Company, however, chose Deloitte, Plender, and Griffiths.[76]

In their roles as objective searchers for the truth, the public accounting firms were constrained. They could not do anything that would bring into question their objectivity or emphasize their differences. Conflict had to be suppressed. Compromise and cooperation were the order of the day.

Thus Sells and his colleagues were able to engineer a compromise. It was a policy that Dickinson had proposed in 1905 for the reorganization of the federation. Under this plan the federation was absorbed by the AAPA, whose original members constituted a special subcategory known as "members at large" and were not associated with any individual state. AAPA members who were not certified were in this manner admitted to a national organization committed to the promotion of state CPA legislation. The NYSSCPA was recognized as the exclusive representative for New York. In this fortuitous manner and after several false starts, the AAPA became the national organization of the accounting profession.[77]

The Fruits of Accord

The primary impetus for national association building had come from the emerging national firms, whose leaders viewed them as useful vehicles in helping to combat efforts by local groups to limit access to particular state markets. Their strategy was to encourage uniform licensing bills. In this respect public accountants were like medical practitioners, but they had different motives.

The efforts to create a national structure became intertwined with state politics and with various interassociational struggles. Only after suffering a series of defeats were the leaders of the NYSSCPA and AAPA persuaded to surrender their particular claims in favor of national cooperation. Even then they adopted a loose federal structure that ensured that power would remain diffused among the member associations. Given the association's experience with various government and business leaders, it was desirable to have a decentralized organization. In that way threats to the profession from external sources could be dealt with on a state-by-state basis. Meanwhile, the federation assured the public that all was well in a unified profession that could provide the objective evaluations needed by a business system under attack from liberal reformers. External pressure was thus the final element needed to overcome the particularism of the practitioners and bring about a successful effort to create a truly national association.

Part 2

Accountants in an Age of Progress, 1900–1916

The creation of a model structure for state governance in New York initially did little to cool the passions of rival professional groups. Instead, this development sparked renewed competition to control professional affairs by establishing new state and national organizations. One motivating factor was the concern about the alleged discrimination against the interests of resident chartered accountants by some of the members of the new licensing agency in New York. The polarization arising from these disputes in the Empire State fueled a renewed competition between chartered accountants and their elite American rivals to obtain legislation favorable to their interests in other states. They also competed by building rival professional associations.

These new structures of state governance, however, threatened to impede the progress of these same elite practitioners, who were also building national practices. To serve efficiently large business clients that operated across state boundaries, these elite firms had to establish nationwide networks of branch offices. What they feared was local legislation that prohibited out-of-state accountants from practicing.

The emergence of state and national governmental authorities to regulate important industries also frustrated the elite accountants' aspiration to play a more important role in these affairs. Leading states, such as New York and Massachusetts, organized regulatory agencies that mandated uniform financial accounting for local insurance companies. On the national level, these trends seemed even more worrisome. The power of the ICC, for instance, to prescribe uniform accounting to support its regulatory activities was substantially broadened. Other federal agencies, such as the Bureau of Corporations in the newly organized Department of Commerce and the Census Bureau, also began to gather economic and financial data to aid regulatory activities. Ultimately, these developments encouraged professional leaders to reorder associational activities so that practitioner interests could be effectively represented before governmental bodies—particularly on the national level.

A growing need for greater practitioner accord was reflected during this period in the AAPA's reorganization into a federation that included all the state professional societies as component units. The federative organization achieved some notable successes. It functioned as a forum for resolving the conflicts that divided practitioners and thus helped to build a broad consensus. As the reconstituted AAPA grew, its ability to shape practitioner values increased through the expansion of its publishing and member-committee activities. The promotion of its model CPA law and state society bylaws also contributed to the standardization of the state structure for professional governance. Finally, the national body was more effective than the individual state organizations both in building public awareness of the profession and its special skills and also in advocating its notions of associational governance over economic affairs.

Defining a
Professional Image

The Problem of Professional Values

Influenced by the activism of a few leading chartered accountants and their American allies, the AAPA became increasingly concerned, after the 1906 reorganization, with the propagation of professional values. The reorganization had denied the elite practitioners the strong powers necessary to control the new profession. As an alternative, they sought to offer guidance to public accountants in their day-to-day activities. Most active in this effort were the two senior partners of Price Waterhouse and Company—Arthur Lowes Dickinson, managing partner of this firm's American practice from 1902 until 1911, and his close associate, Joseph E. Sterrett, an American CPA. The values and role models they advanced had a decidedly British flavor.[1]

The successful promotion of British professional values after 1906 did much to displace the old "science of accounts" as a normative model for professionalism. Practitioner interest in this alternate vision had declined markedly after the deaths of Charles Haskins and his colleague Anson Kittredge in 1903. No other practitioner of comparable prestige emerged to promote the ideas that had so fascinated Haskins. His former partner, Elijah Watt Sells, lacked the powers of persuasion and self-confidence necessary to keep these concepts alive. Another contributing factor in the decline of the idea of the science of accounts was that it failed to provide specific answers to many of the vexing problems encountered in practice. On the other hand, British chartered accountants' ideals, based on over four decades of experience, provided guidance on a wide range of problems encountered in practice. The science of accounts therefore gave way— although it continued to appeal to the emerging community of accounting educators.

Dickinson, Sterrett, and their professional allies worked diligently to transform the AAPA's vague commitment to the ideals of chartered accountancy into a comprehensive and dynamic program of professionalism. For the most part, they would succeed in crystallizing American professional values under Dickinson's able leadership. The elder of the two sons of Lowes Dickinson, a highly successful portrait painter and professional photographer, Arthur Lowes Dickinson was admitted to Kings College, Cambridge, partly on the basis of his father's close personal connections with members of that school's faculty and partly as a result of his own innate abilities. Studying under John Neville Keynes, the young Dickinson achieved great academic success, completing a tripos and becoming a master wrangler in mathematics in 1882. That same year he earned a master's degree and left Cambridge to begin what proved to be a very short-lived career as a business statistician and actuary. Later, attracted by the expanding opportunities in chartered accountancy, he became articled to the firm of Edwards, Jackson, and Browning in London. In 1887 he completed his apprenticeship and successfully passed the last of his professional qualifying exams, tying for first place. He was initially a partner in the small firm of Lovelock, Whittin, and Dickinson, which was merged in 1901 into that of Price Waterhouse. Because of his knowledge of American business conditions, Dickinson was selected by his new partners to develop their practice in the United States.[2]

Assuming his new task during a wave of railroad and industrial consolidations, Dickinson successfully expanded the American firm's practice; he had the strong support of some of Wall Street's top investment bankers, who were anxious to market in Europe the securities they were floating to finance new consolidations. The American bankers needed financial statements that were certified by well-known chartered accountants. Thus it was Dickinson who advised the partners of the House of Morgan and the management of the newly organized United States Steel Corporation, the nation's first billion-dollar company.[3]

Today, if we look at the faded photograph of this slight, meticulously groomed man under his grey homburg, it is easy to sense the detachment and composure but not the deeper emotions that drove him to achieve. The critical dark eyes and the tightly pursed lips convey a slightly disdainful superiority and an impeccable respectability. The control was almost too perfect and perhaps suggests that we should look for hidden fears and misgivings that compelled this remarkable man to try so hard to excel in every task he undertook.[4]

Though Dickinson came from a comfortable middle-class background, he shared with the other chartered accountants of his generation the insecurity of a member of a new professional class in an old ascriptive society. Practitioners such as Dickinson recognized that they needed the active support of the more established elites—lawyers, bankers, landed aristocrats, and the industrial magnates—in order to penetrate the charmed circle of the respectable elements in British society. The original founders of the profession had indeed been able to win acceptance as individuals among leaders in business and government, but it remained to the men of Dickinson's generation to transform their calling into a truly respectable pursuit.

In the course of doing this, Dickinson had cause to be anxious about his own family background. His middling social origins were certainly not impressive to the elite clients he served. Though his father, as a result of his unique gifts, had enjoyed access to those at the highest levels of society, this special status was not a condition that could be transmitted by heredity. Dickinson had to work hard in the world just to preserve the social status his father had achieved.[5]

Dickinson was surely a driven man and a talented one as well; he skillfully overcame the fear and suspicion he encountered from native practitioners when he first went to the United States. Dickinson sketched for his fellow practitioners a convincing portrait of American public accountancy as an important part of a great worldwide movement (with its roots firmly anchored in British chartered accountancy). He used the *Journal of Accountancy*, the official publication of the AAPA, and the proceedings of the association's annual convention to popularize this vision.

The Journal of Accountancy *and the* Technical and Ethical Challenges of Practice

The *Journal of Accountancy* exerted a lasting influence on the thinking of American practitioners. Founded by Dickinson in 1904 as the official publication of the Illinois Society of Certified Public Accountants (ISCPA), it had been transferred to the AAPA at the time of its merger with the federation. This new magazine had helped to fill the void created by the discontinued publication of *Commerce, Accounts, and Finance* a year earlier.[6]

Aided by two of the nation's leading business educators, Dickinson worked diligently to make the journal a first-rate publication. Because of the heavy demands that his practice made on his time, Dickinson engaged as part-time editor Joseph French Johnson, Haskins's successor as dean at NYU's School of Commerce, Accounts, and Finance. The new editor selected his former Wharton colleague, Edward S. Mead (father of anthropologist Margaret Mead), as associate editor.

Although the primary responsibility for preparing the journal for publication rested with the editors, Dickinson and his partner, Joseph E. Sterrett, remained instrumental in defining the magazine's editorial policy, reviewing, for example, the galley proofs for each month's issue.[7]

This effort was so important to Dickinson and his allies that they tolerated substantial financial deficits for several years; subscription revenues were insufficient to cover expenses for the magazine until after 1910. These losses constituted a major drain on the AAPA's funds, yet, to the elite practitioners of the journal committee, they were worth it if the minds of the accounting community were convinced that the magazine and its sponsoring association were the voice of professional opinion. The imaginative and skillful editors succeeded brilliantly. Each month they presented, in an attractive and polished format, a broad selection of articles on accounting and general business topics of interest to contemporary practitioners. As a consequence the elite leaders were happy to close the association's chronic deficits through voluntary contributions.[8]

Through the journal Dickinson and his peers tried to shape outlooks on five major issues. Foremost among these was the need for a more comprehensive and better-defined body of technical knowledge about accounting, auditing, taxation, and financial reporting systems. Second, developments in such related fields as banking, finance, and economics were also of concern. Third were ethical issues involving the relationship between the practitioner and society, and fourth and fifth were education and developments in professional governance, particularly at the state level.

There were few alternatives to the *Journal of Accountancy*. With the exception of federal regulatory agencies such as the Interstate Commerce Commission, no other organization established standards for financial accounting or disclosure for business enterprises. The articles published in the journal on special accounting problems and practices thus served as a valuable reference for busy practitioners. Discussions of the special accounting problems of railroads, brewers, universities and colleges, fertilizer manufacturers and retailers, to name only a few, appeared in the AAPA's magazine. Many of these industry articles provided illustrations of the forms used and discussions of how the accounting systems were organized. There were also more general articles on such accounting problems as the proper treatment of bond discounts and premiums, the determination of the proper carrying costs of manufacturing inventories, and the best form and content of financial statements for commercial, industrial, and municipal enterprises.[9]

Much attention was also focused on federal tax matters, particularly after 1911, when the new federal excise tax was instituted, and 1913, when an amendment to allow for a federal income tax was passed. The editors established a regular monthly column to survey in detail developments in tax regulation and reporting. The column, called "The Tax Corner," was written by John B. Niven, the Scottish-trained managing partner of Touche, Niven and Company.[10]

The periodical also reprinted pieces that provided overviews of current developments in economics, finance, and business. These articles must have been particularly valuable in broadening intellectual horizons in the profession, most of whose practitioners had only a high school education. Some of these articles were drawn from the proceedings of such organizations as the Economics Club of New York and the American Academy of Political and Social Sciences and included selections by steel magnate Andrew Carnegie, political leaders Lyman J. Gage and William Jennings Bryan, and educator Charles W. Mixter of the University of Vermont. Frederick W. Taylor and Louis Brandeis made appearances, as did banker Isaac Seligman. The editors also provided an extensive book review section in each month's issue.[11]

By writing articles for the *Journal of Accountancy*, ambitious practitioners and accounting educators could establish a professional reputation. In a professional organization that frowned on advertising or other forms of touting one's abilities, the publication of an article was one of the few acceptable ways for practitioners to communicate their special competence. The elite of the AAPA contributed extensively to the journal. The partners of Price Waterhouse were particularly prolific, and none was more prodigious than its future managing partner, George O. May.[12]

In addition to selections on technical aspects of accountancy, the journal published a series of provocative articles by important professional leaders on ethical problems faced by the profession.[13] Many of the editorials by French Johnson and his successor as editor, Alphyon P. Richardson (a business journalist and former diplomat in the United States Consular Service), also addressed these matters.

At this time, the profession had only a very limited code of ethics enforceable by either the national or the state organizations. Local practitioners seemed not to be interested in this issue. Elite chartered accountants such as Dickinson, however, felt that a broadening of

enforceable rules of ethics was necessary to draw the American profession up to the level achieved by the British. A broader body of
fundamental rules would reassure the public and also rein in overly
aggressive competition for clients (believed to be a major factor contributing to so-called pernicious practices).

The issue of market control alienated many of the local practitioners
in the association. They had the most to gain through sharp competition and the most to lose through control. The journal, anxious to
encourage emulation of the example set by chartered accountants,
attacked three practices that had long been censured by the British
profession and were not addressed in the AAPA's code of ethics.
These were "touting," which included all types of "unprofessional"
advertising or solicitation for new business; dubious fee arrangements, which undermined the ability of the practitioner to provide an
acceptable quality of service; and the operation of a practice through
an "audit company" structure rather than a partnership.

The chartered accountants' tradition had a strong class component.
Professionals were prohibited from trying to build their practices by
means of crass commercial advertising or direct solicitation of the
clients of fellow practitioners. Instead, the new entrant to the profession was expected to make himself known to his colleagues, who
would help him to build a practice through the referral of clients.
Touting was clearly an activity in which the true gentleman would
never engage; such actions were the sure signs of the braggart and
brazen opportunist.[14]

Unethical fee arrangements was the second concern of the editors of
the journal. The two most frequently noted abuses in this category
were unrealistically low bidding and contingent fee arrangements.
The elite leaders of the national firms, who had to generate adequate
revenues to cover the heavy overheads associated with the maintenance of national networks of branch offices, were sensitive to the
need to prevent price-cutting. An inadequate fee structure, they said,
encouraged marginal practitioners (who might keep their overhead
down by employing such expedients as operating out of their living
rooms). Low fees constrained the ability of the practitioner to spend
enough time on an engagement to perform at a minimum level of
competency.[15] Finally, the willingness to accept a low fee might signal
that the practitioner was susceptible to client economic pressure in the
performance of such important services as audits. In the performance
of an audit, it was critical that practitioners maintain their independence so that they could render to the public, whom they ultimately

served, an objective opinion of the fairness of their client's financial statements.

The other ethical deficiency was conducting practice through a corporation. The use of the "audit company" form of organization was relatively widespread. Haskins and Sells, for instance, had at the time of Haskins's death operated as an audit company and only later reverted to the more conventional partnership form. From the perspective of the chartered accountants, the incorporated practice was unprofessional because it could be organized and controlled by entrepreneurs who were not public accountants. In that case, the judgment of professional accountants would necessarily be subordinated to the desires of profit-seeking boards composed of nonpractitioners.[16]

As one might imagine, the local practitioners saw it otherwise. They had a stake in competition, and they were the least well known and the most in need of advertising. They vehemently opposed the strictures against advertising and other forms of direct client solicitation. They viewed the proposed rules as devices conceived by the elite practitioners on Wall Street and designed to assert their dominance over the entire practitioner community. To a steadily growing number of local certified public accountants (who had achieved their special status by passing an examination administered by their state governments), there seemed to be little need to confer about what were viewed as special regulatory powers of the "foreign" or "eastern" accountants based in New York. In 1915, when the proposal to promulgate additional ethical rules against advertising and solicitation came up for debate at the AAPA's annual meeting, it was defeated by a coalition of local practitioner delegates led by John F. Forbes of San Francisco.[17]

The Journal of Accountancy *and Professional Certification*

Besides the extensive discussion of ethical and technical matters that it provided, the *Journal of Accountancy* during these years was also an important source of accounting education. During the years before World War I, there was neither a professional association for accounting educators nor journal that addressed exclusively their special interests. The journal filled this gap for a time by surveying the curricula being developed in accountancy in the nation's new business schools. Other articles analyzed the educational requirements mandated by state licensing boards and provided the answers to questions appearing on selected qualifying examinations.

Although college training was not inimical to the chartered accountant's tradition, as the career of Dickinson proved, it did represent an exception to the normal pattern. In Britain, the great majority of chartered accountants began their careers immediately after completing their secondary school educations. Although the Universities of London, Birmingham, and Manchester would all begin formal degree programs during the early years of the twentieth century, business education in Britain never experienced the explosive growth that it did in the United States. It is not surprising, therefore, that we find in the journal few articles by chartered accountants on this topic. Even Dickinson, who had written important pieces on technical and ethical topics, remained silent on higher education and its relationship to the American profession.[18]

The accounting educators, however, sought, through the journal, to increase the awareness of the benefits of a business school education—and along the way, to enhance their own status in the academic community. In one candid article, French Johnson discussed the status problems of business educators in the university community during this period. In his view the business educator occupied a position analogous to that of the science teacher, who prior to the 1880s had sought a place in universities long dominated by the humanities and theology. Like the scientists of an earlier generation, Johnson and his professional associates were cognizant of the skepticism and even contempt that business studies aroused among the professors of the older and more established academic disciplines.[19]

In their efforts to heighten an awareness of the progress being made in business education both by practitioners and by academics, the accounting educators periodically published in the journal the findings of a series of mail surveys. These surveys, sponsored by the association's Committee on Education, analyzed the curricula of the nation's new business colleges and also summarized the educational requirements mandated for CPAs by various state licensing boards. In its 1911 report the committee noted that eighteen of the forty-three schools that responded had established formal courses both in accounting and in other business subjects.[20]

As these surveys indicated, the new business schools were modeling their curricula on the programs developed either at the Wharton School or the Harvard Business School. Wharton, whose philosophy had been shaped largely by its second dean, Edmund J. James, trained specialists in specific business functions such as accountancy, finance, marketing, and management. This approach was adopted by most of the schools destined to become major centers of accounting education: New York University, the University of Chicago, Northwestern University, and several major state universities, including those in Illinois, Michigan, California, Wisconsin, and Kansas.[21]

Some schools followed the Harvard Business School model. Under the leadership of Dean Edmund F. Gay, Harvard had created a uniform curriculum designed to provide general training for prospective businessmen. This model shunned training in functional specialties and relied heavily on the case study method borrowed from legal education. The Harvard curriculum was designed to produce a generalist manager who could successfully address the problems arising in a wide range of businesses. Because of its primary concern with providing a general education, it is understandable that the Harvard model had less impact on accounting education than the Wharton model. This result was somewhat ironic in view of the fact that Dean Gay had consulted with Dickinson in 1908 about the Harvard curriculum.[22]

Although the early surveys reflected a wide variation in curricula, by 1913 a consensus was developing about which topics accounting majors should study. The majority of the respondents indicated that they provided training for the specific topics addressed on most states' licensing examinations, including commercial law, auditing, and the theory of accounts. In addition, many indicated that courses were offered on economics, banking, finance, management organization, commercial mathematics, and even penmanship. By training a growing number of their graduates to pass these important qualifying tests, these new schools established a permanent position for educators in the new profession.[23]

Along the same line, the *Journal of Accountancy* ran a special monthly feature that analyzed questions previously asked on state licensing examinations. This column, the "Student's Department," was edited by Seymour Walton, an American practitioner who had helped to establish the accounting program at Northwestern University. He was succeeded by John R. Wildman, who was then serving on the faculty of NYU's School of Commerce. Since 75 to 90 percent of all candidates failed the difficult licensing examinations, the column performed an important service to the profession.[24]

Some educators used the journal as a medium for making practitioners aware of the unique aspects of their colleges' programs. Because these educators were writing for a journal whose readership was made up of practitioners who had for the most part learned their craft

as apprentices and had not enjoyed the benefits of a college education, it is not surprising that most of the educators' articles focused on
pragmatic issues. Typical of this genre was the reprint of the paper
that Dean Edmund Gay of Harvard presented at the 1913 annual
meeting of the AAPA; Gay's paper outlined the accomplishments of
his school's new Bureau of Economic Research. Besides providing a
general description of the activities of the bureau, Gay also explained
how the Boston-based educators had successfully collaborated with
the AAPA's Committee on Federal Legislation in preparing for the
recently organized Federal Trade Commission a model accounting
system for use by shoe retailers. In another article of this sort, Robert
Montgomery described the accountancy "laboratory" that he had first
established at NYU and later introduced at Columbia. Using the financial records of companies dissolved by the bankruptcy courts,
Montgomery provided his students with an opportunity to perform
their exercises using the actual records of once active businesses.[25]

In these ways the *Journal of Accountancy* gradually helped to mold a
particular concept of the profession's objectives. Although the elite
leaders of the AAPA could not translate these ideas into regulatory
powers, they could provide the profession with an attractive and
positive body of thought that would eventually condition the decisions of the practitioners when regulation became reality.

The Annual Meeting and
Accountancy's Emerging Worldview

The AAPA's annual meeting served the same purpose. The elite practitioners structured the rhetoric and symbolism in this annual event to
convey a sense of the close relationships between American developments and a worldwide professional movement. While the annual
meetings had all the other political and social characteristics familiar
to those who are members of any profession, they developed from the
1904 Congress of Accountants this special symbolic aspect. Leaders
such as Arthur Lowes Dickinson guided the program along lines that
bolstered the AAPA's image as a source of authority in important
matters and emphasized the breadth of this professional community.
The meetings also stressed the wide range of the profession's contacts, in part by having a parade of honored guests. The message to
the members and the world at large was that important leaders in
business, government, and law held the AAPA in high esteem. The
list of celebrities included leading bankers such as Jacob Schiff of

Kuhn, Loeb, and Company, government officials such as Henry C. Adams, the chief statistician of the ICC, and prominent businessmen such as Paul S. Morton of the Equitable Life Assurance Society. Lengthy messages of congratulation and visits by prominent representatives of prestigious foreign professional societies demonstrated that an important bond connected American public accountancy with the profession in every part of the world.[26]

The effect that these efforts had on shaping the outlooks of some important American practitioners can be illustrated by the transformation in outlook of Elijah Watt Sells. At first Sells was a strong American nationalist who vigorously opposed what he regarded as the intrusion of the British chartered accountants. Gradually he changed. Ultimately he accepted the professional ideals that the foreign practitioners and their friends were assiduously promoting. As early as 1904, Sells began to comment on how favorably impressed he was by the polish of the meeting Dickinson had organized in St. Louis.[27] In this and other ways, Dickinson and his allies conceptualized and communicated a powerful vision of accounting professionalism.

The peculiar worldview evident in the transcripts of the AAPA's annual meetings reflected a narrowness in outlook not characteristic of many of the other professions emerging during this period. While it was not uncommon to find one national tradition predominant in a particular profession (chemistry in Germany or bacteriology in France), few professions seemed as unconcerned as were public accountants about learning the progress of related professional developments in non-English-speaking countries. Although public accountancy as it developed in Britain differed markedly from the practices in the other industrialized economies of Europe, there was never any strong desire among the AAPA leadership to establish any sort of connections with Continental professional groups. Instead, the AAPA leaders were content to view the profession as having relevance only in the United States, Britain, and the latter's empire. Practice in the rest of the world remained a terra incognita, whose different forms and conditions failed to excite the slightest interest among the AAPA leadership. In many of the other new professions and the natural and social sciences, there was a very significant degree of international cross-fertilization of ideas. But public accountancy, like the legal profession, seemed content to operate within a framework of traditional Anglo-Saxon institutions and values.

This narrow worldview was no doubt very comforting to elite American practitioners. They had much to contend with; traditional values in their society were under pressure as a result of rapid industrialization and large-scale immigration from southern and eastern Europe. Alien religions and cultural traditions were viewed pessimistically by many nativist Americans. There were also great disparities in wealth and status brought about by the changing economic order, disparities that needed to be rationalized in new ways. The professional ethos offered a solution to all of these problems; it explained the individual's relationship to his society, the nature of that social system, and the unity between the present and the past.

For those concerned about the direction of social change in America, professionalism was both a mechanism and a rationale for separating the few possessing special knowledge and training from the rootless masses in the nation's urban slums. The British aristocratic tradition, based on the ownership of land, a scarce commodity in Europe, and transmitted through heredity, had not appealed to nineteenth-century Americans as a good model on which to structure their society, with its ample supply of cheap land. The new professional elitism, however, for which the chartered accountants served as role models, was acceptable to many Americans at the beginning of the century; after all, it was based on individual merit and achievement, characteristics in accord with traditional American values. Our concept of equality was changing, was being applied more to opportunity than to social and economic circumstances. From this new perspective, all that was needed in the good society, after the diligent personal application necessary to gather the scarce resource of special knowledge or expertise, was an equal opportunity to advance. Failure, it was assumed, derived primarily from inferior personal qualities.

The fact that these new professional ideals had been originally developed by Anglo-Saxons, thought to be leaders in creating progress, was also comforting to nativist practitioners who could readily identify with this cultural tradition. The increasing cohesiveness of the British and American leaders of the AAPA was based not only on common professional concerns but also on a heightened awareness of a shared cultural tradition. The code words recited in innumerable toasts raised at annual meetings through the 1930s, "to our brethren across the seas," reflected the AAPA leadership's recognition that the new professionalism they promoted was influenced as much by a common cultural identity as by a common economic function.[28]

The AAPA was thus becoming a social and economic bastion for the magnates of the profession, but they found themselves in conflict with the little men of accounting, of which there were many. The "outs" manned the hundreds of small, local practices proliferating as the nation's economy continued to expand. In firms of this sort, the sons of farmers in the South and the West and the sons of immigrants in the nation's cities found outlets for their professional ambitions. It was these practitioners who would provide the leadership in the state professional societies in the AAPA and would challenge the national firm representatives.

In Search of
Professional Roles

Besides shaping practitioner opinion and defining normative values, the AAPA leadership also worked diligently during the years prior to World War I to enhance the prestige of their members' special skills among government leaders. Potential opportunities emerged as accounting became more important in ordering a society experiencing great changes. Accounting, for instance, played a key role in regulating industries such as insurance and the railroads. This information was useful in evidencing to investors the honesty and effectiveness of managements in their stewardship over corporate assets; it could also be used by government officials to regulate market competition. The development of accounting systems also became critical for the effective direction and control of new bureaus organized as part of a growing national executive state. Finally, accounting measurement was critical in the administration of the new federal income tax.

But the AAPA's success was mixed in its attempts to capitalize on these promising prospects. In the members' drive to grasp the new opportunities, they were most successful in developing accounting systems and engagements and in resolving weighty tax questions. They were least successful in finding outlets in the regulation of market competition. Nor were they able to convince government officials to mandate their audit services as essential elements in corporate governance.

Their frustrations were conditioned by several factors. The relatively small numbers of public accountants and the uncertainties in the public mind about the nature of their skills impeded their acceptance. So too did the attitudes of key officials who favored more direct government intervention in ordering economic affairs. Moreover, although accountants had successfully served as the certifiers of financial statements, nothing in their experience prepared them to play an active role in regulating market competition.

Yet, ironically, some of the seeming setbacks of this period actually helped to win adherents among business leaders concerned about the growing extensions of state power. Public accountants' ideas about corporate governance were beginning to be perceived as preferable to direct government involvement in these matters. Their certifications, it was believed, could enhance investor confidence without directly exposing managers and directors to the state's police powers. Moreover, the model involving private professional groups was amicable to free-market notions many were anxious to preserve during a time of extensive regulatory reform.

This chapter focuses on four episodes in the developing relationship between profession and government in the decades before World War I. First, it evaluates the accountants' role in the Armstrong investigation of the life insurance industry in New York in 1905. Second, it assesses the AAPA's efforts to influence the accounting details of the new regulatory requirements imposed on the railroads under the Hepburn Act and subsequent legislation. Third, it weighs the AAPA's contribution to the Keep Commission's efforts to develop more effective managerial accounting systems for federal executive agencies. Finally, it considers the AAPA's successful advocacy before the Treasury Department in defining preferable practices under the new federal income tax.

Accountants and the Life Insurance
Enterprise in New York

An early involvement with government occurred because of rising public demands for stronger legislation regulating the life insurance industry in New York, a movement that grew out of the Armstrong Committee's investigation in 1905. Much of the public debate concentrated on the need for fuller disclosure of the financial operations of these giant institutions. Many believed that fuller publicity would act as a deterrent to corrupt practices that came to light during the probe of company officials by committee counsel Charles Evans Hughes.[1]

Another focus of criticism was the New York State Insurance Department. Although this agency had required the filing of annual financial statements since the middle of the nineteenth century, these practices had failed to alert regulators to the mounting crisis. This was due in part to the summary nature of the financial reports themselves, which provided insufficient information about the details of the insurance companies' investment practices. Nor did this agency audit these filings to judge their reliability.[2]

The public accountants were first drawn into this crisis by the boards of directors of the companies being investigated. Paul Morton, the former secretary of the navy, had been hired by James Fortune Ryan to head the Equitable Life Assurance Society. Morton believed, along with many business leaders, that the Armstrong findings were undermining the public's confidence in the life insurance enterprises. He decided to restore that faith by engaging well-known American and English public accounting firms to examine the Equitable's condition and its dealings with Wall Street's largest underwriting firms. Other companies followed suit, using Price Waterhouse, Haskins and Sells, and Deloitte, Plender, and Griffiths to provide the requisite services.[3]

Both Dickinson and Sells pressed for the establishment of special committees at both the AAPA and the NYSSCPA to present recommendations at public hearings held in Albany about the form state regulation should take. They argued that annual audits should be required of all insurance companies operating in New York and should be performed by independent public accountants certified in that state. Following requests from their client firms, they also gave testimony about the form and accounting principles that life insurance financial statements should use.[4]

The AAPA's special committee sought to establish between government and the profession a relationship that was unusual in America. In Britain the professional work of chartered accountants satisfied the requirements of the registrar of companies, which mandated the submission of audited financial statements for all registered companies. Government officials there recognized the authority of the chartered accountants. When Dickinson testified as an expert witness representing the AAPA and Sells appeared in the same capacity for the NYSSCPA, they hoped to establish a similar relationship between the profession and the New York State Insurance Department. Their expectations were soon dashed. Although the new legislation strengthened industry reporting requirements, audits by independent accountants were not mandated. The New York State Insurance Department was reaffirmed as the exclusive regulatory agency for this industry.[5]

The problems experienced in New York in winning acceptance for accountancy's special skills in ordering economic affairs would soon be repeated in a national forum. In this second case the extension of the regulatory legislation over the railroad industry seemed to provide new opportunities not only to demonstrate the relevance of their specialized knowledge but also to press for a permanent role in monitoring these affairs. But, as in New York, their primary achievement was limited to educating the public about how their skills could serve corporate governance. They were still unable at this juncture to find a niche for their expertise in the emerging regulatory order.

The AAPA and Railroad Reform, 1906–1908

The Hepburn Act (ratified on June 29, 1906) marked an important transition in the federal government's regulation of the railroad industry. During the two decades since its inception in 1886, the ICC had been only marginally effective in carrying out its two primary responsibilities: assuring the equity of rates and assuring the probity of the financial information provided to investors and other groups interested in railroad operations. Two circumstances had foiled the agency's efforts. First, a series of unfavorable Supreme Court decisions in the 1890s seriously curtailed the ICC's power to regulate tariffs and competitive conditions in this industry.[6] Second, the accounting and statistical data on which both bureaucrats and investors had to rely were deficient in several respects.[7] In this second instance, although the railroads were required to submit annual financial statements using uniform formats, the ICC did not have the authority to prescribe uniform accounting methods. The resultant filings were often prepared inconsistently. Any inferences derived through the analysis of this data were of little use for decision making because they lacked homogeneity and comparability.

Although much of the historical literature on the Hepburn Act has focused on the extension of the ICC's power over rates, the act also had important implications for the accounting practices that informed the regulatory process. By authorizing the agency to prescribe uniform accounting methods, this legislation materially advanced the "self-executory" style of regulation advocated by key bureaucrats such as Chief Statistician Henry Carter Adams. Regulatory limits were to be set so that compliance could easily be monitored through the railroads' financial reports. Since infractions would be readily discoverable, strong incentives existed for obeying the law. Adams thought that by creating a fishbowl environment, large enforcement units might be eliminated and policing left to his small cadre of accountants.[8] Adams explained to the ICC commissioner Wheelock G. Veazey in 1893:

> Now, the easiest way, indeed, the only way by which uniformity of management may be secured is to establish uniformity in

accounts and to take from railway officials the right of adjusting them in an arbitrary manner. Accounts, if they be honest, are true records of administration, and he who controls accounts can, in a large measure, control the policy of management. Should the form of book-keeping be determined by the Commission and all railways be obliged to adjust their accounts to a uniform rule, the Commission would be in a position to impose its ideas on the management of the road. And more than this, uniformity in accounts and strict supervision over them, which may be secured through the agency of the statistical bureau, provides a new way of testing the compliance of the carriers with the rules of the Commission. Statistics properly used and adequately guided are the surest means of detecting any departure from established rules of management.[9]

Uniform accounts would also play a more central role in evaluating rate equity. Tariffs were to be set on the basis of the value of service to consumers rather than the cost of furnishing service. Cost of service was rejected as a basis because of the inability of contemporary accountants to develop economically meaningful methods for allocating the joint costs of common facilities to specific lines of service (a problem that continues to frustrate modern accountants). The key to the method the ICC eventually formulated lay in determining a railroad's financial break-even point. In the ICC's system this information could be estimated from the railroads' reports, thus eliminating the need for any special services from public accountants. As Adams explained further in his letter to Commissioner Veazey:

The first step is to determine the income which a railway corporation actually needs: the second step is to measure the business which rightly belongs to that corporation, and so far as freight traffic is concerned, to classify that business according to a uniform classification: and the third step is to adjust rates to these various classes of freight in such a manner that the required gross income will be secured and the burden of payment rest as lightly as possible on the customers of the railways. The principles which lie at the basis of just railway schedules are derived from a study of the theory of taxation. As in taxation payment for the support of the government should be in proportion to their ability to bear the charges. If this theory of rate making be accepted, or indeed, any theory which regards the problem from the standpoint of the public interest, the determination of rates comes to a purely statistical problem, or at least, a problem that calls for decisions that can only be given on the fullest and completest information as to the facts.[10]

The AAPA's involvement in the public debate over railroad accounting was spasmodic and poorly coordinated. The organization had failed to participate in the important hearings before the Senate Interstate Commerce Committee (chaired by Stephen B. Elkins, senator from West Virginia), which considered the emerging legislation between December 1904 and May 1905.[11] The accountants were too distracted by their as yet unresolved competition among key associations for national leadership, to have been able to mount any major drive for promoting their services.

When the AAPA eventually became involved, its advocacy was understandably limited to the provisions of its twentieth section, which dealt with financial reporting. Arthur Lowes Dickinson, who was chairman of the AAPA's Committee on the ICC, wrote on August 20, 1906, to Chairman Martin A. Knapp of the ICC requesting that the association be allowed to advise the government on the accounting rules for railroads. In this same letter Dickinson called upon the government to mandate that the railroads have their financial records audited annually by independent public accountants. Knapp cautiously replied on October 16 that both he and Professor Adams would be happy to meet with the AAPA's representatives.[12]

At this point, however, the AAPA's effort was again sidetracked by another internal struggle. Elijah Watt Sells defeated Dickinson for the presidency, and the latter relinquished his post on the ICC committee. A new committee, formed early in 1907, was composed not of members with substantial railroad clients but of members who were close in associational affairs to President Sells. They did not pursue with vigor the opening that Dickinson had created. Although no longer on the AAPA committee, Dickinson took it upon himself to stay in touch with Adams about the problems of railway accounting, particularly the difficult problem of capital asset accounting. On March 8, 1907, for instance, he drafted a lengthy appraisal of the various approaches the ICC might follow in accounting for the maintenance and depreciation of capital assets. He also provided the ICC with copies of technical memoranda prepared by members of his firm. Later, after another leadership change in the AAPA, Dickinson returned to the committee and carried forward in a formal capacity his efforts to shape public policy vis-à-vis the railroads and his profession.[13]

Practitioners raised objections to specific details of the ICC's new accounting regulations that were thought to be detrimental to their clients' interests. Even Arthur Lowes Dickinson, who worked closely in 1907 with Adams, was upset by several of the ICC's new requirements. In letters dated April 6 and April 30, 1908, he indicated his dissatisfaction. Dickinson and his colleagues were mindful of the need to protect their clients—especially very large ones.[14]

The strong reactions of the public accountants and their clients surprised Professor Adams, who apparently felt these changes offered substantial benefits to the railroads as well as to the public. Indeed, in his speech to the AAPA at its 1908 annual meeting in Atlantic City, Adams implied that he had originally thought the railroads would welcome the regulations. Had not the railroads' accounting officers themselves debated and ratified all the changes proposed?

But the angry tone of the debates about technical accounting matters reflected a deeper anger and frustration among the accountants gathered at the meeting. At the heart of their problem was the fact that, although a great structure of governance based on accounting information for the nation's largest industry had been created, it provided no role for these experts. Instead, the new ICC regulations seemed to undercut their special claim of authority in matters relating to financial accounting. Individual practitioners, who had for years agreed with railroad managements that the methods they used to measure revenue and expense were proper, now had the rug pulled out from under them. Events seemed to indicate to the public that the real source of authority in these matters was not the public accountant but rather the strong-willed educator turned bureaucrat. They saw themselves as being changed into minor functionaries who conformed unthinkingly to the requirements government set forth in edicts. The rules flew in the face of the English tradition of the gentleman accountant who was perforce a man of good and steady judgment.[15]

The accountants responded by sharply criticizing the ability of the new ICC system to protect investor interests. After the Atlantic City meeting, press reports quoted Dickinson's questioning the ability of the federal agency to attract sufficient numbers of qualified accounting experts to perform its duties efficiently and competently. Naturally, he believed the solution lay in the adoption of the English style of audit.[16]

The ICC's leaders were unimpressed by these arguments. Although the English audit system might assure probity in financial reporting, it did not provide the control over railroad operations that these bureaucrats and their political allies craved. Nor did the federal regulators welcome the accountants' criticisms of uniform accounting as being too rigid and therefore providing potentially misleading summaries of railroad affairs. Moreover, the bureaucrats may also have harbored misgivings about the independence of members of this profession from the interests of their clients. At that time there were no explicit laws or codes of ethics defining the conditions necessary to preserve practitioner independence. Consequently, they, like attorneys, were often perceived as advocates of the businesses they served rather than as autonomous professionals dedicated to the protection of investor interests.

The apparent futility of the profession's efforts from the perspective of the regulators was captured in a poem written by an ICC staff member after the Atlantic City meeting. The piece, entitled "The Public Accountants and the Interstate Commerce Commission," was attached to a newspaper article reporting on Dickinson's critical remarks, which was sent to Professor Adams:

A little dog barked at the big round moon
That smiled in the evening sky,
And neighbors smote him with rocks and shoon
But still he continued his rageful tune
And barked 'til his throat was dry.

The little dog bounced like a rubber ball
For his anger quite drove him wild
And he says "I'm a terror although I am small
And I dare you, you impudent fellow, to fall"
But the moon only smiled and smiled.

So the little dog raged at a terrible rate,
But he challenged the moon in vain,
For calmly and slow as the workings of Fate,
The moon sailed along in a manner sedate,
And smiled at the dog in disdain.

But soon 'neath a hill that encircled the West,
The moon sank out of sight,
And the little dog said as he laid down to rest
"Well, I scared him away, all right."[17]

Needless to say, this negative perception was not quite accurate.

The extension of the powers of the emerging executive state won adherents to the regulatory notions espoused by the AAPA's leaders. The strengthening of the ICC undermined the ability of railroad leaders to control activities in their industry. Although regulation may have helped to stabilize this industry economically through its system of administrative pricing, it stultified innovation and initiative. The vitiating effects of state regulation may well have been reflected, as some historians have argued, in the declining levels of investment capital that railroads attracted or in the lower premiums that this industry's securities commanded in the nation's financial markets after 1906.[18]

Moreover, the new legislation made business leaders personally more vulnerable to governmental sanctions. One telling example was the 1908 investigation into the affairs of Edward H. Harriman, which ultimately led to an antitrust suit forcing the dissolution of his control over the Union and Southern Pacific railroads. A more worrisome presentiment to many was the belief that the rigor of this interrogation contributed to the railroad magnate's declining health and then death in 1909. Unlike the mode of regulation in the days prior to 1906, when managements could better insulate themselves through the court system, the new administrative mode of regulation directly exposed them to the full force of government power. In this context the British model of corporate governance no doubt became more appealing to many business leaders.

Although the accountants failed to achieve a permanent place in regulating either insurance or the railroads, they did achieve a signal success as advisors to several federal executive agencies. As we shall see, these consultations were invaluable in developing accounting systems to manage more effectively several bureaus established during the administration of Theodore Roosevelt.

The AAPA and the Keep Commission, 1906–1908

Through their participation in the work of the Committee on the Department Methods of Government, the AAPA leaders would apply their special skills in helping the Roosevelt administration to solve the problems of establishing adequate controls over the national government's expanding operations. The pressure for administrative reform resulted partly from the sensitivity of the incumbent administration to criticisms of waste, inefficiency, and corruption in the operations of the Post Office Department. An investigation of this major department begun in 1903 led ultimately to the indictment of forty-four postal employees shortly before the 1904 presidential election. What emerged from these investigations and subsequent trials was an embarrassing image of a public agency incompetently led by political favorites who had lost control over its operations. President Theodore Roosevelt was anxious to reorganize management practices and to tighten financial controls at the beleaguered Post Office Department.[19]

Pressure for reform also came from some bureaucrats within the government. Foremost among these was Gifford Pinchot, chief forester of the Department of Agriculture. Pinchot believed that existing management practices impeded critical agencies charged with the execution of some of the administration's most important policies; he included among these agencies the Reclamation Service, the Geological Survey, the Isthmian Canal Commission, the Bureau of Corporations, and his own Forest Service. One of the problems was the inflexibility of the accounting system first installed by Haskins and Sells in 1894 as part of their work for the Dockery Commission. This system was no longer adequate because the procedures it had mandated for the Treasury Department to follow in authorizing disbursements of funds were found to be overly cumbersome and because the financial accounts were not helpful to administrators in planning, controlling, and evaluating the operations of their departments. The accounting system did not, for example, provide detailed information about costs in executive agencies.[20]

Pinchot convinced Roosevelt of the need to form an interagency committee to address these administrative problems. The Committee on the Department Methods of Government, formed in 1906, included James R. Garfield, commissioner of corporations; Frank H. Hitchcock, first assistant postmaster; Lawrence O. May, assistant secretary of commerce; Overton W. Price, chief administrator of the forest service; Charles H. Keep, assistant secretary of the treasury; and Pinchot.[21]

Lacking expertise in accounting matters and dissatisfied with the ability of the Treasury Department to satisfy its needs, the committee turned to Pinchot's old friend and public accountant, Henry A. Niles of the New York firm of Niles and Niles. Niles, in turn, called upon the AAPA (he was a member) to form a special committee to help the federal government. The resultant AAPA committee included Niles as chairman and Arthur Lowes Dickinson, John R. Loomis, and Arthur W. Teele as members. Later, in 1907, E. W. Sells and a British chartered accountant, Francis F. White of the firm of Deloitte, Plender, and Griffiths, were added as members.[22]

For nearly two years the AAPA committee worked in an advisory capacity with the interagency committee (which unofficially took the name of Assistant Secretary Keep) and, later, with another special committee formed to consider improvements in the Treasury Department's bookkeeping procedures. The initial responsibility for collecting information and formulating preliminary recommendations lay with a series of sub- or "assistant" committees that reported directly to the Keep Committee. The AAPA group then reviewed and made suggestions about the work efforts of the subcommittees. This highly successful endeavor resulted in a series of improvements in public administration in the federal government and—not so incidentally— enhanced the prestige of the AAPA and the accounting profession. Later a number of AAPA member firms would provide consultancy services to government agencies interested in improved control of costs.[23]

The recognition of the increasing importance of accountancy in government management would be reflected in the establishment of another specialized professional organization in 1907 to address these problems. The Association of Governmental Accountants, like the AAPA in public accountancy, would serve as an institutional focus for the discussion of common problems confronting professional accountants in the public sector.[24]

In addition to their management advisory services, the accountants also experienced another important success during this period in advising the Treasury Department. This last case, as we shall see, was concerned with the question of what basis of accounting was most economically meaningful in measuring the taxable income of corporations.

The AAPA and Corporate
Income Tax Accounting, 1909–1913

The public debate over the federal income tax legislation passed by Congress in 1913 offered the most important opportunity for the AAPA's leaders to demonstrate the usefulness of their special knowledge. The primary beneficiaries of their contributions to this debate would be their elite business clients—particularly those associated with the nation's largest and most capital-intensive industries. Through their successful advocacy of the natural business year, the AAPA helped to minimize the disruption to corporate clients' internal accounting operations in complying with the new tax. Their success in convincing government to accept the use of accrual accounting in calculating taxable income allowed capital-intensive industries to reduce their liability by deducting substantial charges for the depreciation of their investments in fixed assets. By winning acceptance for the accrual basis as an acceptable alternative to the net-cash-receipts basis (as originally proposed by the Treasury), the AAPA helped to shift the burden of taxation away from clients in such industries as steel, petroleum refining, electric utilities, and the railroads and toward other taxpayer groups.[25]

The AAPA's efforts to influence this and other progressive-era legislation were mounted by a newly organized Committee on Federal Legislation (1909). This group assumed responsibility for the missions of the Committees on the Department Methods of Government, the Interstate Commerce Commission, Federal Recognition, and Standard Schedules for Uniform Reports of Municipal Industries and Public Service Corporations. The charge of the preexisting Committee on Legislation was redefined so that it would monitor developments only in state professional licensing.[26]

The driving force on the Committee on Federal Legislation was Robert H. Montgomery. Except for the years he served as president of the AAPA (1912–13), Montgomery chaired this key committee from 1910 until 1916. Among those who, along with Montgomery, played prominent roles were George O. May, who after 1911 would serve as the managing partner of Price Waterhouse; the Scottish accountant, Arthur Young; Harvey S. Chase, father of social commentator Stuart Chase; former AAPA president J. Porter Joplin; Arthur W. Teele; and Perley Morse.[27]

In their efforts to shape legislation, the committee members dealt directly with government officials (such as Attorney General George S. Wickersham), marshaled the AAPA's members to contact their legislators, and cooperated with the U.S. Chamber of Commerce (of which the AAPA was an early constituent organization). While these techniques of lobbying seem commonplace today, they were new to this profession and were experiencing a remarkable transformation in degree during these years. A new brand of interest-group politics was just beginning to emerge from the party style of political behavior that had characterized the nineteenth century.[28]

Though the public accountants ultimately prevailed in the tax accounting debate, they encountered negative attitudes that reflected how tenuous their authority was in the eyes of some more established professions. To lawyers such as Wickersham, business accounting practices seemed all too often to be artful subterfuges, useful to unscrupulous businessmen in creating misleading impressions. The findings of the Armstrong Committee in New York and the investigation of Harriman by the ICC reinforced this view. Unlike the emerging sciences or the law, accounting could claim no great body of literature defining the basic underlying principles on which practice was based. With the exception of the systems mandated by a few federal agencies such as the ICC, there were no comprehensive rules of accounting that practitioners were compelled to advise their clients to follow.[29]

Nevertheless, once the AAPA succeeded in altering the tax measure, it would go on to establish a permanent and prominent role for public accountants in federal tax regulatory affairs. The Treasury did not initially mandate uniform accounting (as the ICC had sought to do in 1907). The body of acceptable practice would be gradually defined over the subsequent years through the issuance of detailed regulations by the Internal Revenue Service (IRS) and, later, through the rulings by the Board of Tax Appeals, predecessor of the U.S. Tax Court. The profession would play an important role in the process of gradually narrowing the range of acceptable practice in tax matters.[30]

Accountants and Progressive Reform

This survey of the AAPA's involvement with government during the two decades prior to World War I provides a picture that is somewhat different from the one painted by the progressive historians. The new professions are frequently depicted as the natural allies of the reform politicians. In this view the politicians with their idealist visions and the professionals with their technical expertise jointly provided the new values and institutions needed by a changing society. The progressive version of history, however, does a better job of analyzing the experience of the politicians than of treating the motivations and activities of the new professional groups such as the AAPA. The association had objectives different from those of the leaders of progressive reform. Instead, what becomes apparent is the readiness of the new professional groups to form alliances with both "liberal" and "conservative" politicians to achieve their particular objectives.

The primary desire of the new professionals was to use their special knowledge to secure their collective income, wealth, and status in a society that was being radically transformed by industrialization. Among the public accountants, political ideology was not a primary motivator. Rather, they typically considered the political process as a channel that could be used to improve their economic and social condition. The leaders of public accountancy applied four criteria in determining whether or not a particular public issue was worthy of their attention. Public policy initiatives were supported if they offered an opportunity to increase the demand for accountancy and the public's awareness of the value of the public accountant's special knowledge. The AAPA worked closely with governmental leaders when this participation enhanced the image of the AAPA and its members as the most competent source of authority on financial accounting matters. In addition, the AAPA consistently opposed any efforts of government to mandate for technical accounting matters rules that would limit the ability of practitioners to exercise their independent professional judgment. Finally, the AAPA opposed any governmental activities that threatened the vital interests of important client groups.

Only by recognizing the importance of these basic priorities does the involvement of the public accountants in the political developments of this period become comprehensible. The AAPA supported increased regulation of the insurance industry in New York because this proposal would have significantly increased the demand for audit services. The association also worked closely with liberal politicians in their efforts to increase the efficiency of government operations because it advertised to the nation the value of their special knowledge. The group opposed other proposals of liberal leaders when they seemed to undermine the profession's image of authority in financial accounting matters or to restrict too severely the scope of independent professional judgment. They opposed conservative politicians such as Attorney General Wickersham because his tax accounting proposals threatened their authority and would limit their judgment and also because the proposals would have been potentially harmful to the interests of important clients.

Although this analysis of the national political involvement of the AAPA provides some important insights into the motives of this association's elite leadership, it does not address the issues that were of primary concern to the steadily increasing mass of local practitioners scattered throughout the nation. As we shall see, other differences unrelated to national governmental policies acted to divide the elite practitioners from this growing professional lumpen proletariat.

Part 3

Mobilization, Prosperity, and
Autonomous Associationalism,
1917–1929

During this period the accountants radically reorganized their national representative association by replacing its earlier federal structure with one in which authority was more centralized. In 1916 the newly formed American Institute of Accountants (AIA) emerged to take the place of the AAPA. These changes were brought about primarily because of the activism of the elite in response to a series of what seemed worrisome internal and external developments. The external concerns involved the federal government's efforts to widen the scope of economic regulation and the implications that had for this profession. During the first administration of Woodrow Wilson, the accountants worried about proposals to regulate accountancy through the newly organized Federal Reserve Board (FRB) and to establish uniform accounting for industries other than railroads through the Federal Trade Commission (FTC). The internal concerns, on the other hand, related to the uneven quality of professional standards nationwide. This uncertainty detracted from the profession's image as a "learned calling" and invited federal encroachment to order its affairs. Additionally, a growing body of practitioners of social backgrounds and types of practice different from those of the elite opposed many aspects of the new program of professionalization. Finally, many of the elite also desired a more tightly controlled associationalism to assure greater effectiveness in supporting the nation's mobilization effort.

America's entry into war changed the relationship between the profession and the federal government. Although the federal bureaucracy had expanded steadily since the beginning of the century, it was neither sufficiently large nor sufficiently expert to order such a vast undertaking as mobilizing the nation's energies for war. Instead, government relied on private business and professional groups, including public accountants, to marshal the country's resources. Victory later created a public climate favorable to the autonomous and centralized professionalism that the elite first tried to create on the eve of war. The valuable services rendered to the national state by the accountants demonstrated convincingly the importance of their expertise. Furthermore, the nation's success in arms also supported the belief that private groups could be highly effective in resolving even the most serious challenges confronting society. Finally, the memories of wartime restrictions and the curtailment of individual freedoms also made associationalism appear a more attractive alternative for ordering both society and professional affairs.

During the postwar years, several national firm leaders extended the new course first chartered for the profession in 1916. Their actions were influenced in part by the unique problems they were experiencing in serving a large-scale business clientele, problems that further differentiated themselves from the increasing number of small, local public accounting firms. To the elite it seemed necessary to promote research in accountancy, to widen the scope of the rules of professional ethics, to raise entry standards through the establishment of a new qualifying examination, and to begin the process of defining educational standards for university accounting programs. The local practitioners did not see the need for these innovations. Consequently, the national firms' efforts fell far short of their goals, and the profession was left in a seriously fragmented condition.

The profession was also severely damaged because of the loss of public confidence after the 1929 stock market crash. The market's collapse and the resultant public criticism of all the professional groups closely associated with it raised serious questions about the reliability of public accountants' services. A new political regime eager to expand the federal government's powers promoted a public solution to what had heretofore been a private problem. The plans for building the New Jerusalem of professionalism that some leaders thought they had created through the 1916 reorganization would be revealed as sadly lacking during the depression decade. Until they were able to create a broad consensus about the meaning of professionalism in accounting, the AIA leaders were unable to build sufficient political power to control the drive for a governmental solution to these problems.

The Crisis in Professional Governance

The outbreak of war and the end of a period of progressive reform modified the relationship between the national executive state and public accounting. The extension of federal power as part of Woodrow Wilson's "New Freedom" motivated the AAPA's leaders to formulate new strategies and structures to secure a safe haven for their profession. Moreover, opposition within the AAPA to the policies proposed by elite accountants as well as concerns about the European war and its implications for America increased the pressures for an organizational reordering. What ultimately emerged in 1916 was a more centrally controlled association, the American Institute of Accountants. Its impressive contributions to the national defense during the First World War contributed to a favorable public perception about the sort of autonomous professionalism the elite had begun to implement.

The new program of professional governance had three elements. First, the power of the central leadership to control professional affairs was increased by extending the scope of the code of ethics. Second, the elite tried to redefine the boundaries of the practitioner community by developing new methods for certifying competency. Third, boundary concerns also encouraged the formulation of new policies toward the growing body of accounting educators.

A strong ethical code was fundamental to the autonomous professionalism that certain elite practitioners promoted. Such standards were thought vital in establishing a perception that accountants were sensitive to the need for applying their special knowledge only in socially beneficial ways. But many local practitioners suspected less laudable motives. They feared a more robust code would strengthen only the elite, toward whom they felt a remoteness conditioned by differences in the nature of practice and social backgrounds. The locals were also apprehensive that the new rules would curtail their ability to compete through advertising and other direct forms of practice development.

Polarization also heightened when some elite accountants tried to broaden the national association's role in certification. These activists worried that uneven state licensing standards had eroded accountancy's professional image in the eyes of important business and government leaders. Emulating the example of British chartered accountants, they sought federal sanction for their organization's new methods of certification. But this alienated many local practitioners, who feared a displacement of their hard-won badge of merit, the state-granted CPA.

Boundary redefinition also created the need for a policy with respect to the colleges training the growing numbers of entrants to the profession. One aspect of this was the joint development by practitioners and educators of a standard accounting curriculum. A second was the promulgation of ethics rules prohibiting members from maintaining any professional connections with "proprietary" accounting schools. A third concerned the educators' desire to standardize financial accounting along lines that did not allow for practical variation. Finally, some practitioners worried about leadership succession in their firms and sponsored programs to recruit candidates through the national organization for future partnership, candidates who, besides showing educational promise, also satisfied specific social background criteria.

Although the reordering occurred when accountancy's prestige was ascendant, the failure to reach a consensus about these initiatives undermined unity in the 1920s. A growing cadre of local practitioners expressed their dissent by forming a second national association, the American Society of Certified Public Accountants (ASCPA). The resultant split thwarted the advance of the elite's ambitious program and, ironically, weakened accountancy's claim to professional status.

Accountants and the New Freedom

Two reforms advanced by the Wilson administration—the formation of the FRB (1913) and the FTC (1914)—had major impacts on the development of the accounting profession. As in earlier Republican administrations, the motives for promoting this legislation were complex. Its sponsors wanted to bring order to the nation's changing economic scene; they also sought certain political advantages.

The interplay of these related imperatives was evident in the progress of banking reform. Since the dissolution of the Second National Bank of the United States by Andrew Jackson nearly a century earlier, the American economy had grown more vulnerable to disruption from periodic financial panics. Their severity increased as the nation's credit base grew. The new FRB was designed to bring order to the nation's financial markets by serving as a "creditor of last resort" in times of crisis. By assuring liquidity, this agency, it was hoped, could mitigate the disruptions resulting from occasional credit stringencies.

This reform also had its political dimension. On one level the FRB's unique regional structure was responsive to the concerns of country bankers who feared the domination of powerful bankers in the money centers. But, paradoxically, it was also welcomed by magnates such as Jacob H. Schiff and his young partner, Paul M. Warburg. They believed that it would stabilize financial markets and counter the influence of powerful rivals. These financiers had bolted from the Republican party in 1912 and backed Wilson's reforms partly to diminish the political leverage of their competitor J. P. Morgan, who had benefited from a close relationship with previous Republican regimes. Indeed, many of the events leading to this reform suggest that Morgan was a special target of this drive, in much the same way that Harriman had earlier been a target of the railroad reformers. Henry Cabot Lodge, for instance, expressed his belief to Theodore Roosevelt that Jacob Schiff had inspired Louis D. Brandeis to write *Other People's Money and How the Bankers Use It*, a book that built support for reform by attacking some of the House of Morgan's financings. Frank A. Vanderlip, president of the National City Bank, also thought that the Pujo Commission's investigation of the "money trust," which concentrated on the Morgan firm's practices, had been inspired by certain "Hebrew private bankers." Thus, the new regionalized reserve system made the formulation of national banking policy receptive to a broader range of political influences.[1]

The FTC, on the other hand, confronted problems in the nation's industrial sector. One responsibility was to support the administration's antitrust enforcement. Like the old Bureau of Corporations in the Department of Commerce, its staff collected and analyzed economic information to determine whether infractions had arisen as industry became more concentrated. Supporters also hoped it would mandate uniform financial reporting for industrial and merchandising companies along the lines imposed earlier on the railroads.[2]

The FTC was also committed to developing policies to aid business—particularly smaller enterprises, traditionally an important constituency of the Democratic party. These businesses were often vulnerable to the new competitive forces transforming the economy. Innovations in technology and business management often threatened the interests of these groups. Although society broadly benefited from these developments, many small businessmen remained apprehensive. From their perspective, the new industrial economy dominated by giant enterprises frequently disrupted the market conditions necessary for them to prosper. Besides these long-term economic trends, new fiscal policies also disturbed them. Although substitution of a progressive income tax for a protectionist tariff to finance federal operations liberalized America's international trade, its impacts on small business were not entirely clear. Here again was another problem for this business segment for the FTC to address.[3]

Although the AAPA's leaders tracked the legislation authorizing these new agencies, the events that most influenced them occurred later, when the details of administration were being worked out. Because it was a federation of more than a dozen state associations, the AAPA had difficulty in forming a legislative consensus. Instead, it seemed content to follow the lead of the United States Chamber of Commerce, of which it was a member.[4]

The first proposal affecting public accountancy grew out of efforts to assure the liquidity of the commercial paper discounted by the FRB. The regulators wanted member banks to accept only paper whose quality had been evaluated through objective analysis of financial statements audited by independent accountants and not through subjective judgments about a borrower's character.[5]

The central bankers, however, had misgivings about some public accountants. Leading New York note brokers complained about the competence and probity of some practitioners. This negative perception may also have been encouraged by the elite accountants through their contacts in Washington, particularly the FRB's vice-chairman, Frederic Delano, and the FTC's chairman, Joseph E. Davies, and commissioner, Edwin N. Hurley. To screen out the incompetent or dishonest, the FRB in 1915 planned, under its "Circular Thirteen," to judge the credentials of all accountants wishing to practice before it. Those admitted to federal practice were to be signified "zone experts."[6]

The FRB proposal coincided with a FTC plan to mandate uniform accounting for manufacturing and merchandising enterprises. As in the case of the railroads, accounting information was thought vital for effective regulation. Louis D. Brandeis, Woodrow Wilson's key economic advisor before his appointment to the Supreme Court in 1916, recognized the importance of financial disclosure and initially counseled the administration to require industry to provide it. Moreover, uniform accounting, it was thought, would also benefit credit analysts and investors by making financial statements more comprehensible.[7]

Although it supported statement certification, the AAPA did not favor either the zone expert or the uniform accounting plans. Members feared that federal regulation would undermine professional autonomy. Instead of practitioners regulating themselves, politicians with little concern for or understanding of professional accounting matters would control decisions. The accountants abjured uniform reporting because it lacked flexibility. They also protested that many businesses lacked adequate accounting systems to assure timely preparation of the requisite financial statements. Moreover, many clients were reluctant to disclose detailed operating data required by this regulation.[8]

Besides accountants and businessmen, farmers also disclaimed Circular Thirteen. Their representatives argued that few farmers kept elaborate books of account. Preparing financial statements was not a common practice in agriculture, and requiring it for credit purposes was considered too expensive and burdensome.[9]

The Wilson administration subsequently abandoned the original version of Circular Thirteen because of new imperatives associated with the approaching presidential election and concerns about foreign affairs. During its first three years, the regime had expended much of its political capital achieving the New Freedom's primary legislative objectives. Opposition to the FRB's plans, as we have seen in the reactions of accountants, businessmen, and farmers, was beginning to mount against certain aspects of these reforms. The need to build support for the nearing 1916 presidential campaign encouraged the administration to forgo its effort to extend regulation and to concentrate instead on improving relationships with business groups. Furthermore, rising public concern about neutrality and military preparedness began to supplant economic regulation as a national political issue.[10]

Louis Brandeis also prompted a similar change at the FTC. To bolster Wilson's candidacy, he advised the FTC to dedicate more of its limited resources to developing popular programs aiding small business. Soon the FTC's accounting priorities changed radically. The thrust toward uniform financial accounting, potentially helpful in antitrust enforcement, was laid aside as too divisive. New emphasis was placed on projects that helped small businesses determine the costs of their products and services.[11]

The new direction found strong support within the FTC, particularly from Chairman Davies and Commissioner Hurley. The need for improved product costing was stressed in Hurley's book, *Awakening of American Business* (1917), which outlined a strategy for greater American international competitiveness. Both commissioners believed that inadequate cost data were a major cause of small business failure, and they strongly advocated programs providing guidance on cost measurement techniques. They also felt that uniform financial accounting was infeasible until more companies, both large and small, established effective product cost systems. They were supported in this view by Robert H. Montgomery of Lybrand, Ross Brothers and Montgomery and by other members of the AAPA's Committee on Federal Legislation. Moreover, the drive for better cost information also appealed to other FTC bureaucrats, who felt it could be useful in controlling inflation.[12]

The cost accounting emphasis and the desire to draw closer to the AAPA also reflected a growing perception within the FTC of the need for the cooperation of business groups in preparing for possible future involvement in the European war. A few months later, American industry was drawn into a massive mobilization in which business and professional associations played key roles in implementing the policies of the War Industries Board (WIB). By 1916, the AAPA had already formed a special committee to serve the Naval Consulting Board, which presaged its involvement with the WIB.[13]

The accountants' organization accommodated to these public policy changes in two ways. First, they donated their expertise to help the federal agencies achieve their redefined objectives. In 1917, they contributed the publication "Approved Methods of Preparing Balance Sheet Statements," written by John C. Scobie of Price Waterhouse. This bulletin, which the accountants periodically updated, presented standard formats of financial statements for a commercial or industrial enterprise. The AAPA's Committee on Relations with Credit Men also prepared bulletins educating businessmen and bankers about the benefits of statement certification. Another committee prepared for the FTC cost accounting guides for the following industries: lithographers, typesetters, pipe manufacturers, paper and pulp processors, chair manufacturers, and retail merchants.[14]

The second response was a decision reached by the elite leaders to reorder the national organization. Sensitive to the FRB's concerns, Joseph Sterrett in 1915 proposed the formation of the Special Committee on the Form of Organization of the Association. Its mission was to develop a plan to improve the profession's quality by restructuring the AAPA into a more tightly controlled entity, thereby dissuading the government from intruding on professional prerogatives. As we shall see, the elite desired a reorganization both to strengthen their position within the association and to advance the programs they believed critical in winning acceptance for the profession.[15]

Practitioner Division over the Direction
of Professional Development

Although successful in the rudiments of profession building, the AAPA was unable to consolidate its control in the years before America's entry into World War I. The opposition came largely from local firm practitioners. Their attitudes toward the elite had always been ambiguous. Many admired the professional ideals promoted by the leaders and supported their efforts to win recognition for accountancy's useful skills in Washington. Yet they were suspicious, partly because of their own economic interests and partly because of the differences in outlook stemming from their social origins. As their influence grew in the constituent state organizations, the local practitioners successfully opposed the elite's efforts to transform the AAPA into a strong agency of professional governance.

Recognizing that their influence within the federation was declining, the elite sought a radical restructuring in 1916. They pointed to the alleged failure of the state licensing authorities to demark proper boundaries for the profession as the reason for the change. Certification should be transferred, they said, from the state to the professional association. From their perspective, state licensing board appointments had been influenced too often by political considerations and not often enough by candidate qualifications. They were also concerned by the lack of uniformity in the qualifying examinations and the manner in which they were graded. They wanted high barriers to entry in the form of high minimum educational standards.

Before World War I, the AAPA promoted two basic mechanisms for standardizing the profession throughout the United States: the model CPA law and the model state society bylaws. Neither had been a complete success. While the model law was generally followed in the northeastern and north-central states, many of its key elements were not implemented in the South and the West. The high school educational requirement was thought to be overly restrictive in states with poorly developed educational systems. Furthermore, no practice experience was required for licensure in three states: Illinois, Vermont, and Washington. The AAPA experienced frustration in encouraging the creation of nonpartisan licensing boards made up exclusively of practitioners. Many states proved reluctant to grant reciprocity to out-of-state accountants. Nor did the model bylaws solve the perceived problem of excessive diversity in a profession growing rapidly nationwide.[16]

The elite first responded by calling for the establishment of a permanent secretariat in the AAPA. Prominent among those urging this change was Joseph E. Sterrett of Price Waterhouse, who had been elected president in 1908 without incurring the bitter opposition experienced earlier by his British colleague, Dickinson. Because of Sterrett's strong insistence, Alphyon P. Richardson was in 1912 appointed secretary and editor of the *Journal of Accountancy*. Richardson replaced Thomas Cullen Roberts, a local practitioner who had served voluntarily. As editor, he also replaced Professors Joseph F. Johnson and Edward S. Mead.[17]

From Sterrett's perspective, Richardson's engagement enhanced the Executive Committee's effectiveness in implementing association policies. The new secretary-editor could devote all his energies to the AAPA's programs. Because he was a full-time employee dependent upon his salary, he could also be expected to show deference to the committee's members. In the past, if an independent agent such as Roberts had disagreed with committee plans, he could sabotage them by failing to push matters with vigor. But an employee was less likely to run this risk.

Sterrett and his colleagues could not, however, counter the growing influence of the state societies in the AAPA. This shift could be seen in the experiences of the NYSSCPA, the largest state organization. By 1915 membership in the state society grew to 251, about one-quarter of the national association's total membership. The dominance of the local practitioners was reflected by the fact that only seven presidents through 1940 were from national firms. Moreover, in New York a second pattern emerged that was distressing to those among the elite who were concerned about the social backgrounds of those entering the profession. As early as 1906, a significant number of the names of candidates passing the CPA examination there were of eastern European origin. In the following decade, the proportion of these new men among those certified steadily increased. The trends evident in the NYSSCPA were also apparent in varying degrees in other state societies.[18]

By 1914, the growth of the local practitioners' influence threatened the national firm practitioners' ability to promote plans for professional ordering. The locals, for instance, consistently defeated proposals for widening the scope of the rules of ethics. So serious was the tension that in 1916 the national firm leaders demanded that such states as Wisconsin, whose licensing laws were viewed as deficient, be banished from the AAPA.[19] Other incidents during these years reflected the mounting conflict in the profession and mirrored as well the broader conflict taking place in Europe. This too created pressures for reorganization.

Rumors of War and the Pressure for Reorganization

The European war contributed to the mounting sense of urgency among elite practitioners, motivating them to take strong action. Many personally identified with the national and cultural traditions of the Allied powers. They saw their traditions threatened at home and abroad and were encouraged to abandon compromise. They did away with the federalist structure of governance and centralized control. They firmly ensconced power in the hands of the "best men." Furthermore, the restructuring facilitated their plans to draw the association into the national preparedness movement. In accounting, war's pressures convinced practitioners that they should act forcefully to protect their vital interests and those of their clients. Many of them had benefited greatly from the great influx of British investment into America since the 1890s. That stake grew as the war intensified. The House of Morgan served both as Allied agent in managing the Inter-Allied Purchasing Commission and as underwriter for Allied war bonds in America. Price Waterhouse provided accounting and auditing services for various Allied relief programs, while Arthur Young and Company worked for the purchasing commission. In fact, the Young firm was compelled for a time to take over the accounting function of the Winchester Arms Company, which had nearly been driven bankrupt while expanding to satisfy the new Allied demands. That same year the AAPA also selected new attorneys, the firm of Cravath, Henderson, and de Gersdorff, who were also the American legal representatives of the Bank of England. There were also personal reasons for supporting the Allied cause—family and friends in England.[20]

Many of the AAPA's elite leaders became advocates of the preparedness movement, which was largely lead by pro-Allied elements. Former president E. L. Suffern pushed within the Executive Committee in 1915 for direct involvement in the work of the Naval Consulting Board. A special committee including Suffern, Montgomery, and Waldron H. Rand of Massachusetts served as consultants on accounting matters for industrial preparedness and, later, as special advisors to the WIB.[21]

The professional leaders involved in preparedness were, of course,

concerned about what they viewed as the dangerously mixed attitudes of many of their countrymen toward the Allied cause. Many
respectable persons such as Wall Street bankers Jacob H. Schiff and
Paul M. Warburg, identified closely with Germany and urged the
Wilson administration to adopt a more favorable foreign policy toward
the Central Powers. Leaders of German-American groups, whose
members were particularly numerous in the Middle West, were also
opposed to shipment of material and the raising of funds for the
Allies. Others, shocked by the war's terrible destruction, as was indus-
trialist Henry Ford, sponsored peace initiatives to end the fighting.
Moreover, great numbers of Americans were completely apathetic to
the events unfolding in Europe. Morgan partner Thomas C. Lamont,
a strong supporter of the Allies, lamented over the indifference of
southern and western newspapers to the war's progress. Finally, small
terrorist cadres directed by Franz von Papen, military attaché and
future *Reichschancellor*, aided the Central Powers by sabotaging domestic manufacturing and transportation facilities supplying the Allies.
New York's financial community was horrified during July 1915, when
one extremist attempted to assassinate J. P. Morgan, Jr.[22]

During these years, Gilbert Parker of the British Ministry of Information worked diligently to turn American opinion in favor of the
Allies and against the Central Powers. Much of this work involved
the cultivation of support among American professional groups. Although no direct evidence exists of a connection between Gilbert
Parker and the AAPA, there is reason to believe that AAPA leaders
were privately involved in these efforts.[23]

The AAPA was split over this issue, as it was over matters of professional development. In February 1915, for instance, a well-meaning
Elijah Watt Sells used his influence to have the *Journal of Accountancy*
publish his "Plan for International Peace." Sells called for disarma-
ment and the establishment of an arms control system based on the
relative size of each nation's population. A respectful but critical editorial appearing in the same issue indicated that other professional
leaders did not share Sells's hopeful view.[24]

Other prominent practitioners were not committed to the Allied
cause. Typical of this element of the profession were A. C. Ernst and
Durand Springer. Like Sells, both were Middle Westerners of Ger-
manic or Scandinavian background who seemed reluctant to see their
nation take up arms against a country with which they must have felt
a cultural affinity. Ernst, founder of the growing firm of Ernst and
Ernst, resented the AAPA leadership for the rest of his life for being
too "English." Durand Springer, for many years secretary of Michi-

gan's board of accountancy, also became disenchanted with the tone of the New York–based leadership.[25]

The Reorganization

Nervous about dissension in the AAPA ranks, the elite pushed for tighter central control. The chief architects of change were the members of Sterrett's Special Committee on the Form of Organization of the Association, including W. Sanders Davies of New York, Carl Nau of Ohio, Waldron H. Rand of Massachusetts, and Elijah Watt Sells of New York.[26]

The Sterrett plan, first presented to the board of trustees on April 10, 1916, substituted a more centrally controlled structure for the decentralized one that had been in place since 1903. Instead of membership based on a state society affiliation or inclusion in the category of unaffiliated "society members," there were only two classes of members, fellows and associates. The state societies were completely spun off from the new entity. Dues were one hundred dollars a year, and local members found themselves paying to be in two organizations. Accountants no longer in practice, such as those in industry or education, were reduced in status to nonvoting associates. Existing state society members continued as members of the new association, but its ruling council was no longer selected by the state organizations. Thus the new structure eliminated the need to build a broad consensus among the leaders of what were viewed as meddling and obstructionist state society organizations.[27]

There was, of course, opposition to this new course. There were those in the organization who harbored misgivings. Some, such as John F. Forbes of San Francisco and the Scottish accountant John B. Niven of Touche, Niven, and Company, frankly questioned whether the reorganization might not create serious future problems. Forbes, who had for years worked diligently to keep the rival practitioners of San Francisco and Los Angeles united in the California Society of Certified Public Accountants, understood the dangers of not providing adequate representation from different geographic regions and types of practice. On the other hand, Niven, who was mindful of the disruptive competition that grew between the chartered and incorporated accountants in Britain, prophesied quite accurately that the Sterrett plan would contribute to the development of the same sort of bitter intraprofessional rivalry in America.[28]

The opposition to the new plan was poorly organized, however, and the AAPA's trustees adopted the proposal at its September 1916 meeting. The new entity, to be known as the Institute of Accountants in the United States of America—later as the American Institute of Accountants—was chartered in Washington, D.C., on September 19, 1916. Its first president was W. Sanders Davies, the first chartered accountant to be elected to this office since 1899. In addition to its president's background, the composition of its first council was another sign of this organization's nature: ten of its thirty-five members had been born in Britain or Canada. They, of course, rejected the CPA conception that Haskins had promoted in 1897. They tried, instead, to reorder the American profession along the lines previously developed by the chartered accountants. This radical change split the profession in the 1920s, seriously undermining its ability to govern its own affairs or to serve the public interest.[29]

But in the short run the new association and its leaders enhanced their prestige through their services in the nation's war effort. AIA committees aided the national defense by helping the War Department to create accounting systems for cantonments and the WIB to develop methods for cost-plus procurement contracts. The United States Civil Service Commission accepted the institute's evaluation of the credentials of all who applied to serve as government accountants during the war. The new food administrator, Herbert Hoover, appealed to this association to recommend a practitioner to help his agency establish financial reporting systems to control the distribution of domestic food supplies. Several leaders also served in key wartime positions: George O. May of Price Waterhouse served on the war loan staff of the Treasury; his partner, Joseph Sterrett, served on the Advisory Tax Board; Charles S. Ludlam of Haskins and Sells served as the American representative to the Inter-Allied Transactions Committee; and Robert Montgomery served at the WIB.[30]

The prestige garnered for accountancy and its national representative association during the war made its leaders more confident of the professional programs they aggressively advanced with the return of peace. There were three elements in the elites' revised pattern of professional governance. Two elements, a new certifying examination and new policies toward educational institutions, aimed at redefining professional boundaries. The other element involved the strengthening of the association's central leadership through a stronger code of professional ethics.

Ethics Revision and the Revolt
of the Local Practitioners

Public accountants' moral role had long been a difficult matter for the AIA's leaders to define. They had, however, tried to address this problem by widening the scope of professional ethics after the 1916 reorganization. Leaders such as Sterrett wanted to make these rules a key part of the new structure of professionalism. Other successful and prestigious professional and business groups already had mandated similar rules. The AIA frequently cited the examples of law and medicine. Even business and trade associations, which rarely made claims to professional status, were infatuated with the idea of promulgating codes of behavior.[31]

A strong code seemed essential to legitimize the AIA's claim to the power to regulate professional activities. It communicated to the public the good intentions of the association. The accountant's special knowledge would thus be used selflessly in the public's interest.

A strong code might also minimize professional competition and secure the positions of the better-established firms. New rules mandated in 1921, for instance, prohibited advertising and the direct solicitation of clients, thus blunting the expansion of aggressive newcomers. It was, in fact, this aspect of the rules that undercut the AIA's attempt to centralize control of the profession. The rules sparked the rebellion of many local practitioners and contributed to the formation of yet another rival national organization.[32]

Though debated for years, concerns about "unethical" competition did not become a central item on the AIA's policy agenda until 1918. That year the Special Committee on Ethical Publicity was formed to make recommendations to the Council about the propriety of solicitation and advertising. Although many of the chartered accountants abhorred "touting," some on the Council disagreed. Consequently, the Council's initial reaction in 1919 was a compromise. It merely issued a resolution, at George O. May's behest, expressing its disapproval of circular letters promising prospective clients substantial tax savings.[33]

The debate, however, was resolved in the following years after the formation of an alliance between practitioner leaders in New York and Ohio. The primary movers were May, his partner Sterrett, and Carl H. Nau of the Cleveland firm of Swearingen, Nau, and Rusk. These practitioners seem clearly to have been motivated by a desire to contain the disruptive market competition of aggressive professional rivals. Carl Nau had connections with the Swearingen family of Cleve-

land and with the Standard Oil interests in that city. He was elected
AIA president in 1920 after completing a two-year term as chairman of
its Committee on Professional Ethics. There had been hope that this
midwesterner with a German surname and a local firm affiliation
would rebut the criticism that the association was too "eastern," "English," and "big-firm" oriented.[34]

While the firm was indeed small, even more important was that it
was close to one of the new profession's most flamboyant practice
developers, the Cleveland-based firm of Ernst and Ernst. The Ernst
brothers, A. C. and T. C., represented just the type of brash outsiders
that those in the inner circle of the AIA wished to contain. Starting in
1903, they had rapidly built a large Ohio practice both by advertising
in newspapers and by employing a staff of salesmen. Nor did the
retirement of T. C. from the partnership in 1906 discourage A. C. from
his ambition to expand far beyond the confines of Ohio. By 1928, Ernst
and Ernst controlled a network of thirty-nine offices and, by this
measure, was the largest practice operating in the United States.[35]

Nau's allies in New York, May and Sterrett, were also distressed by
what they viewed as abusive advertising. They were concerned about
what they thought was the unfair competition of former IRS employees who set themselves up as "tax experts" and implied in their
advertising that they enjoyed special influence at the service. To check
this competition, the AIA in 1920 supported an unsuccessful proposal
to bar former revenue agents from practicing before the IRS for two
years after resigning from the service. Still disturbed, the two accountants traveled to Washington in 1923 to discuss their concerns with
the assistant secretary of the Treasury, Seymour Parker Gilbert. Shortly thereafter, Gilbert was admitted as a partner to the law firm of
Cravath, Henderson, and de Gersdorff, attorneys to both Price Waterhouse and the AIA. Later, he joined Sterrett on the staff of the Dawes
Reparations Committee as agent general for reparation payments until 1930. Another ally that May enlisted in this battle was Professor
Thomas S. Adams of Yale University, who served as economic advisor
to the solicitor general of the IRS.[36]

The AIA and the Treasury Department shared an interest in an
improved code. At the annual meeting in 1921, Fred G. Angevine, an
assistant solicitor at the IRS, delivered the keynote address and urged
the AIA to follow the example of the American Bar Association and to
adopt ethical rules prohibiting advertising and other forms of "unethical" behavior. Angevine pointed out that the Treasury's Committee on
Enrollment and Disbarment was combating the abusive advertising of

self-proclaimed "tax experts" by prohibiting them from practice before the agency.[37]

In the subsequent discussion of this speech, Edward E. Gore, president in 1922, proposed that the rules barring advertising, previously drafted by the Committee on Professional Ethics, should now be adopted. A debate ensued in which many local practitioners voiced their opposition. Prominent in the opposition were Durand W. Springer, secretary of the Michigan State Board of Certified Public Accountants and the auditor of the University of Michigan; Charles W. Main, the managing partner of a regional firm based in Pittsburgh; Charles Hecht, a local practitioner from New York who was active in that state's professional society activities; Clinton H. Scovell of Massachusetts; and William B. Castenholz of Illinois.[38]

Their arguments were varied. Some charged that the prohibition should be limited only to tax practice to satisfy the IRS. Others claimed that advertising was necessary to explain the benefits of accounting services to small business operators. Durand Springer attacked the contention that a code of ethics was a necessary aspect of professionalism; he boldly asserted the unpopular notion that public accountancy was not a profession at all but a higher class of business. In his view the average level of educational attainment among both national and local firm practitioners was too low to classify them in the same category as doctors and lawyers. Springer, who had earned a bachelor's degree at Albion College in Michigan and a master's degree in economics at the University of Michigan, ranked among the very few whose education had extended beyond the secondary school level. From his perspective the claims to professional status were not justified.[39]

But these last-minute objections could not dissuade the majority from later voting in favor of the rules prohibiting advertising. Gore's proposal passed 150 to 68. This action had several immediate consequences, one of which was quite unforeseen by the AIA's leadership.[40]

The Executive Committee immediately confronted A. C. Ernst and sought to compel him to curtail his unethical behavior. Receiving little satisfaction from the strong-willed Ernst, the Executive Committee, functioning as a trial board, summoned Ernst and his two partners, Horace Manning and Lester W. Blyth, to New York to face charges of unprofessional conduct. The trial never took place. Ernst, who had long believed that the AIA was too strongly influenced by English professional customs, resigned from its membership, as did his two partners.[41]

This situation drove out many local practitioners. It was becoming clear that the AIA was changing in ways they did not favor. The advertising ban was viewed as a first step in the emergence of the unwelcome program of professionalism fostered by national firm practitioners. Soon there were disturbing hints about discontinuing the coveted CPA badge of competency and substituting a new mode of national licensing administered by the AIA. These threats to the status of the state-certified public accountants resulted in the formation of a rival body, the American Society of Certified Public Accountants, during December 1921.[42] By 1936 the ASCPA would grow to 2,135 members, as compared to the AIA's 2,239.[43]

But the advertising rule did prompt the AIA to provide publicity about the special services offered by public accountants to the business community. The association-sponsored publicity tried to defuse local practitioner's criticism that the advertising ban denied small businesses information about the benefits of accountants' services. A newly organized Bureau of Public Affairs responded by distributing about a dozen circular letters to as many as half a million businessmen (in each case) on topics ranging from "The Crime Tendency" to "Federal Tax Simplification."[44]

Ultimately, the publicity program failed because it did not interest the AIA's elite leadership. They had been tapped twice within the decade to make contributions for establishing a research library and purchasing a headquarters building. The elite members whose practices were already flourishing saw little need to finance publicity aimed primarily at small and marginal businesses. As George O. May stated, practitioners had more than enough business, and what was really needed was a greater emphasis on assuring high quality practice. By 1926, it was obvious the days of the Bureau of Public Affairs were numbered. Soon its sole employee resigned.[45]

The disruption of practitioner unity resulting from the revision of the ethics code was soon amplified by discordant reactions to other aspects of the elites' vision of professional governance. One such response resulted from the efforts to redefine the methods used to certify practitioner competency.

Redefining Professional Boundaries:
New Modes of Certifying Competency

The second element in the AIA's postwar program involved a revision in the ways competency would be certified. An early step taken by this organization was the establishment of its own examination and board of examiners. It was vital for an association that sought greater autonomy in ordering professional affairs to provide the public with assurances about member competency. One explanation for the reorganization was the perceived inadequacies of the state boards in excluding the incompetent. Developing a more challenging examination, it was thought, would also legitimize efforts to obtain a congressional charter broadening the AIA's powers to control professional activities nationally and displacing the state agencies as validators of practitioner skills.

The new board of examiners was responsible for establishing minimum educational and experience requirements. The basic standard established in 1917 included successfully completing "a satisfactory preliminary education," generally interpreted to mean secondary school. Candidates also needed five years of practice experience, but this was reduced to three years for college graduates. The examination tested the same four topics addressed by the state boards.[46]

The AIA first proffered its examination to all states at the 1917 annual meeting of the Association of Certified Public Accountant Examiners (ACPAE). Many welcomed this offer, particularly those whose boards were pressed to provide the administrative support necessary for the operation of a professional examination. In 1917, three states adopted the AIA examination; by 1921, this number rose to thirty-six. However, some states with large practitioner communities and well-organized licensing bureaucracies, including New York and Massachusetts, continued their own examinations until after World War II.[47]

Ironically, the broad acceptance of the new examination was soon used to justify efforts to substitute AIA membership for state licensing as the sole badge of professional authority. The shift away from CPA licensing first became apparent in 1917. At the annual meeting in Washington, D.C., Carl Nau gave an address, "Comparative Value of Personal Reputation and Conferred Degrees," which belittled the importance of "degrees" in judging the worth of a professional man. Nau's remarks remained purposely ambiguous and could be interpreted as an attack on the CPA designation (which was commonly referred to as a degree) or on a university degree. It was clear to his listeners that his remarks were primarily directed at the CPA license.[48]

Nau's words were followed by revealing actions. Soon the AIA's representatives lobbied the Senate for a national charter allowing it to certify public accountants throughout the United States. These actions further alienated those who had earned their CPAs and had a vested interest in its continuation as the primary symbol of competency. Nau's policy induced many practitioners to join Springer's ASCPA, which was committed to defending state licensure.[49]

Although the ASCPA was the AIA's major antagonist, there emerged yet another association, one whose brief history also shaped the course of professional development. This group, the National Association of Certified Public Accountants (NACPA), was founded in the District of Columbia during the early 1920s by former IRS employees. It sought both CPA legislation in the District of Columbia, which had no licensing law until 1922, and also a congressional charter.

Though the NACPA appealed to accountants unable to pass their states' licensing examinations, concerns about its standards undermined its credibility. Initially, members were granted diplomas identifying them as "certified public accountants" merely by paying the requisite fee. Later, after receiving criticism for operating a "diploma mill" and selling "bogus degrees," the NACPA engaged Frank Broaker to develop an examination. To Broaker, this assignment represented a welcome chance to get back into the limelight. Ignored by the new generation of AIA leaders, Broaker had resigned from the association he had served earlier as president. Though he continued to be active in the NYSSCPA, the damage done to his reputation in 1898 by charges of conflict of interest in his role as CPA examiner apparently tainted his later efforts to maintain professional leadership.[50]

The NACPA's plans soon collapsed under the combined attacks of the AIA and the ASCPA. The AIA engaged J. Harry Covington, of the Washington law firm of Covington and Rublee, who won a federal injunction prohibiting the NACPA from issuing its bogus credentials.[51]

After squelching the NACPA, the AIA's leaders renewed their efforts to establish their organization as the national certifier of practitioner competency. Like the now defunct NACPA, they also sought licensing in the District of Columbia and a federal charter. In the first matter, the AIA formed an alliance with the District of Columbia Institute of Public Accountants to support the Capper Bill (1922), which, among other objectives, ratified several professional licensing laws in the district. Secondly, President Edward E. Gore, a partner in the Chicago firm of Smart and Gore, lead the effort in 1922 to charter the Institute of Chartered Accountants in America. In petitioning Congress, the AIA patterned its actions on the examples of the Carnegie Foundation and the American Institute of Biology. This lobbying, however, eventually proved futile. The plan had too many enemies to succeed in a locally oriented institution such as Congress.[52]

The AIA's program, however, was economically unacceptable and socially distasteful to many local practitioners, some of whom resented the British ties of the chartered accountants. The perception of the AIA as the bastion of those of Anglo-Saxon background was reinforced by two provisions of its new examination. First was the 1917 exemption allowing some prospective members to bypass written examinations and to be admitted, instead, on the basis of oral questioning by the board. The second suspect exception, introduced in 1922, allowed the board to accept members who either had passed a state CPA examination not administered by the AIA or were members of a foreign professional society. These alternatives had presumably been designed to accommodate seasoned practitioners lacking the time to study for the AIA's rigorous examination. But like the waiver provisions of the various states, these exemptions were viewed as devices to admit those with connections to the leadership.[53]

Animosity heightened when it became apparent that several firms had sponsored the admission of increasing numbers of chartered accountants. Many of them who came to America after 1916 did not sit for state CPA examinations. (Many did not wish to become citizens, a nearly universal requirement.) In 1926, for instance, twenty-nine individuals (twenty as full members and nine as associates) were admitted without taking the written examination. At Price Waterhouse's New York office during the previous year, ten (eight members and two associates) of the thirty-one of the firm's personnel listed on the AIA's roll were not CPAs.[54]

Many AIA leaders doubtless wished to admit seasoned chartered accountants who experienced difficulty in obtaining employment in postwar Britain. Leaders such as May, who traveled annually to the old country, were aware of the poor employment prospects in Britain. In contrast, the United States was experiencing great prosperity, with many opportunities for trained accountants.[55]

The AIA's apparent cultural bias and its ambiguous attitude toward the CPA credential persuaded many practitioners to join the rival ASCPA. This association became the focus of an odd social ecumenism among disparate groups considered marginal by many of the AIA's leaders. The ASCPA attracted local practitioners from the South and the West, men who thought the AIA too "eastern" and too closely allied with big-city bankers. A large contingent of German-Americans led by Durand Springer of Michigan, W. B. Castenholz of Illinois, Jean Paul Muller of Washington, D.C., Edwin Ober Pride of Boston, and A. C. Ernst of Cleveland were also attracted; they found the AIA too "English." Charles Hecht of New York also helped to recruit a substantial number of practitioners who were Jewish and of eastern European origin. Moreover, many Irish Catholic practitioners were drawn in through the leadership of Charles L. Hughes of Jersey City, New Jersey, and Dean John T. Madden of New York University. The ASCPA thus became a formidable rival of the AIA.[56]

While the elites' ambitious program alienated many local practitioners, they were more successful in forming cooperative relationships with the growing body of accounting educators.

Redefining Professional Boundaries: Changing Relations with Educators

The AIA reopened its full membership to educators in 1923. This initiative was partly facilitated by the important roles of some leading practitioners in advancing accounting education, including Robert H. Montgomery at NYU and Columbia, John R. Wildman at NYU, James O. McKinsey at the University of Chicago, Arthur Andersen at Northwestern University, Waldron H. Rand at Boston University, Eric L. Kohler at Northwestern University, and J. Hugh Jackson at Harvard University.[57]

Moreover, the AIA's leadership was worried about the ASCPA's active courting of educators. They responded by increasing educator membership on its Committee on Education and by identifying two issues for them to address. First, like its AAPA predecessor, the committee surveyed college accounting curricula to advise the board of examiners which were of university caliber. Later, in 1924, it drafted a standard accounting curriculum. Second, the educators classified the types of services practitioners rendered in order to define better the body of knowledge that their pedagogy should address.[58]

The AIA's leaders also drew the educators closer by promulgating an ethical rule prohibiting members from associating with proprietary schools of accounting. The collegiate educators were concerned about these schools. Like the Packard Institute of the 1890s, they were run for profit and were considered to be of low academic standing. In 1929, the AIA's Executive Committee expelled Andrew J. Quigley, the operator of the American University of Commerce in Illinois (on the charge of advertising for prospective students). This expulsion led to a new rule forbidding members to associate with schools advertising or soliciting students. Besides directing members away from proprietary schools, this action was an indirect slap at some ASCPA leaders, such as W. B. Castenholz, who operated the LaSalle Extension Institute, a Chicago-based correspondence school.[59]

With a similar goal in mind, the AIA conducted a profit study for the National Bureau of Economic Research (NBER). The impetus came from George O. May, whom Professor Edmund F. Gay induced to serve in 1924 as a NBER director. Data were gathered by mailing confidential questionnaires to members about their largest clients' profitability. Thus the AIA acquired for the first time an extensive body of information prepared on a consistent basis and suitable for comparative analyses. Professor William A. Paton of the University of Michigan's Accounting Department prepared the summarization published in 1935 under the title of *Corporate Profits as Shown by Audit Reports*.[60]

In spite of the educators' growing involvement, the AIA's leaders remained reluctant to allow them to participate in the deliberations of the committees addressing technical accounting matters. Not until the 1929 stock market crash and the emergence of the threat of governmental regulation would the leadership, trying to restore morale and build a consensus in a badly divided profession, accept educators as participants in the discussion of important technical issues.[61]

They did, however, involve the educators in their efforts to recruit candidates from acceptable social backgrounds for future leadership in the profession's most elite firms. Foremost in this development was F. W. Nissley, a Princeton graduate and a partner at Arthur Young and Company's New York office. As chairman of the Committee on Education, Nissley recommended to the Council that the AIA help member firms recruit candidates from the nation's most prestigious universities—that is, candidates who trained in the liberal arts rather than in business disciplines. Nissley and others who shared his upper-middle-class background were concerned about the caliber of the graduates from the flourishing business schools. Some thought these graduates were trained too narrowly as accounting technicians. Candidates were needed, it was believed, who had a broader cultural grounding and could easily interact with Wall Street's sophisticated bankers and lawyers. The prestige of an Ivy League education was becoming greatly respected by many of the elite. Montgomery sent his sons to Princeton; Arthur Young preferred to recruit there. May sent his son to Yale; the AIA would hire its new assistant secretary, John Lansing Carey, from that university in 1924.[62] As Nissley explained:

Very few of the present members of the Institute have had a formal education in those subjects which are generally supposed to develop the mind to its full possibilities, for example, English composition and literature, modern languages, higher mathematics, history, Latin and Greek, physics and chemistry, political economy, philosophy, economics and related subjects.

Despite the above statistics which give evidence that many men have succeeded as public accountants in the past without a formal general education, your committee is of the opinion that the public accountant of the future would be materially benefited by a study of some of these subjects before he takes up his technical education or concurrently with the latter, and judging from the letters which have been received most of the successful firms throughout the country concur in this opinion.[63]

There was concern about social background as well as training. The second-generation Americans graduating from accounting programs at schools such as NYU, CCNY, and Wharton, though useful as staff accountants, were not the sort of men whom many of the elite felt should be groomed for leadership. NYU, for instance, a school with a large enrollment of students of recent immigrant origins, provided 57 of the 179 college-educated American practitioners admitted to the AIA from 1917 to 1926. Accepting such men as partners was believed unwise for fear that they might alienate elite clients. It was the ambitious Monroe Stahrs of this world—stereotyped by Nissley's fellow Princetonian, F. Scott Fitzgerald, in *The Last Tycoon*—that the new plan sought to screen out. The AIA established an Office of Placements to identify acceptable candidates and arrange their interviews with interested firms. By 1930 the program had placed 223 candidates. That year, AIA representatives conferred with students at many colleges and universities: Carleton, Chicago, Franklin and Marshall, Hamilton, Harvard, Hobart, Illinois, Princeton, Syracuse, Tufts, Union, William and Mary, and Yale. With the exception of Illinois, all were prestigious private institutions whose traditional liberal arts programs drew students largely from middle-class, native American backgrounds.[64]

Prospective employers were expected to provide these candidates with guarantees of full-time employment, even during the slow summer seasons. One reason for the disinterest among the upper-middle-class students whom leading firms wanted to attract was the uncertainty of employment. It was common for even the largest firms to lay off most of their staffs at the end of the traditional "busy season" each spring. Moreover, these special graduates could develop greater proficiency by perfecting their professional skills uninterrupted for the entire year. It is unclear how many educators actively supported the Nissley program, but there can be little doubt as to what kinds of social background they had.

Technical Challenges and Professionalization

The major technical accounting and auditing problems encountered during these years by the top accountants of the AIA grew out of the expanded roles they were called upon to play as intermediaries between clients, investors, and federal tax authorities. The demand for their special services heightened as the public's interest in investing grew and as the federal governmental operations were financed increasingly through tax revenues. As so often is the case, making the transition to this new set proved difficult. There was a wide diversity of opinion on the principles underlying both financial and tax accounting. Nor was there consensus about accountants' responsibilities in reporting their findings to investors relying on the financial statements they examined. Growing public criticism of these shortcomings encouraged practitioner leaders to collaborate with allied professional and business elements in addressing these problems. These efforts, however, progressed too slowly to deflect the undesired intervention by federal regulators during the financial debacle of the 1930s.

Accounting and the Challenges of the 1920s

The economic expansion of the 1920s generated strong demands for accounting data by both government and investors. As American society became more complex and interdependent, the need increased for effective modes of communicating economic information. Business continued to prosper through the successful exploitation of new technologies and methods of finance and management. These innovations, in turn, frequently required the formulation of new forms of accounting expression to measure accurately their economic effects. The sage counsel of experienced practitioners about accounting technical matters therefore became highly prized by business and government leaders charged with the responsibility of reporting financial results.

But the failure to develop a comprehensible framework for accountancy seriously undermined public accountants' intermediation between important social groups during this period. Unlike information in such professions as law and medicine, in which expert knowledge was beneficial while remaining essentially a mystery to the public, information in accounting was valuable only if it could be comprehended by such informed users as bankers, brokers, government bureaucrats, and investors. What was critical to users was that it be based on well-defined principles.

But the accounting profession during the 1920s was a house divided on questions of best practice. Substantial variations still existed even in the definitions of many basic terms. In fact, dissatisfaction over the definitions provided by the old AAPA's original Committee on Terminology prompted Walter Mucklow, a Florida practitioner, to urge the AIA's governing council to extend this effort. By 1929, the new Committee on Terminology, chaired by Mucklow, finally published a "tentative" list of definitions for over six thousand accounting terms. Given the extreme variations in basic nomenclature, it is not surprising that this profession's efforts to provide guidance in technical accounting matters seemed so unsatisfying.[1]

While substantial progress was achieved by the government in standardizing tax accounting, major financial accounting issues of vital concern to investors remained unresolved. In taxation, the IRS demanded prompt resolution of important accounting issues affecting its operations. But there was no comparable authority for financial reporting for investors or creditors. Though some bureaucrats at the FTC and the FRB may have desired these powers, there was no chance that they would get them when conservative political regimes dedicated to a free market economy were in office. Moreover, the curtailment of individual liberties during World War I made many Americans leery of proposals to expand federal power. Instead, many believed that the public-spirited volunteerism of business and professional associations, which had seemingly worked so effectively during the recent conflict, represented a more attractive alternative for both ordering society and preserving democratic traditions.

Though many among the investing public remained oblivious to these issues, an increasing number of sophisticated users of financial data began to register concerns about the insufficiency of information provided to investors. The criticisms came from three sources in particular. First were those from allied occupations such as banking and the law, where professionals were hindered in the execution of their professional obligations because of uncertainties about important accounting issues. Other critics were accounting and economics scholars who sought greater order in the body of accounting technical knowledge or who were concerned about the moral dimensions of the profession.

The wide variations in the form and content of financial statements became targets for educators' criticisms. The academic theoreticians were frustrated, however, in trying to establish a sounder intellectual basis for accounting knowledge. What complicated their efforts was the fact that there were many possible alternatives that, under particular circumstances, might satisfy the objectives of financial reporting. What was lacking was a consensus as to what these objectives should be and what information was needed by various statement users.

Though the educational moralists frequently referred to technical details to illustrate their points, they were less concerned with theory. Instead, they pressed for new institutions, preferably governmental, to standardize financial reporting. Unlike their more theoretically oriented colleagues, these critics did not confine their charges to scholarly journals or symposia addressed primarily to a narrow community of experts. Rather, they directed their calls to the broad investing public and thus sought to build a strong political base for more vigorous governmental intervention.

In their efforts to accommodate the concerns of outsiders, the leaders of the AIA were most sensitive initially to the criticisms of those in allied professional groups. It was not until late in the decade, after the problems of financial reporting assumed crisis proportions, that they came to terms with statements being made by their critics.

The Emergence of a Tax Accounting Framework

Early in the decade, when the future looked bright, the AIA's leaders formed close personal relationships with key Treasury Department bureaucrats and members of Congress. This gave the association a voice in shaping the content of federal tax legislation. Since its successful agitation in 1911 for allowing corporate filers to use the accrual basis of accounting, individual leaders of the AIA had maintained close contacts with important legislators and bureaucrats concerned with tax matters. Robert H. Montgomery was a friend of Cordell Hull, chairman of the House Ways and Means Subcommittee, and had advised him about accounting in the drafting of the 1913 legislation. Joseph E. Sterrett of Price Waterhouse had served under Professor Thomas S. Adams of Yale University as vice-chairman of the Advisory Tax Board during the world war. His partner, May, cultivated a close working relationship with Secretary William G. MacAdoo while serving as an advisor to the Treasury and was very close to the under secretaries who had been partners in the law firm of Cravath, Henderson, and de Gersdorff, attorneys to both Price Waterhouse and the AIA. These included Russell C. Leffingwell, who had served as under secretary of the Treasury and after the war had joined the firm of J. P. Morgan as partner. Another was Seymour Parker Gilbert, who eventually succeeded his mentor Leffingwell as under secretary and, as noted above, was instrumental in convincing the AIA to broaden the scope of its code of ethics in 1921.[2]

The AIA leaders, in addition to cultivating these informal channels of communication, tried to influence tax legislation through the testimony of their association's specialist committees and also through the publication of articles on specific tax matters. Committees of the AIA made presentations both to legislative committees and to Treasury officials about proposed law changes. The association built support for its positions by publishing articles or editorials in the *Journal of Accountancy*. Its representatives also contributed to congressional debates over the proper calculation of capital gains, the recognition of profits on installment sales and on the sale of real estate, and the revocation of the tax on capital stock distributions in lieu of cash dividends.[3]

The interaction between the public accountants and the IRS gave rise to new modalities within the Treasury Department to determine what constituted proper tax accounting. Since judging what was acceptable in some tax disputes required official interpretations of the sometimes ambiguous wording of the revenue code, the AIA proposed that the agency publish summaries of its rulings for the public benefit. In 1925 the IRS began issuing its "Revenue Regulations" bulletins, which communicated significant changes in its policies or interpretation of the tax code. In addition, the increasing number of confrontations between taxpayers, their representatives, and the IRS bolstered demands for an oversight board to which the public might ultimately appeal. Working initially with Senator Warren G. Harding of Ohio and, later, Senator Boies Penrose of Pennsylvania, the AIA pressed successfully for the creation of the Board of Tax Appeals. The AIA then was successful in seeing that the board's members were appointed by the president rather than the secretary of the treasury as the IRS had recommended. It also supported the successful nomination of attorney Charles D. Hamel as the board's first chairman.[4]

The AIA was an effective spokesman within the United States Chamber of Commerce. The leaders of the chamber, along with some FTC members, had long been interested in improving cost accounting to help American industry operate more efficiently. The chamber's staff set up a series of committees of volunteer experts drawn from business and government to study various aspects of this problem and to publish their recommendations. Two AIA representatives, E. E. Gore, its president from 1922 until 1924, and David L. Grey, served on the Committee on Cost Accounting. One important accomplishment of this committee was the FTC's depreciation study.[5]

The impetus for this particular project grew out of a survey of sixty thousand corporations (1916) which indicated that nearly one-half of the companies sampled did not estimate the depreciation of their capital assets in calculating profits. Later, the IRS, anxious to standardize practice with respect to depreciation deductions and eager to achieve the Hoover administration's goal of strengthening American industry by reducing corporate tax burdens, began in 1928 to develop depreciation guidelines for specific industries.[6]

Financial Accounting and the Information Needs of Shareholders

The growing number of investors in corporate equities also became increasingly dependent upon the financial statements that the public accountants were certifying. What were especially needed in these summaries were more comprehensive measures of changes in the wealth of equity investors. The estimation of future dividends became the critical determinant of the market value of securities. There was greater emphasis on the problem of measuring profit, and, therefore, the standardization of the accounting for transactions affecting owners' equity accounts became vital. Moreover, many states required that sufficient "earned surplus" exist, above the contribution of investors, before dividends might legally be paid. Financial statements had to provide for all classes of preferred and common stockholders an accurate measure of the surplus earned from the entity's operations. Though many state laws mandated this requirement, none provided any guidance on how "earned surplus" should be measured. Indeed, many "innovative" and often misleading adjustments were being made to these accounts by the managers of some public companies.[7]

At the AIA the primary focus for the discussion of these technical matters was the Committee on Procedure, chaired by Henry B. Fernald of the firm of Loomis, Suffern, and Fernald. This committee and its offshoot, the Special Committee on Earned Surplus, encouraged discussion on what constituted the best practice for recording each particular transaction. While these conferences were usually limited to elite technicians, comments were sometimes solicited by mail from the entire AIA membership. During this period the committee drafted recommendations on such matters as accounting for holding-company and consolidated operations and for the issuance of no-par common stock. When the committees determined that a consensus existed, they communicated their findings to the AIA's ruling council and had one of the members write an article for the *Journal of Accountancy*. No efforts were made, however, to compel the practitioner community to conform to the preferred practice. The judgment of the practitioner was too important to allow social control on any recommendation made by a committee, no matter how well qualified.[8]

In 1926 one issue became so time consuming that it was assigned to a special subcommittee that worked closely with the United States Chamber of Commerce, the American Bankers Association, and the American Bar Association. Accountants, it was clear, were making all kinds of special adjustments for revaluation of assets; moreover, the issuance of no-par stock in corporate reorganization and the establishment of contingency reserves frequently had material impacts on earned surplus. The dilemma facing the profession was that no one really knew whether or not all these variations in practice were consistent with the intent of the state laws. Nor were the committee efforts successful in solving the problem. The profession was too fragmented, the laws too variable to allow for consensus.[9]

Progress in providing guidance was slow because of the small scale of the AIA's research capabilities, the limited time busy members could devote to these questions, and the substantial differences in opinion that divided the practitioners. Inevitably, the resolution of complex problems of accounting expression was left to practitioners and their clients to work out as they thought best. Concern about this lack of progress may have been what motivated May (in 1926) to step down as the managing partner at Price Waterhouse and to devote all his energies to the affairs of the AIA. In any event, the demands from those external to the profession for better and more comprehensive accounting would not wait.[10]

*Educators and the Problem of Establishing a
Theoretical Foundation for Financial Accounting*

The accounting educators pressed hard to place the profession on a firm theoretical base. When the AIA had been reorganized in 1916, all those not engaged full-time in practice had been reduced in status. Cost accountants, financial controllers, and accounting educators were allowed to participate only as nonvoting associates. As a consequence, the cost accountants organized in 1919 the National Association of Cost Accountants, and the financial controllers banded together in 1931 in the Controllers' Institute (the predecessor of the modern Financial Executives' Institute). The educators responded by forming their own national association. In 1917 John R. Wildman, chairman of the Department of Accounting at NYU's School of Commerce and later a partner at Haskins and Sells, Fayette H. Elwell of the University of Wisconsin, Charles C. Huntington of Ohio State University, Martin J. Shugrue of MIT, John Bauer of Princeton University, and John E. Trevelen of the University of Texas founded the American Association of University Instructors of Accounting (AAUIA). The AIA later tried to reverse field and bring the educators back into its fold, but to no avail.[11]

The AAUIA steadily increased in size and influence. Starting with a membership of only seventeen in 1917, it grew to six hundred by 1928. In 1926 the association also began to publish a journal, the *Accounting Review*. Under its second editor, Eric L. Kohler of Northwestern University, the review encouraged serious research into the important but unresolved accounting issues of that day. Through the journal and the association's symposia, the AAUIA attracted attention to the lack of agreement on such crucial issues as how to value assets on a balance sheet—should one use the historic cost of acquisition, the replacement cost, the discounted value of its estimated future economic benefits, or a price-level adjusted basis? Thus the academics drew attention to the inconsistency of application that characterized the profession.[12]

Though many educators wished to work closely with the AIA on such problems, few practitioner leaders were anxious to reciprocate. Many practitioners resisted the idea that accounting could be standardized, fearing that it would eliminate the need for professional judgment. They saw standardization as equivalent to rigidity, which would, they feared, destroy the viability of this medium for communicating the results of complex and changing economic processes. This had been a basic concern earlier when this association opposed the uniform accounting proposals of both the ICC and the FTC. From the standpoint of a man such as May, accounting was not a science based on a fixed set of underlying first principles. If principles existed, they were more akin to those of the law, where changes in practice were based on the successful interpretation of precedent-setting events.[13]

Many accountants also harbored misgivings about the potential value of the educators' contribution to resolving the problems of financial accounting. Few academics had the range of practical experience of the leading practitioners. Moreover, the educators' criticisms may have seemed too brashly stated to many in practice, who, because of their need to maintain client goodwill, were necessarily more circumspect in publicly expressing their professional opinions. Many practitioners also perceived educators as instructors dedicated to teaching basic skills rather than as scholars dedicated to extending through research the horizons of accounting knowledge. Unconstrained by clearly defined obligations to clients, the financial markets, government, or the general public, the intervention of the collegiate accountants was viewed by some as bordering on irresponsibility. Still piqued years later by the aggressive advocacy of some academicians like Eric Kohler, George O. May would subtly rebuke these critics by entitling his two volumes of collected writings *Twenty-five Years of Accounting Responsibility*.[14]

A growing feeling of bitterness toward the AIA eventually developed among the educators. In 1931, Kohler became chairman of the AAUIA's Committee on Accounting Research and Education, a group jointly sponsored by the AIA's rival, the ASCPA. Finally, in December 1934, Kohler called upon the accounting educators to promulgate principles for financial accounting.[15] Writing in the *Accounting Review*, Kohler stated:

For years [the editor] has assailed the smugness of the profession and its inability to set standards for its own conduct and for the information of the public that relies on its findings. . . . For years it has failed to see the problem before it: problems for the complexity of which it alone has been responsible. . . .

To instructors in accounting, this condition of affairs should offer a challenge. Now, more than ever, the voice of enlightened opinion within the profession is needed. Shall we as accountants recognize that the responsibilities of the profession are large, particularly to third persons? Or shall we drift as we have done in the past, waiting, at first hopefully and now fearfully, for someone else to tell us what to do? Is it impossible for us to take any initial responsibility for defining our accountability to the business and financial world and to the investing public?[16]

What Kohler did not appreciate was that important practitioners such as May were also anxious to solve these problems, but in cooperation with outside organizations whose interests were thought congruent with the AIA's. May was not eager, however, to cooperate with Kohler and other research oriented educators viewed as allies of the rival ASCPA. May, instead, wanted to cooperate with client groups. For instance, he worked diligently to bring the AIA and the New York Stock Exchange (NYSE) together to address such matters. Although this choice was a logical one, it did not still the growing public clamor for more rigorous standards.

Financial Accounting's Moral Dilemma

Another source of academic criticism—one that probably did much to heighten the general public's concern about accounting practice—was William Z. Ripley, Ropes Professor of Economics at Harvard University. Ripley had originally been trained as a civil engineer at MIT; interested in economics and sociology, he had earned a doctorate at Columbia in the former subject in 1893.[17]

Ripley's writings in both sociology and economics were pervaded by a strong concern with value. He was worried that traditional American virtues were in danger of being subverted by industrialization and massive immigration. In his first major work after receiving his doctorate, *The Races of Europe: A Sociological Study* (1899), he imputed different personal and moral characteristics to the races and expressed concern for a country whose northern European stock was being diluted. This same concern about the need to preserve traditional values was implicit in his extensive writings on corporate finance.[18]

Though basically committed to free market economics, Ripley thought that government regulation and an informed public made important contributions to a massive, interdependent society. Great concentrations of economic power were developing, he said, and men of dubious backgrounds were rising to positions of leadership. Government was needed to control these new and disturbing forces. In this regard the outlook of the economist was similar to that of his friend Theodore Roosevelt, whose use of governmental power in the earlier Harriman case he had stoutly defended. Moreover, Ripley practiced what he preached. He was active in many federal agencies including the United States Industrial Commission, the War Department, the FTC, and the ICC. The need for governmental regulation to preserve order and value was a theme that ran through all his major works: *Trusts, Pools, and Corporations* (1905), *Railroads: Rates and Regulation* (1912), and *Railroads: Finance and Organization* (1915).[19]

In 1926 Ripley presented in the *Atlantic Monthly* a series of highly critical articles about the insufficient information and inadequate accounting provided to the public about the industrial and utility companies. These essays were published that year as a book entitled *Main Street and Wall Street*. The articles gave specific examples of deficient financial practices. Research alone, he implied, would not solve these problems. What was necessary was the active intervention of the federal government to compel uniform and timely reporting by all corporations whose securities were publicly traded.[20]

Ripley's stinging criticisms brought forth angry rebuttals from George O. May. In a letter to the editor of the *New York Times* on August 27, 1926, and in a keynote speech given before the AIA's annual meeting the next month, May questioned the professor's motives and his conclusions. From May's standpoint, Ripley was again "fronting" for those in the federal bureaucracy, in this case the FTC, who wanted greater powers over business. While May's rejoinders may have soothed the pride of the faithful, they did little to counter the public response to Ripley's arguments.[21]

Criticism of Accountants' Communications

Besides accounting principles, another aspect of contemporary practice that vitiated the AIA's efforts to socialize their members' expertise involved the assurances provided about the fairness of the financial statements they certified. Although all agreed that reporting on the probity of clients' financial statements was a primary service of this profession, there was much less agreement about the form and content of these attestations. This too eroded the profession's prestige during this period.

Though the code of professional ethics prohibited AIA members from certifying statements containing material misstatements or omitting material facts important to investors, this rule was too broad and inexact to prevent abuses. One important group concerned about the need for more standardized expressions was the nation's commercial bankers. It was often difficult for lending officers to judge the information presented in particular financial statements. Extreme variability in the wording of accountants' reports undermined the credibility of the audit services that practitioners were eagerly promoting. These reports too often seemed designed to avoid the expression of a clear-cut and unambiguous opinion by the practitioner about the fairness of financial statements.[22]

The bankers' dissatisfaction had led to the earlier suggestions that the FRB and FTC begin to regulate professional activities by registering all acceptable practitioners. The tightening of standards for admission into the reorganized AIA and the subsequent revision of the FRB bulletin on the preparation of balance sheet statements were early efforts to respond to these criticisms. But these measures failed to satisfy critical bankers. During the early 1920s, they began to articulate their concerns through the Robert Morris Associates, the national representative organization of credit executives and bank lending officers.[23]

The specific issue that first engendered the bankers' criticism was the growing practice of certifying *pro forma* statements instead of ones that reflected an enterprise's actual financial condition. These statements frequently purported to reflect the condition of a borrower after a proposed financing was consummated. The presentation of prospective, rather than actual, conditions was thought by many bankers to be misleading. Although the practice of certifying *pro forma* statements had already been censured by the AIA's Committee on Procedure, it was not formally prohibited.[24]

By 1923, this and related problems led Harvey E. Whitney, president of the Bankers' Trust Company, to call for the organization of a special joint committee of the AIA and the Robert Morris Associates. The AIA's Special Committee on Cooperation with Bankers was chaired by William B. Campbell (May's successor in 1926 as the managing partner at Price Waterhouse), whose firm audited Whitney's bank. But their efforts failed. It soon became apparent that there was little consensus among the practitioners. They could agree about neither the classification of the attestations they provided the public nor the responsibilities they were assuming in providing them. Only the stock market crash would precipitate action—but this would come too late to forestall the drive for regulation.[25]

As these efforts revealed, most practitioners had little leverage that they could use to compel unscrupulous clients to eschew misleading accounting. Even honest managements were frequently reluctant to be forthcoming for fear of revealing valuable proprietary information that might be used to the advantage of competitors. Although many practitioners bravely proclaimed that they would resign an engagement rather than be associated with false or misleading statements, few really had the fortitude to do this. The potentially adverse economic consequences, particularly in cases where a client was a source of substantial fees, were too great to bear. Accountants thus lacked the independent status they needed to become a fully developed profession.

Practitioners such as George O. May saw the dilemma and responded by initiating new policies within their firms. May believed practice problems were best avoided if accountants concentrated on doing better professional work and also on being more selective about the clients they agreed to serve. In 1925, he communicated this view to the members of his firm: "Two essential points in the firm's policy have been, first, that mere volume of business was not in itself attractive and that therefore its policy should be directed towards a constant improvement in the quality of the firm's connections and work, and not to the increase of volume; second, that the firm should never deliberately expand its activities except as the senior personnel of the organization should be adequate to cope with increased responsibilities."[26]

By the 1920s, Price Waterhouse could in this way afford to limit its practice, but less established firms could not. The partners in these less prestigious practices were often willing to accommodate to the high degree of risk implied by the acceptance of assignments from clients who were either economically marginal or thought to be of dubious integrity. It was the practitioners in the great number of firms of this caliber who faced daily the sobering reality of the limits of their powers to compel clients to provide sufficient disclosure. They were reluctant to be pinned down by fewer and less ambiguous choices in framing their reports. It was not until after the Great Crash in 1929 that these circumstances undermining the effectiveness of the profession's basic function changed.

Part of the changing definition of accountants' responsibilities was also determined by the actions of the courts. The primary issue for which the judiciary was slowly beginning to provide guidance during this period was the practitioners' liability to third parties for negligence. In the cases of *Landell v. Lybrand* (1919) and *Craig v. Anyon* (1925), the courts applied the old doctrine that the accountants had no liability to any parties not enjoying "privity of contract" with them. What this meant was that public accountants could be sued for their negligent acts only by their clients; generally, third parties not specifically mentioned in a contract for professional services could not sue except in cases of fraud. If the practitioner knowingly certified false financial statements, then third parties who had experienced losses as a result of their reliance on this false information could sue.[27]

This doctrine, however, did not remain static. In 1931, Benjamin N. Cardozo, chief judge of the New York Court of Appeals, rendered an opinion in the case of *Ultramares Corporation v. Touche* that marked the beginning of an important change in the definition of practitioner responsibilities. In this case (in which the AIA served as an amicus curiae), the plaintiffs argued that the defendant, the firm of Touche, Niven, and Company, had operated fraudulently in the audit of Fred Stern and Company, a bankrupt firm. Though the plaintiffs failed to prove their charges, Judge Cardozo ruled that the public accountant's negligence had been so gross as to constitute "constructive fraud" and ruled in favor of the plaintiffs. This decision, in effect broadened the scope of the practitioners' liability to third parties. Under this new doctrine, accountants were potentially liable for gross negligence to all third parties who relied upon their professional work. They were also potentially liable for ordinary negligence to all "primary beneficiaries," that is, third parties previously identified as recipients of the auditors' reports.[28]

Toward a New Model of Market Governance

Recognizing the worrisome implications these trends had for the future of the accounting profession, George O. May had as early as 1926 begun to formulate a strategy to address the public's concerns about the governance of the financial markets.[29] In this effort he first joined with other leaders in business, government, and education who were interested in sponsoring research aimed at identifying solutions to these problems. This work first centered in the Committee on Corporate Relations of the Social Science Research Council.[30] May had become active in this organization as a consequence of his friendship with Edmund F. Gay, first dean of the Harvard Business School.[31] As chairman of this committee, he helped to define the objectives of research designed to assess the implications for America of the increased public ownership of investment securities. This project also drew him closer to Professor William Ripley, who had been designated by the Rockefeller Foundation as the administrator of its grant supporting this project.[32] Attorney Adolf A. Berle, who taught part-time at the Columbia University Law School, and Gardiner C. Means, a graduate student in economics at Harvard, conducted this study.

They published their findings in 1931 in *The Modern Corporation and Private Property*.[33]

Although the committee's membership originally included many who favored a more active role for government in regulating the financial markets, it gradually changed to one dominated by those who favored an associationalist solution. Besides Ripley, Isaiah L. Sharfman, professor of economics at George Washington University and former student and ICC colleague of Henry Carter Adams, favored a greater governmental role. Ripley, however, left the committee because of serious injuries he sustained in 1927 in an automobile accident in New York City. He was replaced that year by another educator, James C. Bonbright, professor of finance at Columbia University, who also favored greater governmental activism.[34]

Those who seemed not to favor broadening government's role became a majority by 1928. All were friends or professional associates of Chairman May. They were united, largely through their war experience, in the belief that private institutions were appropriate for solving society's most serious problems. Most had either served in or had close contacts during the war with associational committees involved in military mobilization. Waddill Catchings of Goldman, Sachs, had been the chairman of the War Committee of the United States Chamber of Commerce; Henry G. Dalton of Pickland, Mathers, and Company had served on the Steel Committee of the WIB; and attorney Nicholas Kelley had worked with May on the War Loan Staff of the Treasury.[35]

Although the work of Berle and Means is probably best remembered for its analysis of wealth distribution in America in the 1920s and the implications of the growing separation of ownership and control in the modern corporation, it also stressed the need for more objective financial information to assure the equitable and efficient functioning of the financial markets. Their book argued that the groups primarily responsible for adequate financial disclosure were investment bankers in the flotation of new securities and corporate directors and managers in the case of secondary sales of "seasoned" securities. To assure that these groups operated in the public interest, the authors called for increased regulatory powers for the NYSE. Specifically, they cited the need for requiring large public companies to file audited financial statements and for mandating some accounting principles to prevent the most flagrant abuses plaguing contemporary financial reporting. Public accountants were also identified as key agents in assuring that this regulatory mechanism functioned efficiently. In addition to providing statement certification, they would also advise the NYSE about accounting matters.[36]

Given the outlooks of the steering committee, it is not surprising that the study they sponsored did not envision any significant regulatory role for the federal government. The only body other than the NYSE thought relevant to this process was the courts. Aggrieved investors might, it was suggested, seek redress from a firm's investment bankers, directors, or management under a common-law suit for either fraud or violation of the disclosure requirements of particular states' blue sky laws regulating the sale of securities.[37]

It was this vision of market governance that May and his AIA colleagues tried to implement. In 1926, the AIA made an initial overture to the NYSE to develop jointly minimal disclosure standards for listed companies. Initially, however, the stock exchange's leadership (reluctant, it seems, to alienate the boards of directors of listed companies) rebuffed the AIA. After all, rigorous requirements might have induced some companies to delist their securities and register at exchanges that were not so demanding. Instead, the NYSE merely engaged May's firm to act as special accounting advisors to its own Committee on the Stock List.[38]

The Great Crash finally convinced the NYSE that something should be done. The stock exchange reversed their decision in 1930 and agreed again to work with the AIA on the problems of financial reporting. At that year's annual meeting, J. M. B. Hoxsey, an executive assistant to the Committee on the Stock List, read a paper ("Accounting for Investors") in which he, with May's help, identified the major abuses concerning the investing community. He invited the AIA to help develop new accounting standards that would remedy these problems. By that time, however, the public was too convinced to be tolerant of yet another careful study by private parties.[39]

The *Ultramares* case indicated just how weak and poorly focused had been the AIA's efforts to order activities within the profession had been during this decade. The overemphasis on rules to moderate competition and the slowness in developing definitions of professional responsibilities to the public left the association vulnerable to the new criticisms raised after 1929. The tide was beginning to run out on the AIA's efforts to create a new spirit of professionalism. Weakened by the rebellion of the local practitioners and operating in an environment in which practitioners enjoyed little leverage against unscrupulous clients, the AIA had little power to resist the drive of the activist government that came to power during the crisis of the Great Depression.

Part 4

Economic Crisis and Countervailing Associationalism, 1929–1940

The unresolved problems of professional roles and governance apparent in the 1920s came to a head in the atmosphere of crisis during the 1930s. The criticisms of financial reporting gradually became more worrisome as a new political regime came to power in Washington, D.C. Though key leaders of the AIA tried to assist the reformers in the Roosevelt administration, they were unable to prevent the promulgation of sweeping new legislation subjecting practitioners to stricter federal accountability.

The profession was unable to block or substantially amend this legislation in part because it was seriously divided. The differences that separated the AIA and the ASCPA were now deep and seemingly unbridgeable. The AIA had during the 1920s killed off the spirit of compromise with a program that opposed the vital economic and social interests of the ASCPA's members. Relations with educators and others had become similarly frayed, leaving accountancy poorly organized for the political struggle that was to transform the modern profession.

The disturbing flux of this period, however, eventually gave way to a new pattern of government-professional relationships that better protected the interests of both practitioners and the public. This involved the development of new strategies and structures on the part of the accountants to countervail the undesired encroachments of government. It also involved a greater sensitivity on the part of government planners to how the expertise of professional groups might be better applied in maintaining social order.

A New Structure of
Financial Market Governance,
1929–1934

Demoralized by the crash and divided internally, public accountants were unable to influence significantly the New Deal's drive to regulate the nation's securities markets. Cognizant of the complexity of market operations, the draftsmen of the Securities Acts of 1933 and 1934 tried both to strengthen the existing system and to assure probity by defining stricter accountabilities. Their main focus was the many interdependent professional groups, including public accountants, on which the markets depended. By reinforcing functional relationships that contributed to equity and efficiency, the securities acts had a more lasting legacy than other important legislation of the "Hundred Days" that tried unsuccessfully to administer prices.

But the passage of these sweeping laws initially precipitated a series of problems for the AIA's members. The greater power accorded federal regulators inevitably threatened practitioner autonomy. Government bureaucrats were now authorized to evaluate the professional work of accountants. Equally vexing was the widening exposure of practitioners to investor malpractice suits.

These acts also threatened the AIA's image as the nation's authority in financial accounting. The lack of substantial guidance in financial accounting exacerbated relations between the practitioners and the SEC. Soon the federal agency began mandating new accounting rules for corporate registrants. Moreover, expanded federal regulation encouraged another rival professional organization, the one representing accounting educators, to challenge the AIA's leadership for promoting research to determine what constituted "generally accepted accounting principles."

These disturbing trends, in turn, intensified the debate within the AIA as to the proper boundaries of the profession. The decline in the association's ability to shape the outcome of these events convinced many that its claim to leadership could be retrieved only by broadening its membership base and, consequently, its political power. Besides legitimizing its claim to leadership, the reunification of the practitioner community would reduce the confusion of important outsiders, who had frequently been bewildered by the competing claims to authority.

The AIA and the Emergence of the Securities Acts

The AIA played a minor role in the public debate over the New Deal's securities market legislation in 1933 and 1934. This was partially conditioned by the association's preference for centering the regulatory process in private institutions such as the NYSE. Its leaders' reluctance to send an official representative to testify in the various congressional hearings was also probably influenced by their correct anticipation that these deliberations would be hostile to professional groups involved in the operation of the collapsed financial markets. Such an appearance ran the risk that the image of the profession might be further undermined by harsh and critical questioning.[1]

Although a few of the profession's leaders appeared before Congress, they did not do so as the AIA's representatives. Except for Colonel Arthur H. Carter of Haskins and Sells, none addressed in his testimony the content of the emerging legislation. May, for instance, whose firm had been engaged to examine the records of the collapsed Krueger and Toll, largely limited his testimony before the Senate Banking Committee to describing how the "Match King" had deceived the public about his companies' financial condition. His predecessor before this committee, a representative of Ernst and Ernst, Krueger and Toll's auditors, explained why the fraudulent transactions contributing to this client's insolvency had not been discovered earlier. Little testimony focused on the deficiencies of financial reporting. Instead, much attention was devoted to explaining how "pools" and other manipulative devices for influencing stock prices worked.[2]

One exception, however, was May's fellow committeeman from the Social Science Research Council, Professor William Z. Ripley. Though only partially recovered from severe injuries sustained in a New York taxi accident, Ripley stressed the need for more adequate financial disclosure to reduce the opportunities for fraud and to restore the public's confidence in the stock market. In his view, much of the dangerous speculation, particularly in the securities of industrial and public utility companies, might have been prevented if these industries were required, as were the railroads, to file financial reports periodically with the federal government. Had this been done, he felt, much of the unjustifiable rumormongering, on which the wild speculation fed before October 1929, would have been greatly diminished. He praised the financial reports prepared by the United States Steel Corporation, audited by May's firm, as an example that all public companies should be required to follow. Finally, he recommended that Congress be guided in drafting future legislation by the conclusions of Adolf A. Berle and Gardiner C. Means in their book *The Modern Corporation and Private Property*.[3]

Soon after the Roosevelt administration came to power in 1933, several unsuccessful efforts were made by different individuals to draft securities market legislation. This task had first been assigned to Samuel Untermyer, the attorney to the 1913 "money trust" investigation. By March 1933, dissatisfied with Untermyer's proposal to regulate the securities markets by widening the scope of the laws against mail fraud, Roosevelt turned to Daniel C. Roper, the secretary of commerce and longtime political protégé of conservative financier Bernard M. Baruch, to prepare a new bill.[4]

This second draft was completed by March 19, 1933, and was known as the Thompson bill, after one of its primary drafters, Huston Thompson, a former member of the FTC. This second bill was essentially a financial disclosure law, embodying many of Berle and Means's recommendations. It was also advantageous to the public accountants for several reasons, which may explain their quiescence as it progressed through Congress.[5] The public interest was to be protected under this bill by requiring the managements of public companies to file audited financial statements with the FTC for each new security issue they brought to market. Corporate directors and executives found guilty of filing false financial statements would be subject to federal prosecution. This potential liability for filing false statements provided a potent lever for practitioners in restraining the desires of clients who might seek to profit by misleading the public. As a consequence, public accountants' reports about the fairness of their clients' financial statements would assume a far greater importance to directors and managers than hitherto had been the case.[6]

Though the AIA maintained a low profile during the public discussion of the Thompson bill, it recommended in a letter to the House Committee on Interstate Commerce (chaired by Congressman Sam Rayburn of Texas) that the requisite financial statements be audited by independent public accountants. One writer has suggested that this proposal was ultimately adopted by the house committee because of the effective lobbying efforts of the association's legal representative, Judge J. Harry Covington. Besides being a partner of George Rublee and the rising Dean Acheson, he also served as Mrs. Woodrow Wilson's personal attorney. Thus he maintained excellent connections within the hierarchy of the Democratic party and certainly enjoyed entrée with Chairman Rayburn and his committee.[7]

While the AIA worked quietly and indirectly, other prominent practitioners who did not number among its inner circle were more outspoken in support of the Thompson legislation. On March 30, 1933, Colonel Arthur H. Carter, son-in-law of Elijah Watt Sells and then managing partner of Haskins and Sells, wired the chairman of the Senate Committee on Commerce and Banking to congratulate him on behalf of the NYSSCPA on the emerging legislation. Carter asked permission to provide his testimony. In volunteering to testify, he was probably trying to lend support to the position of those close to the current political administration (such as his friend Colonel Montgomery, who would begin to serve on the staff of the National Recovery Administration [NRA] in 1934). This proposed legislation placed authority for regulating the nation's financial markets in the hands of the FTC, an agency with which Montgomery had worked closely at its inception in 1913. Montgomery had also subsequently maintained close relations with the agency's leadership. May, for instance, described Montgomery as a "protégé" of FTC chairman and career civil servant George Mathews.[8]

One potential problem with the new legislation, however, was that it did not indicate who would bear the responsibility for auditing the financial statements required by the FTC. What Carter may have feared was that serious consideration might be given to the idea of forming a large corps of federal examiners (as had been previously done at the ICC and the IRS) to perform these duties. In an effort to involve the profession more intimately, Carter argued that the government should, as a matter of economy, mandate the use of independent certified public accountants for these examinations.[9]

The ironic outcome was that this legislation was soon transformed into a bill highly distasteful to all factions of the profession's leadership. Both investment bankers and spokesmen for various corporations strongly opposed the heavy legal penalties that could be imposed on directors who filed false information. This legislation apparently was also poorly drafted and seemed to imply that directors might be held liable for assertions made in filings that were based on the opinions of such experts as accountants, engineers, and attorneys. Critics argued that the legislation should be modeled more along the lines of the British companies acts, which exonerated directors from any liability if they could prove they had acted with "due diligence" or had relied on the opinions of experts.[10]

By April 5, 1933, the opposition to the Thompson bill had grown so intense that Congressman Rayburn indicated privately to presidential advisor Raymond Moley that a new effort would have to be made. As a consequence, Moley convinced Roosevelt on April 7 that a new team headed by Harvard law professor Felix Frankfurter and assisted by three former students—Benjamin V. Cohen, Thomas G. Corcoran, and James M. Landis—should undertake the task.[11]

In drafting the final version of the legislation, these attorneys introduced new requirements that realistically reflected the complexities of bringing securities issues to the market. These provisions had important implications for public accountants. In the view of Frankfurter and his associates, the issuance of new corporate securities was a complex process involving not only companies, their managements, and directors but also a host of such expert advisors as accountants, attorneys, engineers, appraisers, and investment bankers. From the lawyers' perspective, since fair disclosure depended upon the proper functioning of all these interdependent parties, each professional group should be held liable for its individual contribution. In the drafts presented to Congress on April 10, the essential change, from the perspective of the public accountants, was the broadening of their potential liability to the public for their professional negligence.[12]

Though the legislation signed into law on May 27, 1933, required that registrants file financial statements certified by independent public accountants, it also mandated severe sanctions for practitioners who negligently failed to discover "untrue statements or omissions of material facts." Section 11a of the "Truth in Securities" Act stated: "In case any part of the registration statement, when such part becomes effective, contained an untrue statement of a material fact or omitted to state a material fact required to be stated therein or necessary to make the statements therein not misleading, any person acquiring such security. . . may sue . . . every accountant . . . who has with his consent been named as having prepared or certified any part of the registration statement."[13]

The practitioners' vulnerability to legal suits was far greater than they had previously experienced under the common law. Under the new federal statute a plaintiff purchaser had to prove only that he had experienced a loss as a result of the purchase and that the financial statements the public accountant had certified were misstated. The practitioner, on the other hand, contrary to the common-law tradition requiring plaintiffs to prove the guilt of defendants, had to prove either the purchaser's loss resulted from his reliance on information other than that contained in the registration statement or that the practitioner had acted in "good faith." Under this second defense a practitioner might avoid liability if he could prove that he acted with "due diligence" in his performance of his work.[14]

The liability provision of the Securities Act of 1933 shocked many practitioners. The new law defined their roles and responsibilities in the economic order in terms that few had previously imagined. Though the law certainly helped in developing countervailing power against the improper desires of some clients, it also threatened practitioners who failed in their responsibilities with sanctions that seemed incredibly severe and arbitrary. George O. May noted:

> I cannot believe that a law is just, or can be long maintained in effect, which deliberately contemplates the possibility that a purchaser may recover from a person from whom he has not bought, in respect of a statement which at the time of his purchase he had not read, contained in a document which he did not then know to exist, a sum which is not to be measured by injury resulting from falsity in such statement. Yet, under the Securities Act as it stands, once a material misstatement or omission is proved, it is no defense to show that the plaintiff had no knowledge of the statement in question or of the document in which it was contained, or that the fall in the value of the security which he has purchased is due, not to the misstatement or omission complained of, but to quite different causes, such as the natural progress of invention, or even fire or earthquake. The Securities Act not only abandons the old rule that the burden of proof is on the plaintiff, but the doctrine of contributory negligence and the seemingly sound theory that there should be some relation between the injury caused and the sum to be recovered.[15]

This law was soon followed by the Securities Act of 1934, or the Securities Exchange Act, which, among other requirements, mandated the filing of annual audited financial statements for all companies whose investment securities had previously been issued to the public. Its broad objective was to assure continuous financial disclosure for all public companies. Under this second act, practitioner vulnerability to purchasers' legal suits was lessened. Besides having to prove their losses and the fact that the financial statements were false, plaintiffs also had to prove that these losses had resulted from their reliance on the false information. Furthermore, practitioners could be sued under this act only for gross negligence or fraud and not for ordinary negligence, as was the case under the 1933 law. Though less vulnerable under this second law, accountants nevertheless found that their legal status was a far cry from that of the years prior to the crash.[16]

In addition to defining malpractice penalties, the securities acts also created other disturbing conditions that troubled practitioners. One involved the powers, earlier denied the FTC during the Wilson administration, to establish uniform rules of accounting on an industrywide basis if necessary. Many of the AIA's leaders now feared that rigid new accounting rules would be mandated, as many thought had been the case in 1906 when the ICC extended its powers over railroad accounting. The scope of federal authority was also extended beyond the bounds first contemplated in 1916; these new laws vested this agency with the authority to promulgate specific auditing procedures that accountants might be required to apply in their examinations. Though the FTC did not immediately exercise these broad powers, they were viewed by many practitioners as encroachments on some of their most fundamental professional prerogatives. Some of the most vital judgments that public accountants were called on to make, it was now feared, could be dictated by federal bureaucrats.[17]

Another power the FTC exercised vigorously—to the chagrin and frustration of many practitioners—was its right to reject filings that its staff deemed deficient, especially with respect to the accounting principles employed. In these cases the FTC staff could issue refusal orders requiring filers to revise portions of their filings or, in extreme cases, stop orders effectively prohibiting companies from completing their registration statements. This soon became a serious source of friction between practitioners and regulators.[18]

With no well-defined body of accepted accounting principles to which all could refer, the instances of explosive and rancorous confrontation soon multiplied. The experience of receiving a refusal order or, worse yet, a stop order was frequently very demoralizing to the experienced practitioners who received them. One former Price Waterhouse accountant, who had subsequently opened his own practice in the state of Washington, wrote to May about his unhappy experience in a filing in which he and the government's agent disagreed about what constituted generally accepted accounting. He complained about the damage done to his professional reputation after his honest differences of opinion with the government received coverage in the press. To many readers who did not understand the technical issues in question, it might have appeared that this controversy was evidence of the accountant's wrongdoing.[19]

Finally, the FTC, in a further effort to define practitioner responsibilities, started to issue the first of a series of new rules prohibiting client relationships that might destroy their independence and objectivity. This reflected a new consciousness that the practitioners' ultimate responsibility was to the general investing public. Unlike the old days, when many practitioners closely identified with the interests of management or investment bankers, new situations stressed the moral obligation of their role as an intermediary between the public and client firms. The accountants were, in effect, being forced to be more independent and in a sense more professional than some wanted to be.[20]

Yet in spite of the expansion of government power, the relations between the National Securities Commission of the FTC, its successor, the Securities and Exchange Commission (SEC), and the public accountants' representative organizations were cooperative, if not cordial, well into 1935. The new agency's first five commissioners—Joseph P. Kennedy, James M. Landis, Ferdinand Pecora, George Mathews and Robert M. Healy—depended upon volunteer practitioners to help design the various forms and schedules that public companies were required to file. Both the AIA and the ASCPA formed committees to advise the federal government on these matters.[21]

The new federal agency also turned to the accounting associations for advice about whom might be appointed as its chief accountant and also its consulting accountant. For the post of consulting accountant, the commission selected a candidate whom May favored, Thomas H. Sanders of the Harvard Business School. For the post of chief accountant, it selected a relatively unknown professor from the University of North Dakota and former graduate student at Harvard Business School, Carman G. Blough, who was no doubt closer to the leadership of the ASCPA.[22]

The AIA was able to respond effectively to the demands, made by Commissioners Kennedy and Healy during June 1935, that more uniform wording be developed to guide practitioners in cases where they wished to qualify their opinions about the fairness of client financial statements. To date, the only formal examples provided by the AIA of the wording to be used in an accountant's report had been its standard unqualified opinions presented in the various bulletins prepared for the FRB. Yet many conditions could represent valid causes for the practitioner to qualify this standard wording, including an unresolved

uncertainty at the report date that might have a material impact on the
client's financial position, a change in the accounting principles employed by the client during the period covered by the auditor's examination, or a limitation in the scope of the audit.

What were worrisome to Kennedy and Healy, however, were the
misuses of this reporting convention. There were valid reasons for
qualification, such as those just mentioned, but some unscrupulous
practitioners were thought to use this type of report to evade their
responsibilities under the securities acts. Through the use of complex
and ambiguous wording, some practitioners had hedged their reports
so as to make them virtually meaningless.

In his letter of June 28, 1935, Rodney F. Starkey (a partner in Price
Waterhouse who had met with the SEC commissioners and with other
representatives of the AIA) reported to the vacationing May:

> During the same meeting Messrs. Kennedy and Healy also
> raised the question of accountants' certificates. They stated that
> they were quite dissatisfied with many of the certificates which
> had been received because they felt that they were entirely too
> full of "hedge" clauses and said that they frequently received
> certificates which after a long dissertation on the scope of the
> examination stated that, in the opinion of the accountant and
> subject to the notes on Pages 1——, the statements set forth, etc.
> Judge Healy objected to this very strenuously and Mr. Kennedy
> said that if necessary they would put out new regulations to force
> the accountants to express clearly their opinion on the statements
> where possible. He pointed out that this would in reality be a help
> to the accountant and would enable him to clear any disputed
> points with his client.[23]

A year earlier, at a meeting of representatives of the eleven largest
AIA firms held at the Broad Street Club in New York, May had already
convinced his colleagues of the need to address the problem of report
wording. This issue had also become a source of concern to both the
governors of the stock exchange and the commercial bankers of the
Robert Morris Associates. To provide counsel in the selection of the
proper wording for these reports, the AIA leaders agreed to engage
three firms of attorneys: Cravath, de Gersdorff, Swaine, and Wood;
Sullivan and Cromwell; and Cook, Nathan, and Lehman. The lawyers' draft was completed in May 1935, a month before Chairman
Kennedy's initial demand for action. The AIA satisfied this demand by
incorporating examples of these qualified reports in a 1936 revision of
the Federal Reserve Board Bulletin on auditing entitled "Examination

of Financial Statements by Certified Public Accountants." At this point cooperation between the government and the profession was at a high tide.[24]

The interlude of cooperation and accord with the SEC, however, did not last long. The government's efforts to enforce the securities acts more vigorously soon threatened to undermine the credibility of the AIA's claim to authority in public accountancy.

The Mid-Life Crisis of a Profession

Concerned about the vulnerable position in which the division between the AIA and the ASCPA had placed the profession during these critical years, some accounting leaders became more sensitive to the need for greater practitioner cohesion. One of the first was Montgomery's partner, Walter A. Staub, who in 1933 lead an effort to restore professional unity through the merger of the two rival national associations. In a letter considered at the AIA's Council meeting in April 1933, Staub proposed that the association form a committee to consider a merger. Although his recommendation was rejected, Staub and his allies persisted.[25]

At the October 16 meeting of the Council, Staub was granted permission to speak and enumerated the disadvantages of having two competing associations. He pointed out how the competition between the two national associations had slowed the profession's response to important changes. In addition, neither national organization commanded the strong support of the various state professional societies, which were anxious to remain neutral in this rivalry. Division also confused regulators trying to formulate policies that affected the profession. To the federal officials, the competition was disruptive and frustrating. It was this confusion of opinion, Staub contended, that had caused the chairman of the FTC to ask pointedly why the national associations did not get together. In concluding, he echoed his call for a special committee to consider the substantial advantages to be realized from a merger.[26]

The Staub initiative strengthened the position of those in the Council who felt that a more accommodating membership policy was overdue. After heated debate, the Staub proposal was (in essence) adopted. The Council agreed to form a new Special Committee on Relations with Outside Organizations, whose charge was to consider the feasibility of merger. Through the activities of this subcommittee, much of the groundwork for reunification was laid.[27]

An important concern not addressed by Staub, but nevertheless worrisome to those within the AIA who favored merger, was the need to contain their association's slippage in membership. After a decade of sluggish growth, its roll had peaked at 2,196. At that same date, however, there were about 13,000 CPAs, of whom about 2,100 were members of the ASCPA. The primary organizational allegiance for the majority of practitioners remained the state societies, which collectively included some 6,000 CPA members.[28]

In the following year, however, the AIA's membership decreased to 2,182. Though this shrinkage was no doubt due more to the depression than to a loss of interest in the AIA's programs, it disturbed the leadership. To combat this downturn, President John F. Forbes undertook an aggressive drive for new members. He reduced the application fee from fifty dollars to twenty-five dollars. Moreover, he successfully proposed that a committee of fifty members be established to represent different sections of the nation in canvassing for new members. The rules for readmission of members who had previously failed to pay their dues were eased. Though the membership fell to a low of 2,169 in 1933, Forbes's efforts helped to assure a rebound to 2,312 in 1934. In addition to contributing to the association's economic viability, the new emphasis was important to those favoring merger. It provided an opportunity to enlist more members who desired unity.[29]

Furthermore, the emergence of new rivals who challenged the AIA's claim to be the primary source of sound opinion in financial accounting matters increased pressures for change. This new challenge came from the accounting educators' association, the American Association of University Instructors of Accounting. Many educators, concerned in part by the low regard for their specialization in scholarly circles, were anxious to raise their status by promoting research aimed at solving major social problems. The task thought most worthy of their efforts was the development of a framework of principles for financial accounting to help a demoralized investing public. Because of these concerns, a successor organization to the AAUIA was formed in 1935—the American Accounting Association (AAA), which emphasized the importance of research and scholarly endeavor as professional objectives for accounting educators.[30]

The strongest opposition to the research-oriented AAA came from educators closely allied with May and Professor Gay. At the last annual meeting of the old AAUIA, held in December 1935 at the Hotel Commodore in New York, two of the most vocal of the critics of the proposal to merge this organization into the new AAA were Professor Thomas H. Sanders of the Harvard Business School and Professor

Henry Rand Hatfield of the University of California at Berkeley. Hatfield had been a key associate of Professor Gay in the wartime Central Bureau of Planning and Statistics. Sanders and Hatfield were also at that time quietly working as coauthors, along with attorney Underwood Moore, on a study under a grant from the Haskins and Sells Foundation; their work would be published by the AIA in 1938 as *A Statement of Accounting Principles*. Later, in 1939, May supported Sanders's appointment to the post of the director of accounting research at the AIA. Besides opposing the proposed merger, the two dissidents argued that the primary focus of academic research should be on improving classroom teaching techniques. In their view, accounting research should remain the responsibility of the practitioner organization.[31]

Their arguments gained little support among the majority of their fellow educators, who favored the proposal to transform their association into one that encouraged serious research in financial accounting. As a consequence, the vast majority of the members of the old AAUIA voted in favor of its merger with the new AAA.[32]

During the tenure of its first president, the practitioner-educator Eric L. Kohler, the AAA began to challenge the leadership of the AIA as a source of authority. The AAA's publication in the June 1936 issue of the *Accounting Review* of a paper entitled "A Tentative Statement of Accounting Principles" represented a first attempt to define a comprehensive framework of principles for financial accounting. This was praised by important regulatory officials. SEC commissioner George Mathews indicated to the AAA's executive committee how great was the government's need for this sort of guidance in helping to administer the securities acts.[33]

For practitioners such as May, the formation of a research-oriented educators' association created a host of problems. The AAA's new course upstaged the quiet efforts of Professors Sanders and Hatfield, which the AIA encouraged. Because it was strongly supported by important SEC officials, the AAA's initiative made the AIA's efforts to develop accounting principles in conjunction with the NYSE seem redundant and irrelevant. In the closeness of some of the organizations' leaders loomed the danger that the AAA and the ASCPA might further fortify their active alliance in support of accounting research. This would enhance their prestige at the AIA's expense.

May was also worried about the growing number of clashes between practitioners and the SEC's staff over the adequacy of client filings. The era of good feeling came to an end in 1935. No longer called upon to help the regulatory agency design its documents or sharpen the focus of its administrative regulations, the practitioners began experiencing challenges to their professional judgments in the form of refusal and stop orders. Practitioner defensiveness was further heightened by blunt public criticisms of their roles by SEC officials.[34] At the twenty-fifth annual conference of the Investment Bankers Association of America in Augusta, Georgia, Commissioner James M. Landis remarked: "The impact of almost daily tilts with accountants, some of them called leaders in their profession, often leaves little doubt that their loyalties to management are stronger than their sense of responsibility to the investor."[35]

Chief Accountant Carman G. Blough also sharply criticized the inadequacy of contemporary accounting practices. In addresses before practitioner associations in Ohio and New York, he cited dozens of examples of accounting practices rejected by the SEC.[36] More to the point was his criticism, in a speech before the NYSSCPA, of the lack of any clear definition of what was "generally accepted" in accounting.

> The term "generally accepted accounting principles" has been widely used in accounting literature, particularly by the American Institute of Accountants and the Securities and Exchange Commission; yet I do not know of any satisfactory definition of the term. . . . Almost daily, principles that for years I had thought were definitely accepted among the members of the profession are violated in a registration statement prepared by some accountant in whom I have high confidence. Indeed, an examination of hundreds of statements filed with our Commission almost leads one to the conclusion that aside from the simple rules of double-entry bookkeeping, there are very few principles of accounting upon which the accountants of this country are in agreement-
> . . . . I have been forced to the conclusion that procedures so generally followed among accountants as to constitute substantial precedent are not always fundamentally sound.[37]

Though the SEC, shortly after Commissioner Landis's critical speech, entered into an informal arrangement allowing the AIA an opportunity to address all accounting matters with which the agency had taken issue, the bureaucrats were not, through this action, beginning a policy of deferring to the practitioners. This agency soon exercised its right to promulgate accounting rules by issuing, during January 1937, the first of its administrative directives, known as Accounting Series Releases (ASRs), prescribing acceptable accounting for federal income taxes, excess profits taxes, and surtaxes on undistributed profits.[38]

The resolution of these growing crises was influenced by important external events that helped to form a new consensus among Wall Street's rival professional groups. The drive for accommodation was also influenced by important patrons of the competing practitioner leaders. These magnates, deeply concerned by what they viewed as radical economic and tax policies at home and by the disturbing trend of political events in Europe, began to seek accord with their business rivals to preserve threatened values and institutions they mutually cherished. The primary evidence of this growing accord among rival elements among New York's business leadership can be seen in their successful opposition to the Roosevelt administration's undistributed profits tax proposal of 1936.

Though some of the events with respect to the tax debate occurred after the AIA's reunification, it is important to analyze their historical significance to understand what happened in the accounting profession. The key connection between these parallel, and in many ways closely related, developments was George O. May. It is his change in attitude about the benefits of a merger that is most critical to understanding why the AIA suddenly reversed its policy of nearly two decades and sought an alliance with the ASCPA. But May's motives cannot be understood without first understanding why he played such a crucial role in the 1936 tax debate. The factors compelling him to action in defeating the Morgenthau tax plan were the same ones that led him to abandon the old conception of a narrow profession and to accept, instead, the strong demands made by many of his associates for widening the AIA's boundaries.

A New Structure
of Professional Governance,
1935–1940

Dissatisfaction over the new circumstances brought about by the New Deal's securities legislation eventually motivated public accountants to formulate new strategies and structures for ordering their affairs. Though many played active roles in this transformation, my analysis focuses on the actions of the two practitioners who had hitherto lead the most important of the competing factions within the divided profession: George O. May and Robert H. Montgomery. By mid-decade, both became anxious to accept compromise in matters of organization and governance, in part so that the profession would be in a stronger position to ward off the unwelcome encroachments of government. The willingness of these two leaders to accept a compromise was, as we shall see, also conditioned by the pressures imposed by politically influential patrons. What ultimately emerged was a united and vigorous professional association that obtained a safe harbor for its members' expertise in America's changing social milieu.

The "Second New Deal" and
New Directions in Public Policy

By 1936, the period some writers have characterized as the "First New Deal" had drawn to a close. A time of frenzied activity in Washington, it resulted in a substantial expansion of the government's involvement in the nation's economic life. Its basic economic objectives had been to stabilize prices and to restore confidence in the nation's seriously depressed commodities and financial markets. Five agencies had played key roles in the New Deal's initial efforts to restore the nation's prosperity, and virtually all of the leaders of these agencies had been either protégés or allies of conservative business leader and Democratic party benefactor Bernard M. Baruch.[1]

Toward the close of 1935, however, the influence of Baruch and his allies was on the wane. Their policies, designed to restore prices and also to maintain balanced federal budgets, had not solved the nation's economic woes. That year the Supreme Court ruled the NRA unconstitutional and thereby ended the Roosevelt administration's first effort to fix industrial prices. Early in the following year, the AAA suffered a similar fate.[2]

Consequently, the president began to redirect his administration's economic policy toward a greater emphasis on restoring demand by redistributing national income. Faced with the new problem of how to finance the politically popular social insurance programs, Roosevelt became more receptive to the ideas of Henry M. Morgenthau, the secretary of the Treasury, and Herman M. Oliphant, his department's chief counsel. What disturbed conservatives such as Baruch about these new advisors were their proposals that the government achieve its new objectives by increasing the tax burdens of both wealthy individuals and business corporations. By closing loopholes and reducing retained earnings, the advisors hoped to speed recovery and achieve other social objectives.[3]

The desire of these Treasury Department officials to tap the vast pool of earnings retained each year by corporations heightened as a result of two unexpected reverses that the administration experienced in fiscal matters early in 1936. The Supreme Court's decision that the AAA was unconstitutional put an end to the nearly one-half billion dollars in revenue the government had previously received from that agency's processing tax. Worse yet was Congress's override of Roosevelt's veto of the two-billion-dollar bonus payment to the veterans of the world war. These events threatened to throw the federal budget into an embarrassingly substantial deficit.[4]

During January 1936, Secretary Morgenthau, at the behest of Herman Oliphant, had proposed to increase tax revenues by raising the rate of estate taxes and establishing new taxes on inheritances and also on the undistributed earnings of corporations. Of these three, the tax on undistributed profits was expected to be the major generator of additional funds and also an important mechanism in achieving the administration's broader social and economic objectives.[5]

These proposed tax changes were anathema to conservative leaders such as Baruch. From his perspective, the danger lay in the resurgence of inflation, a prospect that had worried many financial leaders in the years immediately before October 1929. Baruch feared that inflation, once started, would be very difficult to quell, and he thought that what was necessary was a decline in prices to a level that would again encourage businessmen to invest. The conception of a liquidity trap and permanently lower levels of demand—something warned of by his old rival from the peace conference days, John Maynard Keynes—did not seem credible to America's most successful speculator. Consequently, Baruch began to work diligently within the Democratic party and in alliance with conservative business leaders to combat the tax proposals.[6]

The Second New Deal and
Changing Business-Government Alignments

George O. May, like many others in Wall Street's professional community, was also concerned about the direction of the New Deal's social and economic policies, and he would soon be drawn closer to Baruch and his circle of conservative business leaders. May had long felt that the tax burden in America was inequitable because it was not broadly based. From his perspective, the progressive income tax structure was ill conceived and had failed to achieve its basic objectives. Those who were supposed to pay the major portion of the nation's tax typically escaped completely through investment in municipal securities or the formation of such devices as personal holding companies. What was needed was a tax system that required all elements in society to bear their fair share of the cost of public finance. What that essentially meant was a shifting of the burden more to the middle classes. May favored reducing the tax rates on the wealthy and also closing the many loopholes the rich used to avoid paying taxes.[7]

May did not favor increased rates on business. In his view, business enterprises, on which the nation's financial health ultimately depended, could be viable only if they were allowed to retain a substantial portion of their profits to finance future operations and growth. Indeed, the policies of the New Deal seemed to smack too much of a "soak the rich" mentality of the sort exhibited in the essentially political attack on Secretary Mellon (whom Price Waterhouse served indirectly as auditors of the Gulf Oil Company). This outlook, he felt, could only discourage the increase in investment that the nation needed to end its present slump.[8]

Like many of his professional colleagues, May initially seemed overwhelmed by the New Deal. The rapidity and degree of change, particularly with respect to ordering activities in the financial markets, kept the profession's leadership in a defensive position. By 1934, however, May's ideas were crystallizing. He could now see how professionals might contain the excesses of the federal government and provide the leadership needed to redirect its focus to less radical and more constructive policies.

May sought a trained economist to provide research support in the forthcoming public debate. Writing to Professor Gay, he said: "There is today an extraordinary opportunity for a man with some background in economics and statistics and some interest in accounting to take an important part in determining the form of the new development. I hope to play some part in the matter myself, but there is a job that requires much more continuous labor than I am either able or willing to devote to the problem. At the same time, there is evidence of widening the scope of the work of accountants—I think, if I cared to do so, I could employ a large part of my time entirely outside the ordinary range but within the legitimate range of the accountant's work."[9]

The former student selected for this assignment was Professor Bishop Carlton Hunt, chairman of the Department of Economics at Dalhousie University in Canada. Price Waterhouse engaged Hunt in New York from 1935 to 1940. Though their initial concern was the problem of developing principles for financial accounting, Hunt apparently assisted May in the analysis of the probable impacts of the administration's new tax policies, particularly the proposed tax on unearned income.[10]

May also began to cement a closer relationship with the conservative leadership of the Democratic party through his connection with Bernard Baruch's friend and colleague, Sidney J. Weinberg of Goldman, Sachs, and Company. At Weinberg's insistence, Secretary Roper invited May on November 20, 1934, to serve on the Committee on the Revenue Act of the Commerce Department's Advisory and Planning Council. The revenue act committee was one of many through which the council operated to build support in the business community for the administration's economic policies. Ironically, it was from this quarter that some of the strongest opposition to the Treasury Department's proposed tax changes emanated.[11]

The acceptance of May as a member of the committee in 1934 was significant, because it represented the coming together of the essentially conservative Wall Street elements, which hitherto had been separated by differences in ethnic background, national origin, and religion. May, whose firm during the 1920s had been ranked among the staunchest allies of such establishment figures as the Cravath firm, the House of Morgan, the Mellons, and the Rockefellers, was now establishing a bridge between these elements and such new men as Baruch,

Kennedy, and Weinberg. Roosevelt's New Deal policies made new bedfellows on Wall Street as they did on Main Streets throughout America.

The disturbing political developments in Europe also encouraged cooperation. The emergence of a racialist and increasingly aggressive fascist regime in Germany had important negative implications for many in New York's financial community. The security of Britain and France seemed threatened, and many of the street's old-line, nativist elite bankers, attorneys, and accountants were as concerned as the new men. Bernard Baruch was especially anxious about these developments. In view of these broader concerns, he felt that a new impost such as the undistributed profits tax was a proposal to be resisted, because it would weaken industry and consequently America's power to countervail against foreign threats.[12]

The Significance of the Debate
on the Undistributed Earnings Tax

The initial focus of the efforts of the conservative business elements in New York to counter the disturbing trends abroad and at home was the debate on the undistributed earnings tax, a debate in which George O. May played a key role. May's telling criticism centered on the validity of the Treasury's estimate of the revenue to be derived from this proposed tax. He concluded that the net increase in receipts projected by the government—receipts taken in after this new impost was levied and both the simultaneous repeal of the "corporate income, capital stock and excess profit tax, and the elimination of . . . exemption of dividends from normal tax"—was based on an erroneous and misleading projection of past data on dividends and profits withheld by corporations. He wrote:

> It is evident from the President's message that he fell into this natural misinterpretation—otherwise, he would not have made the statement which appears on page 3 of the hearings: "Thus the Treasury estimates that during the calendar year 1936 over four and one-half billion dollars of corporate income will be withheld from stockholders." Either the Treasury made an erroneous estimate or the President was completely misled as to the nature of its estimate. It seems to me to constitute a serious reflection on the Treasury that it should put out statements open to such a natural and grossly incorrect interpretation and should have put the

President in the position of creating a clearly unfounded impression on a matter of so much importance. While the table in question was put in evidence by a witness described as "a statistician of the Treasury," the higher officials of the Treasury would no doubt assume the responsibility for the form of the presentation.[13]

May decided to testify at the hearings held by the Senate Finance Committee. At the behest, apparently, of Senator Peter G. Gerry of New York, May and a representative of the AIA, Victor H. Stempf, were placed on the agenda. On May 6, May delivered a blunt challenge to the validity of the Treasury's projections. The following day, Stempf echoed some of the criticisms of the Treasury's statistical methods and also argued that the proposals would favor large companies at the expense of smaller business enterprises.[14]

Although other business leaders, including Bernard Baruch, expressed their opposition in the hearings, May's was by far the most devastating assault. His testimony cast doubt on the credibility of the administration's assertions about the benefits of what appeared to many to be a radical departure in public finance. The targets of his criticism were those within Morgenthau's department, particularly Herman Oliphant, who advocated this reordering of the traditional modes of financing business. In a letter to Senator Gerry written the day after his appearance, May made this clear: "I meant to have mentioned to you yesterday that when I spoke of the Secretary's advisers permitting him to make the unfortunate misstatement I had particularly in mind the testimony of Mr. Oliphant on page 618 of the House hearings, in which he stated he had examined the estimates personally and approved them, and added that the Treasury took responsibility for those estimates. This seems to me to indicate pretty clearly where the blame should fall."[15]

On May 8, a distraught Secretary Morgenthau, embarrassed by the criticisms in the press and in Congress, invited May and other experts to meet with him in Washington, privately and without his staff's knowledge, to discuss the apparent inadequacies of his department's estimates. Later, on May 26, May was one of several business leaders summoned again by Secretary Morgenthau to advise the Treasury on how to strengthen its estimating techniques. Both meetings apparently proved inconclusive and did not dissipate the secretary's unease about his staff's inability to prepare projections that would stand up under rigorous public scrutiny.[16]

The outcome of these events was an embarrassing defeat for the administration's tax proposals for 1937. Congress passed a greatly diluted undistributed profits tax, aimed primarily at reducing the attractiveness of the personal holding company as a tax avoidance device. The corporate income tax was essentially retained in its previous form. The efforts of the administration to restructure the economy by way of tax legislation were abandoned.[17]

May's success was one manifestation of an emergent sense of unity among conservatives in the nation's financial capital. Though these groups earlier had remained divided largely due to their differing social and economic backgrounds, threats to the prevailing order at home and abroad had drawn them together to preserve institutions and values they all cherished. Another manifestation would be the AIA's transformation into a broad-based national association. One key actor in this rapprochement would be George O. May, whose attitude about the role of professional organizations in a modern industrial society had changed greatly since 1933.

The Reemergence of Practitioner Unity

The coalescence of Wall Street's rival factions through their victory in the undistributed profits tax debate contributed to the reestablishment of a unified accounting profession. Part of the groundwork seems to have been laid in the informal discussions between business and professional members of the various committees of the Department of Commerce's Advisory and Planning Council. Through this committee service George O. May was drawn closer to Baruch's protégés, whose ideas about the proper relationship between the government and the professions had been shaped by their experiences on the War Industries Board. These informal contacts with important patrons enjoying access to the highest levels of government helped to reconcile May's and Montgomery's differing conceptions of professionalism. This decade's events had demonstrated how important practitioner cohesiveness was in preserving professional autonomy.[18]

This change in attitude among the AIA's leaders was reflected in the Council's activities during 1934–35. At its annual meeting during October 1934, one month before Sidney Weinberg tapped May for his committee of the Advisory and Planning Council, the AIA defeated Montgomery's proposal that it merge with the ASCPA. The cessation of the opposition to these merger proposals, however, seems to have first occurred early in February 1935, when May was first drawn closer to Baruch's friends. Besides participating on Sidney Weinberg's tax committee, May was invited on February 18 to discuss the securities acts before the Council. The invitation came from Walter P. Gifford, president of AT&T, former lieutenant of Baruch at the WIB, and valued client of Colonel Montgomery's firm. Though May in preparing for this meeting was primarily concerned with the technical details of the new legislation, the most significant outcome seems to have been his conversion to the idea of broadening the AIA's membership.[19]

The opportunity to serve in the elite circle was invaluable to May, especially in light of the New Deal's sweeping securities legislation. Whatever influence he enjoyed in shaping developments in government depended to a large extent on the support and cooperation of his new associates. He in turn was influenced by his new allies. The primary change in May's outlook was his acceptance of what might best be termed "the War Industries Board conception of associationalism." This soon had a major impact on the AIA's policies.[20]

Baruch, Gifford, Montgomery, and the other business leaders advocated a more cohesive associationalism than that followed in accounting during the 1920s. Their outlooks had been shaped by the earlier crisis of the First World War. They had embraced a concept of the corporate state in which the critical interactions between government and industry were channeled through representative associations capable of fully mustering the varied elements of their particular industries or professions. In marshaling America's industrial resources, the WIB had relied heavily on the cooperation of specialist business organizations, including the AIA.

They also believed that the depression could be best cured through a closer collaboration between business and government. This attitude pervaded the National Recovery Administration, in which two old WIB veterans, General Hugh L. Johnson and Colonel Robert H. Montgomery, held senior posts. Like the WIB, the ill-fated "Blue Eagle" tried to achieve its basic mission of stabilizing prices by eliciting the cooperation of hundreds of representative business organizations. Through government-sanctioned codes of fair competition, these groups sought to restore prosperity. From the perspective of leaders such as Gifford, who perpetuated this spirit in the Council, the factionalism that divided accountancy threatened to hinder government's efforts to mobilize the profession and to coordinate the activities of its members in pursuing plans for national economic recovery. What they thought was needed was a single representative association reflective of all this profession's constituencies.

Though these leaders respected May's virtuosity in accounting and tax matters, they found it difficult to accept his desire to keep the accountants' association small and exclusive. The AIA's earlier efforts to block their associate Montgomery's plan to form a broadly representative organization seemed incomprehensible to them, and May could not help being influenced by their feelings.[21]

May's growing receptivity to this alternative associationalist vision was doubtless also encouraged by a recognition of other favorable possibilities. First, a larger and more cohesive association would enhance the profession's leverage in dealing with political leaders. Increased political power would be useful in trying to countervail against the unwelcomed encroachments of an activist federal bureaucracy. Furthermore, by eliminating public confusion about the proper source of authority in accounting matters, reunification would also legitimize the AIA's demands for greater autonomy in ordering professional affairs.

As May's view shifted, the AIA changed course. By its annual meeting in October 1935, it had revised its bylaws to allow a merger with the ASCPA and had elected Robert Montgomery to its presidency. Though some within the AIA bitterly fought these developments, their opposition was in vain. May's leadership and the change in the political environment of the 1930s drove the conservatives from the field.[22]

The initial efforts to promote a merger centered in the AIA's Committee on Relations with Outside Organizations, whose chairman, Frederick H. Hurdman, negotiated with the ASCPA. Hurdman presented the six conditions acceptable to both negotiating committees at the AIA's Council in April 1935. These were (1) the AIA would be the surviving entity; (2) all ASCPA members in good standing would automatically become members of the AIA; (3) all future applicants for membership had to be CPAs; (4) the practice experience of prospective associate members would be reduced to two years; (5) an advisory council of state society representatives would be established to head off the possibility that yet another national organization would be formed; and (6) all of the ASCPA's assets would be transferred to the AIA.[23]

Hurdman's proposals aroused some strong opposition in the Executive Committee of the AIA (responsible for overseeing the association's daily functioning on behalf of the Council). In fact, this committee blocked efforts to distribute Hurdman's report to the Council's members prior to the April 1935 meeting. The nucleus of the opposition included James Hall of Peat, Marwick, Mitchell, and Company, Arthur W. Teele of the New York firm of Patterson, Teele, and Dennis, and Will A. Clader, the managing partner of an important Pennsylvania practice bearing his name. A floor fight broke out in the Council. Motions made to discharge the special committee were defeated, but so too were the calls to submit its recommendations to the full membership for a vote.[24]

Hurdman's opponents on the Council feared that the proposed agreement was unfair to the AIA's current membership and also ran the risk of having control pass into the hands of the ASCPA leadership. The plan, it was pointed out, granted full membership status to the ASCPA members without requiring them to pass the AIA's admissions examination. The admission of all the ASCPA members would result in their constituting about 58 percent of the merged entity's total membership. The ASCPA could dominate the successor organization. Objections were also raised about the legality of transferring the ownership of the substantial assets of the AIA through the proposed merger.[25]

Those who supported the Hurdman proposals argued that the alternative recommendation made by the Executive Committee of allowing the ASCPA members to apply for membership in the AIA, instead of guaranteeing their acceptance, would be viewed as an insult. Hurdman argued strongly against this action for it would be humiliating to the ASCPA membership and would wreck any opportunity for reunification: "I think that we have got to put ourselves in the position of the American Society members. You can't just consider that they are just dirt, that they don't amount to anything. They think they are something. Just put yourself in their place. What would you think if a suggestion was made to you and you are a member of the American Society? I think it is perfectly ridiculous to think that we could get anywhere in this plan by any such move as this."[26]

Former AIA president John F. Forbes, a strong supporter of the merger, indirectly attacked those whose opposition may have been motivated by a reluctance to be associated with practitioners of differing (presumably lower) social backgrounds. From his perspective, he said, the question of social origins should not be an important one. Of much greater moment for the progress of the profession was the establishment of one representative organization for the entire community of practitioners: "I think for the benefit of the profession, the members ought to know whether they can hope for amalgamation. There is a strong feeling throughout the whole country that they ought to know one thing or another. The question is whether we want to take the Society in. Somebody asked me today whether we wanted to take in all these East Side 'kikes' and all that sort of thing. I haven't any idea whether we do or not, but I know this: That in the interest of the profession, there ought to be one large organization."[27]

Those who supported the Hurdman proposal argued that if the AIA failed, others would soon act to unite the profession nationally. President George A. Armistead pointed out that if this association did not approve an acceptable plan of merger, there was a group of practitioners who would try to unify the various state societies into an organization similar to the old AAPA. Such a union, he noted, might include up to six thousand of the fourteen thousand CPAs in America. Armistead warned that two of the national firms had agreed to finance the ASCPA in the event that the AIA failed to agree to the merger.[28]

The outcome of this debate was compromise. The Executive and Hurdman committees met the next day to resolve their differences. Meanwhile, the Council voted its general approval of the task that the Hurdman committee was performing.[29]

Hurdman's opponents on the Executive Committee finally agreed to recommendations quite close to his original proposals. Several factors conditioned their acquiescence. Besides maintaining unity within the AIA, the compromise provided the elite leaders with a flexible position from which they could respond to future changes. Acceptance helped to dissipate the AIA's negative image. By endorsing the recommendations, the AIA made itself the leading force in bringing the profession together.[30]

There was a new sensitivity about the desirability of involving men of different social backgrounds in the AIA's affairs. To some extent it must have been due to the influence of politically powerful allies such as Baruch and Weinberg. In January 1935, for example, the AIA's leadership addressed the problem of ambiguously worded audit reports. They decided that the AIA's Committee on Cooperation with the Stock Exchange would develop reports with standard wording for each type of opinion a practitioner might issue. Mindful of the legal implications of such assertions, the AIA leadership decided to engage three firms of attorneys to draft these documents.[31] In writing to Colonel Arthur Carter of Haskins and Sells about which firms should be selected for this assignment, May said: "Upon the first, I think we are agreed that on account of the services that they have all rendered gratuitously and their knowledge of the subject, Alex Henderson's firm and Arthur Dean's should be included among the counsel. I think one more should be sufficient, and my own inclination is to go into quite a different group. I am disposed to suggest Cook, Nathan and Lehman."[32]

The spirit of compromise was also promoted by the emergence of the new research-oriented American Association of Accountants. This group challenged the AIA for leadership as the main source of sound opinion in financial accounting matters.

May had become aware of this threat in 1934, when he received a letter from Lewis Ashman of the Chicago firm of Ashman, Reedy and Company. Ashman, who had served as a member of the AIA's Special Committee on the Development of Accounting Principles, reported the growing feeling among the membership of the Illinois society that formal standards for financial accounting had to be established. He commented as well on the aforementioned attack made by Eric L. Kohler in the *Accounting Review* on the AIA's efforts in this sphere. The ASCPA, he said, might soon join with the AAA to take over this important function: "It is apparent that the position of the Institute on the subject of accounting standards will be subjected to very strong criticism. If the American Society of Certified Public Accountants takes up this subject and exploits it vigorously, I think they can do the Institute considerable harm and gain a great deal of prestige for themselves. With a cause such as this, I believe they can rally a great many converts. By failing to adopt a more aggressive policy, I think the Institute is furnishing a weapon for offense which, if skillfully wielded, may do it irreparable harm."[33]

The newly invigorated accounting educators did not have close relations to the AIA. Kohler had been a longtime protégé of the ASCPA's executive director, Durand Springer. In establishing the AAA, Kohler was assisted by two other midwestern educators, Howard C. Greer of the University of Chicago and Russell A. Stevenson of the University of Minnesota. Neither had much previous involvement with the AIA. More troubling yet was the fact that Colonel Montgomery's colleague from Columbia University, Roy B. Kester, was supporting the AAA. Finally, Carman Blough, the SEC's chief accountant, was supportive of the AAA's efforts to set standards.[34]

May was upset by these developments; he wanted to keep control of accounting standards in the hands of the practitioners who faced daily the problems of applying accounting information in serving client needs. Writing to his friend Thomas H. Sanders of the Harvard Business School (who was serving as an advisor to the SEC on accounting matters), May complained: "I am wondering whether the accounting instructors would be well advised to set themselves up in opposition to the Institute in an attempt to define accounting standards, or whether it is a correct conception of their proper sphere that they should take the leadership in professional affairs. I should have thought the more far-seeing members of the group would have been content to exercise their influence indirectly through their students, as the wisest law professors have done in the past, and through work as you have recently done."[35]

The ability of May to influence this new and disturbing course of events through the actions of his close allies in academe was, as one might imagine, slight. In Sanders's letter of response, he offered little hope that he could deflect the AAA from its desired course of becoming intimately involved in the establishment of accounting standards. In fact, he characterized this new activism as a manifestation of a broader midwestern reaction against the traditional leadership of eastern institutions.

> The career of the American Association of University Instructors in Accounting has not in some ways been very satisfactory. It has been largely dominated by Middle Western sentiment, which has taken the course it usually does with respect to matters affecting the industrial and financial East. I assume Professor Kohler himself wrote the editorial, and if so it would indicate that, in spite of his being able and attractive personally, he has surrendered too much to that influence.
>
> This group is disposed to adopt towards Harvard the same attitude as towards the American Institute, which sets me at some disadvantage in addressing them. But I should like to see what can be done in preparing a reasonable statement on the matters under discussion.[36]

The elite leaders of the AIA responded to these worrisome new activities of the educators in two ways. First, it had supported the research of Sanders, Moore, and Hatfield for their study, *A Statement of Accounting Principles*. Second, their concerns about the activities of the research-minded educators contributed to their willingness to accept the proposed merger with elements in the profession from whom they had long sought to remain at arm's length. Besides heading off the possibility of an educators-ASCPA alliance, a merger with the ASCPA would strengthen the AIA's claim to ultimate authority in accounting matters and the credibility of its research activities. Furthermore, a single national association representing a united profession would have more political clout to use against any further SEC encroachments on professional prerogatives and would have a stronger claim for a greater degree of self-governance.[37]

The culmination of this process occurred at the AIA's annual meeting in Boston in October 1935. At this conclave the Executive Committee initially mounted a weak opposition to proposals to amend the bylaws to facilitate the merger with the ASCPA. But this opposition soon faded. The nominating committee selected Colonel Montgomery as the official candidate for president. Though some of the diehards nominated Will-A. Clader as an alternate, this last-ditch effort ended in failure. Montgomery won by a margin of 1,210 to 438. At the next annual meeting in Dallas in 1936, the merger was finally consummated and the profession reunited.[38]

The Emergence of the Mature Profession

The last phase in the formation of the structure for the modern public accountancy profession was completed within four years of the 1936 merger of the ASCPA and the AIA. The previous fifty years had seen the development of an array of new institutions to aid the growing practitioner community as it sought to govern its internal affairs and to come to terms with other groups in American society. The code of ethics, qualifying examinations, state licensing, university training, and the promotion of technical publications and research had all contributed to profession building. During the twenties and thirties, the earlier mechanisms for control were rounded out by the development of new programs in the AIA for the definition of both accounting and auditing standards. This process of socialization was further extended by developing new ethical rules on independence that defined more sharply the responsibilities of public accountants to the investing public. These years also saw the achievement of special recognition in the eyes of governmental regulators of the AIA's authority in public accountancy.

Although its committees on Cooperation with the Stock Exchange and on the Development of Accounting Principles had tried to enhance the AIA's image of authority during the early 1930s, progress had at first been slow. The committees depended on the volunteer efforts of busy practitioners who, unlike the retired May, found it difficult to devote substantial time to these matters. Furthermore, the setting of standards involved time-consuming conferences between representatives of as many as ten firms, who often found it difficult to iron out their differences in philosophy and to reach consensus. Progress was slow too because the New Deal's securities and tax legislation and the reunification of the profession distracted the AIA's leaders. The decline in firm incomes because of the Great Depression initially ruled out the soliciting of member contributions to finance these activities, as had been done in creating the library and the national headquarters building.[39]

Yet the press of events forced the AIA leadership to address these fundamental matters. The research-oriented AAA in 1936 issued its "Tentative Statement" document. More disturbing, however, were the critical public comments about the work of practitioners by high SEC officials, including Commissioner Landis and Chief Accountant Blough. Tensions heightened as the regulators challenged the adequacy of the financial disclosures of many public companies. Frustrated by the wide divergence of opinion about what was "generally accepted accounting," the SEC in 1937 started to issue ASRs, or Accounting Series Releases, specifying rules for all registrants.[40]

The now unified AIA took a series of steps in response to these developments. In 1938, the AIA issued *A Statement of Accounting Principles* to recapture the initiative in these matters and assigned to the Committee on Accounting Procedure (CAP) the task of promulgating accounting standards. The AIA's Council funded a full-time research staff, headed by Professor Sanders and his Harvard colleague W. Arnold Hosmer, to aid the CAP's practitioner members. Though George O. May served as CAP vice-chairman, he in effect directed its activities until his retirement in 1941.[41]

The CAP's organizers legitimized their new standards setting by including representatives of all the important elements of the expanded AIA, and its initial membership was therefore a somewhat unwieldly twenty-two. It included three leading educators: William A. Paton of the University of Michigan; A. C. Littleton of the University of Illinois; and Colonel Montgomery's Columbia University colleague, Roy B. Kester. This committee also included longtime AIA critic Eric L. Kohler and former SEC chief accountant Carman Blough (who had recently left government service to join Arthur Andersen and Company). Through the CAP, the AIA drew back in the fold the large national firm of Ernst and Ernst by including George D. Bailey, one of its senior partners, as a member. The committee was expanded to accommodate representatives of some of the more successful local firms, including Frederick B. Andrews of Chicago, Clem W. Collins of Denver, and A. S. Fedde and Henry A. Horne of New York. Later, this list was widened to give better representation to members with immigrant backgrounds. During September 1939 the CAP issued the first three of its new Accounting Research Bulletins (ARBs).[42]

The SEC recognized the AIA's efforts. Though this federal agency continued to issue its ASRs, its second chief accountant, Willard W. Werntz (a former accounting instructor at Yale Law School), established the policy of conditionally accepting the guidance provided through the AIA's ARB pronouncements. The SEC deferred in these matters as long as the AIA's actions were viewed as being intended to guard the public's interest. In effect, the AIA was accorded a substantial power for self-regulation in this vital aspect of professional governance. In the future, threatened governmental encroachments in accounting might be successfully warded off if its standards seemed effective in protecting the public.[43]

Besides standardizing financial accounting, the AIA also began to standardize auditing. May and the other leaders had initially been much less concerned about auditing guidance. What direction the AIA did provide had been limited to the bulletins it had authored since 1917 for the Federal Reserve Board. The latest revision, appearing in 1936 under the title of "Examinations of Financial Statements by Independent Public Accountants," provided a fuller expression of the basic objectives and inherent limitations of the audit process. Although these guides discussed specific audit procedures, they left their selection ultimately to the judgment of the practitioner. In that sense, they fell far short of the standards that government agencies were trying to develop.[44]

Soon tighter controls were applied. The revelations of a major fraud perpetrated by a senior corporate official (it induced the management of the McKesson Robbins Company to file for protection under the bankruptcy law during December 1938) at last motivated the leadership of the AIA to establish standards in auditing. The shocking revelations of how the financial records of this old and respected company—on whose board of directors Sidney Weinberg served as chairman and to which Price Waterhouse served as auditors—had been falsified called into question the adequacy of the audit practices employed by the nation's leading accounting firms. The failure to discover the overstatement of $19 million in this company's accounts-receivable and inventory balances was attributed, in part, to the poor procedures employed by the public accountants in verifying these accounts. During the hearings conducted by the New York State attorney general and the SEC, it was revealed that the accountants did not confirm the validity of the firm's accounts-receivable balances with its customers or observe the physical count of its inventories. Both procedures, though well recognized in the auditing literature, were considered to be optional in the cases of large companies, which presumably maintained strong controls over their internal accounting function. In this case the auditors had been misled.[45]

What the public accountants had failed to anticipate was the ability of key managers of their client firm to override the controls in the accounting system. McKesson's president, F. Donald Coster (who, it was revealed after his suicide, was in fact a former felon named Philip Musica), had twice earlier been incarcerated for perpetrating business frauds. The bizarre tale of how Musica and his brothers were able to infiltrate this company and to ward off the threat of bankruptcy during the early days of the depression shocked and demoralized the financial community—much as the collapses of Krueger and Toll and the Insull Companies had earlier.[46]

These findings had a significant impact on the AIA. Concerns over the threat of government's mandating of specific auditing procedures motivated the AIA's governing council to approve during May 1939 the publication of its "Extensions of Auditing Procedures." This document provided more explicit guidance with respect to accounts-receivable confirmations and inventory observations. Moreover, the growing awareness of the need for auditing standards led to the organization during the following year of a new Committee on Auditing Procedure under the chairmanship of Samuel J. Broad of Peat, Marwick, Mitchell, and Company. This body began to provide direction through the issuance of its "Statements on Auditing Procedures."[47]

Another change within the AIA was the initiation of rules of ethics detailing the conditions that public accountants should satisfy to assure their professional independence. The SEC had earlier started this development through the issuance on May 6, 1937, of its second ASR, which prohibited public accountants from maintaining "substantial" investments in client companies. By this regulation, the SEC was forcefully reminding public accountants that their primary responsibility in certifying financial statements was to the shareholders.[48]

The issue of independence became an important matter in the McKesson case. In its investigative report, the SEC questioned whether the public accountants had been sufficiently independent of their client's management to maintain an objective and unbiased view in this engagement. Noting that the accountants had been appointed by the firm's president and controller, the SEC cautioned that in the future they should be appointed by the boards of directors who had a fiduciary responsibility to an enterprise's shareholders.[49]

Sensitive to the criticism of Price Waterhouse's independence in the McKesson case, the AIA in 1941 began to broaden its code of ethics to include rules that closely paralleled the SEC's requirements. The leaders of the now united profession were increasingly aware of the need for a high degree of public confidence in the unbiased and selfless character of the public accountant's work, and this growing awareness gave rise to future extensions of these rules on independence. Practitioners were beginning to understand that the public's perception of their independence and objectivity was vital in legitimizing the profession's claim of a special place in the social order. Not surprisingly, during the following two decades many of the extensions of the AIA's code of ethics mandated more explicit rules with respect to independence.[50]

The SEC, in its final report on McKesson Robbins in December 1941, did not recommend that the government exercise its power to define detailed regulations to control the procedures that practitioners should employ in examining financial statements. Instead, the regulators noted that the accounting profession had already adopted some of the auditing procedures the SEC had found wanting in this case. The report also indicated that it was the SEC's belief that the profession would continue to widen the scope of these new auditing standards in response to new conditions.[51]

The willingness of the SEC to defer to the AIA's efforts to regulate these matters had been conditioned by the success that the association had achieved in establishing itself as the legitimate national representative of the entire community of public accountants. The SEC would have been unable to accept the authority of the Committee on Auditing Procedure prior to 1936. Such action then would have sparked a rancorous public debate as competing professional groups registered their objections both to the SEC and to their political representatives. Because of the successful transformation of the AIA into a representative association—one concerned more with questions of professional function than with partisan economic advantage or social origins—its leaders eventually received from government the powers they had long sought for ordering professional affairs. But without a broad base of support among state-certified accountants, the drive could not have succeeded.

The crisis of the 1930s had given birth to a new AIA that in the years that followed served as the primary vehicle for socializing the activities of public accountants in American society. By the end of this decade, the AIA had become transformed into the type of professional association that Baruch and his colleagues at the War Industries Board had encouraged. This model for business-government interaction, first widely exploited during World War I, was also found to be an effective mechanism for helping to bring order in a maturing industrial economy facing different challenges during the Great Depression.

Conclusion

On the morning of January 10, 1903, public accountants looked for the announcement of the wake for the recently deceased Charles Waldo Haskins. In the obituary section of the *New York Tribune*, their attention may have been attracted by an advertisement on the same page for a new play appearing on Broadway. *The Wizard of Oz*, by L. Frank Baum, was an allegory about the problem of providing order in the new industrial society. In Baum's view, society's problems stemmed primarily from the character defects of its major components: the heartless tin man of industry; the brainless scarecrow of agriculture; and the cowardly lion of government. Society's only hope for salvation from this flawed leadership depended upon the optimism and energy of youth—Dorothy aided by the worldly wisdom of the medicine-man wizard.[1] For the public accountants, however, the route to their Emerald City was obscure. Their journey was characterized by competition between many wizards, each of whom claimed to know the direction to the yellow brick road.

The accountants recognized early the importance of organization in achieving a special place in the new industrial society. Their professional associations became the primary focus for socializing their activities. Through their collective efforts, these new knowledge specialists hoped to obtain income, wealth, and status in the changing social order. Through their organizations, they also tried to order activities in their new profession and to ally themselves with other elites in business and government who were helpful in achieving their objectives.

Though many were in agreement about broad objectives, there was little consensus in these early years about the specific measures necessary to achieve them. Few models existed to guide the profession's leaders in integrating their special skills into a changing American society. This problem was made more complex because of substantial economic, regional, and cultural differences separating public accountants practicing across America.

What they ultimately discovered was that the key to achieving social integration was their ability to establish a consensus about the nature of professionalism. No single wizard had an answer acceptable to all. Though Haskins, Dickinson, May, and Montgomery all had insights, no one perspective was comprehensive. Wisdom, as the course of events revealed, was discoverable only through debate and compromise.

Strategies and Structures for Ordering Professional Affairs

As in business and government, in accountancy questions of appropriate professional strategies and organizational structures were closely intertwined. The AIA ultimately discovered that a federal form was most effective in advancing its program of professionalization. Only through a federal structure could the leaders accommodate accountancy's diverse factions. Earlier efforts to operate through a centralized structure akin to that of the British profession had failed because it alienated many practitioners who were geographically remote from the center of power. This structure had provided few opportunities for practitioners to come together to resolve their differences and to develop policies acceptable to all. Though suitable for a small European country such as Britain, a centralized structure was poorly suited for a large and diverse American profession practicing across a vast continent.

Most surprising is how long it took for federalism to become permanently established. This slowness seems unusual in light of the widespread use of federalism in American politics. Federations had also been used by other professions, including law and medicine. Decentralized structures were commonly used in business and government for coordinating national operations. What factors, then, compelled the AIA leaders to prefer for such a long period the centralization that so poorly served American conditions?[2]

One factor was the appeal of the model of British chartered accountancy, which excited the imaginations of the American elitists who led the AIA. Other American practitioners also eagerly aped British traditions, believing that the success achieved by their foreign colleagues could be attained simply by following closely their forms and practices.[3]

Many American leaders found British traditions appealing because of the social changes resulting from the influx of new immigrants.

British traditions reinforced feelings of superiority and reassured the elite. They hoped to keep the "good people" in control and traditional values intact in America.[4]

British traditions also persisted because of the role that London's capital market played in financing American industrial expansion prior to World War I. Public accountants functioned as key agents in transferring economic information to European investors, particularly those based in Britain. Through this important connection, British business forms and practices became well established in America.[5]

Moreover, a highly centralized structure worked fairly well in the first stage of professionalism, when the community of practitioners was small and centered in a few northeastern states. Later, the profession's widening geographical scope strained this form of organization and increased the difficulty of achieving consensus. The problem became acute as new professional communities flourished throughout America.

Accountants were slow to adjust, in part because the domestic profession grew rather slowly. Business education developed at a slow pace, and the number of well-trained candidates for admission to the profession remained limited well into the 1920s. This shortfall was partially made up by British chartered accountants who emigrated to this country because of limited employment opportunities in their home country. These elite immigrants helped to convince the AIA's leadership that a centralized organizational structure was still suitable.

In other professions influenced by European models, World War I was a clear breaking point, but this was not the case in public accountancy. The relations between American and British accountants were actually strengthened because of wartime political and economic ties. Leading British-American firms made important contributions to the Allies' economic mobilization.

Besides the British traditions, economic concerns shaped the preference for centralization. The leaders of the national firms were concerned about protecting strong positions in the markets for public accountancy services. It was hoped that concentrating power would minimize disruptive market competition, but this did not happen.

Because they had tried to assure their control by specifying narrow membership boundaries, the AIA's leaders encouraged the rise of dissident groups. They competed aggressively for professional leadership. The rivalry, however, confused outsiders as to the proper focus of professional authority. Public confidence eroded because of the internecine squabbling over which association represented the true source of sound opinion. Ultimately, this dissension left the profession vulnerable to the expansion of federal authority during the Great Depression.

Ironically, these events encouraged the AIA to broaden its membership and adopt a federal structure. These changes actually stabilized the position of the national firms and enhanced the AIA's political influence. Sharing power with the local practitioners did not diminish the national firms' market leadership. Because of their number and largess in financing associational activities, the national firm leaders continued to dominate policy formation in the AIA. The greater political strength associated with federalism enabled the AIA to resist government's attempts either to disrupt the status quo or to regulate professional activities more closely.

Federalism also enabled accountancy to overcome the differences separating the many small practitioners from the few large ones. Each category served different clienteles. The largest business organizations were usually served by the multioffice accounting firms. Among the national accounting firms, research and innovation played a central role in satisfying clients' needs. These practitioners devoted more time to researching solutions for their clients' new and sometimes baffling accounting problems. The large scale of client operations also provided challenges in tax practice and in the development of financial and cost accounting systems.

Consequently, many national firm practitioners became, in effect, narrow specialists. In this type of practice, public accountants gradually discovered that they could devote their time almost exclusively to auditing, tax, or management advisory services. Specialization enhanced their image as authorities and leaders.

To many elite accountants, the concerns of their local colleagues appeared so foreign as to constitute a different profession. Local practitioners usually served small clients whose service requirements seemed routine. Unlike their national firm colleagues, they functioned as generalists rather than as specialists. Often it was not economically feasible for them to concentrate on the mastery of only one aspect of practice.

Tensions between elite specialists and general practitioners also developed in other American professions. As Abbott has convincingly argued, professional prestige is enhanced in the eyes of colleagues largely on the basis of how the practitioner applies special knowledge. Within medicine, for instance, the university-based researcher developing new surgical techniques enjoys greater prestige than does the general practitioner. Moreover, increased specialization has given rise to new and prestigious fields of professional endeavor. New specialties such as surgery, pediatrics, obstetrics, and psychiatry emerged in medicine; engineering branched out into electrical, mechanical, civil, and chemical engineering. Specialization led to the development of what were effectively new professions.[6]

Similar spin-offs did not occur in accountancy largely because national firms wanted to provide a full range of services. Clients found it more efficient to obtain these services from one source rather than from a host of individual providers. Aware of this competitive advantage, few national firm partners wished to promote new modes of certifying specialization, thereby encouraging the formation of specialist practice units. In addition, further fragmentation of public accountancy was unappealing because it might have encouraged the formation of new specialist associations, thus diluting the AIA's influence and power. In this respect public accountancy was similar to law: specialization developed without giving rise to specialist associations.

In accounting, consensus eventually formed over the basic nature of the body of knowledge in the field. Many early practitioners viewed accountancy as essentially an art providing useful approximations of economic conditions and events. Others, however, thought accountancy a precise science. In medicine, such differences gave rise to competing professional organizations. But this was not the case in accountancy. The dominant viewpoint and the one the AIA expressed was that the profession's valuable truths derived from the good judgment and right action of the practitioner-artist. This position left the profession vulnerable to political and intellectual assaults; the AIA was gradually forced to accommodate to the pressure for developing specific practice guidelines. But by the time this was done, the federal plan had been implemented, and the united profession could handle the call for formulating definite practice standards.

Unity was eventually achieved in spite of the diversity of social backgrounds and social concerns. The elite had been nervous about both large-scale immigration and a decline in American values. The small local practitioners identified with the new men on the make—when they were not themselves the new men. For a time it appeared that these differences were irreconcilable. But New Deal regulations had the wonderful effect of encouraging tolerance. Associational unity was achieved under the threat of more drastic federal regulation. Not all the elite changed their minds on this issue under duress—witness the educations of George May and Robert Montgomery. But political pressure was in this case the necessary cause of the institutional unity that overrode social concerns.

To achieve consensus, accountants had to resolve their differing opinions on certifying practitioner competency. The issue of determining who was a valid member of the community was vital in providing important assurances to the public. There were two broad questions. Should the state or the professional association be the certifier of practitioner competency? Should the collegiate business schools or the public accounting firms have responsibility for training prospective candidates?

Though state licensing became the predominant mode, the AIA's leaders were anxious for their association to play an active role in certification. Because it was necessary for the top firms to maintain networks of local offices to serve clients, their leaders wanted to standardize this process. This would minimize the barriers that might exclude them from particular state markets.[7]

Like many of their business clients, the national firms favored establishing uniform national standards. To achieve this, the AIA and its predecessor lobbied the various states to adopt its model licensing law. In this, public accountancy differed from law and medicine. Though the leaders of law and medicine used similar devices, such as model laws, to standardize professional regulation, they were not as adversely affected by limitations on access to local markets. State and local tribunals were not of primary importance to Wall Street attorneys. Their pleading was done through the federal court system or in the courts in their home states. Physicians usually operated through individual hospitals. Patients seeking services traveled to the practitioner.[8]

The attorneys' state legislative activities differed from those of the public accountants in that they were not limited solely to establishing standards for admission to practice. During this period the American Bar Association promoted uniform state laws for commerce. It lobbied state legislatures to adopt its uniform bills for such matters as negotiable instruments, warehouse receipts, bills of lading, stock transfers, and conditional sales. By 1940 these and other aspects of commercial law constituted the Uniform Commercial Code, which the American Bar Association eventually succeeded in persuading all the states to adopt. No state legislative activities undertaken by the public accountants corresponded to this aspect of the political efforts of attorneys.[9]

In extending their authority over examining prospective practitioners, accountants followed the example of their counterparts in law and medicine. In public accountancy and other licensed professions, the influence was evidenced by the state licensing agencies accepting uniform examinations prepared and evaluated by the respective national professional organizations. In all professions, these associations assured minimal and uniform standards of competency among practitioners nationwide. The efforts during the 1920s to replace state certification either by national licensing or by membership in the AIA were contrary to the main trend and ultimately failed.[10]

The second debate centered on whether the new collegiate business schools or the individual public accounting firms should be the proper focus for the preliminary training of candidates. As in law, medicine, and engineering, in accountancy the problem was partially one of reconciling an older apprenticeship tradition with modes of training candidates through formal instruction in colleges and universities. In virtually all of the major American professions, the universities steadily supplanted apprentice programs for basic training. The transition in accountancy occurred more slowly than it did in other professions. The apprentice tradition hung on, but even among accountants it finally gave way.

In these and other regards, including those involving professional ethics, conflict gradually gave way to cooperation. Without the intervention of federal power, however, consensus would have been difficult to achieve.

Accountants and the National Executive State

Connections between government and professional groups became vital strands in the intricate web holding together the new American society that emerged during the last quarter of the nineteenth century. The small size and limited scope of the national government encouraged federal officials to draw closer to professional groups possessing new forms of knowledge useful in controlling the extensive changes evident in contemporary America. Unlike the professions in certain European nations, the professions in this country were not viewed as heretical, subversive, or merely eccentric. Instead of encountering alienation, the American harbingers of revolutionary forms of knowledge achieved actualization through their mutually beneficial alliances with the leaders of the emerging executive state.

But several factors initially inhibited the willingness of government leaders to accept all of the unique skills that public accountants promoted for ordering the nation's economic life. One involved the suitability of accountants' services to the types of regulatory structures government officials wanted to establish. Although accountants were eagerly recruited as expert advisors in creating reporting systems to assure the efficiency of governmental operations during this early period, they won few adherents for the role they wished to play in corporate governance. This was clearly illustrated in their experiences with the ICC. The key players in the accounting-based regulatory framework that Professor Adams erected were government bureaucrats and railroad accountants. He was optimistic that a judicious blending of accounting information and administrative law could provide strong incentives for private groups to operate honestly and equitably, thus minimizing the need for federal intervention. Although public accountants claimed that their professional services were highly relevant for assuring probity in financial reporting, their skills had never been applied as a mechanism for regulating rates. Public accountants were creatures of the free market. They could not advance their professional services among private business groups if they were perceived as agents of price control.

Public accountants were not engaged by government leaders for regulatory purposes during this early period for other reasons as well. Many were concerned about the uneven level of practitioner competency in this infant profession and its ability to play an effective role in regulating America's premier industry. Moreover, the community of practitioners was minuscule, numbering only about eight hundred in 1907. Public accountants were also unsuitable because they were vocal critics of the federal government's uniform accounting systems, which were thought essential in regulation. Furthermore, some in government were skeptical about the accountants' independence from client interests and consequently about their ability to resolve equitably contentious disputes over transportation tariffs.

The style of corporate governance pioneered at the ICC, however, was not widely imitated for regulating other types of economic activity and was extended later only to the special case of monopolistic industries. It was not applied in more competitive industries partly because it seemed inconsistent with traditional beliefs about the sanctity of private property and the limits of government power in controlling free markets. Moreover, contrary to the hopes of its architects, the ICC's system was never truly "self-executory." The expansion of its power correlated with an increase in the instances of its hostile clashes with the railroad industry. Furthermore, because of its central role in controlling railroad activities, this agency's effectiveness depended heavily on the quality and commitment of its leadership. But by 1911, Professor Adams had already moved on to serve as consultant to China's national railroads. Subsequent administrations, following revised political agendas, appointed less dynamic successors. Finally, the prestige that the ICC built up through its achievements, particularly during Theodore Roosevelt's administration, was gradually eclipsed by a series of failures with which it was associated: the steady decline in railroad profitability and the quality of service, the collapse of the Commerce Court, and the industry's poor performance during World War I.[11]

Because of its failures, the ICC remained to many business leaders a worrisome example that influenced later reforms involving accounting. Concerns about the purposes of accounting contributed to the modification of the FTC's and the FRB's plans on the eve of America's entry into World War I. In addition to the objections of bankers and farmers, another reason that the drive to standardize industrial accounting failed was because it would have compelled reluctant businessmen to provide government with data useful in antitrust enforcement. But the pressures of an impending political campaign and the heightening of international tensions induced the Wilson administration to lay aside these potentially controversial accounting matters. Members' bank reports were the only ones that the Federal Reserve Board standardized during this period: they were essential in controlling the nation's money supply.

The 1920s represented the high-water mark of autonomous associationalism. The enhanced prestige of these groups because of their war service made more credible their demands for a more central role in corporate governance. No longer were they visionaries operating at society's periphery. They were part of the mainstream, having won acceptance by demonstrating the power of their knowledge in ordering practical affairs. But by deferring too much to the technical experts, political leaders during this period encouraged the rise of professional structures wanting in the protection they afforded the public. Their plans were often found deficient: they were defined primarily with the interests of the profession's memberships in mind but failed to consider adequately the interests of consumer groups.

In extending government's authority to restore the national economy, the New Deal crafted new programs that both utilized and revitalized professional associations. This was achieved partly by tying professions in more closely to a broadened scope of federal regulation. This helped to restore the tarnished authority of the experts and strengthened their capacity for effective self-regulation. The sanctions defined in the new federal legislation also assured that these groups became more accountable to the public.

The New Deal's ordering of accounting regulation differed markedly from earlier patterns. Unlike the ICC, the SEC drew in the public accountants as key elements in its structure of governance. The SEC also generally deferred to the efforts of the accountants to standardize financial accounting and sparingly exercised its powers to intervene over these matters. The accounting standards that the AIA prepared with the concurrence of the SEC were formulated through debate among practitioners; they allowed greater flexibility in application than did the rigid rules prescribed earlier by the ICC. In this way the accountants created a reporting model that provided useful information to investors about enterprise liquidity, solvency, and profitability, but this information was limited as a basis for developing industry comparisons helpful to those wishing to evaluate market competition and concentration. The different choices made by the SEC were no doubt influenced by the growing size of the profession. By 1933 the number of practitioners had grown to over seventeen thousand. Furthermore, by operating through existing institutional structures, the New Deal helped to defuse some of the political opposition its reform efforts might have engendered. Opposition did eventually emerge, as we have seen, but only after the legislative framework of reform was well in place.[12]

Although the SEC seemed a fulfillment of the plans of the earlier, Wilsonian reformers at the FTC, it differed in one important respect. The proposed financial reporting requirements of the FTC were conceived partly as tools to monitor industrial concentration. In this regard the FTC's mission was an extension of the efforts of the Bureau of Corporations and the ICC's efforts to combat monopoly. It was probably this agency's close identification with antitrust enforcement that created political opposition to its regulation of financial reporting for industry and commerce. Instead, this function was vested with the SEC, whose sole purpose was the protection of investor interests.

Nor was the FRB the appropriate vehicle for regulating accounting. This possibility had been closed off earlier through the Glass-Steagall Act (1932), which separated commercial and investment banking. This legislation sought to prevent the assets of the Federal Reserve System from being used to fuel stock market speculation. Federally chartered commercial banks remained within the purview of the Federal Reserve and the comptroller of the currency, while the investment banking industry was to be regulated by the SEC.

Accountancy's success contrasted favorably with the other associationalist experiment of the Hundred Days, the creation of the National Recovery Administration. The Blue Eagle failed, in part, because it operated through an administrative apparatus that became too complex and unwieldy. The SEC, on the other hand, remained small by utilizing more effectively the existing associationalist frameworks to carry out its policies. The National Recovery Administration's regulatory activities also aggravated tensions within the industries it regulated; the SEC's actions, on the other hand, contributed to the building of practitioner unity. Finally, the National Recovery Administration failed because it tried to stabilize prices using means that had been long rejected in American constitutional history. The Supreme Court ruled that its efforts to limit competition were in violation of the antitrust statutes. The SEC, on the other hand, extended government power in order not to restrain market competition but rather to enhance probity. By so doing, it helped to restore public confidence and strengthened the functioning of the market system.[13]

The emphasis on defining functional relationships, which was central to the New Deal's reforms, also promoted social integration. Political leaders were able to dissipate potentially disruptive tensions associated with region, ethnicity, or class by emphasizing in their recovery programs functional groupings that cut across these social lines. To leaders of the American state, history seemed to abound with examples of how ascriptive concerns could operate to disturb social tranquility. Less than a century earlier, regional competition had led this nation into a devastating civil war; similar anxieties seemed to be drawing contemporary Europe to the brink of another great cataclysm. By focusing the debate on issues relating to occupational roles, America's leaders sought to transcend these particularlistic concerns, which were difficult to resolve and potentially corrosive to social harmony. Moreover, the changing tone of the public dialogue provided a strong incentive for the professions to reconcile their internal differences and to build cohesive organizations that were effective in protecting their members' interests. Organization and function became the vital touchstones on which these groups' future strategies for professional advancement would be based.

Recognition of the central role of function in the new society shaped moral standards, and this too helped to build accord. The reforms conceived by key New Deal advisors such as Frankfurter and Landis were strongly influenced by their perceptions about the nature of the new American society. From their perspectives, its success depended upon the effective coordination of a host of complex and interdependent functions. In this context, merit derived from the competency, cooperativeness, and social responsiveness of its various specialized groups. Religion, race, ethnicity, gender, and national or regional origins were no longer relevant evaluative criteria. In their efforts to

restore their nation's economy, Americans had discovered how perti-
nent functional considerations were in assessing social value.

Accountants and the Problem
of Historical Interpretation

The profession of public accountancy thus experienced dramatic
changes in the decades examined in this study, and this experience
casts some light on the way historians have interpreted their country's
modern history. With respect to the progressive interpretation, the
experience of public accountants suggests that the connection between the new professions and the various political reform movements was relatively tenuous until the 1930s. Many historians of this
school equated the rise of professionalism with the rise of political and
social reform movements. The new professionals were depicted as the
natural allies of the reform leaders in their battle to promote progress,
efficiency, and civic virtue in American society. My research suggests
that though both these movements seemed to develop in tandem, it is
inaccurate to say that they were derived from similar concerns about
society. Indeed, the history of the elite public accounting association
indicates that professionals could, depending on the circumstances,
operate either in support of or in opposition to political reform. The
public accountants were primarily interested in not political ideology
but pursuit of opportunities to secure a safe and profitable place for
their special expertise in the new industrial society. They sought their
opportunities by forming temporary alliances with groups of all political hues—liberals and conservatives, Democrats and Republicans.

The history of public accountants also calls into question the manner in which the corporate-liberal historians have characterized social
change in twentieth-century America. Least convincing in their interpretation is the view that social reforms were essentially shrewd concessions made by conservative business interests to preserve tranquility and their own privileged status. In the struggle between the
classes, these scholars argue, protest and conflict were effectively
defused.

However, in this study of organizational change and of the development of professional strategies among public accountants, a somewhat different interpretation seems necessary. The experience of the
public accountants suggests that political action resulted most often
from the competition between rival groups of businessmen. The cen-

tral tension for change in society did not appear to derive from a horizontal split between the upper and lower classes; nor did any one class or group ever have political change completely under control. Rather, society was split vertically into loosely knit social pyramids whose leaders vied for dominance over the nation's most important businesses and political institutions. Faction was more important than class. In fact, a competition between an old and a new order such as the one envisioned by the liberal historian Arthur Schlesinger, Jr., in his *Crisis of the Old Order* aptly characterizes these developments. In this study change occurred because of the competition. There were, on the one hand, the older, eastern, middle-class elite backed by their British professional allies and, on the other, the representatives of more recently arrived ethnic and national groups with a rather vague middle-class or lower-middle-class orientation. These groups were loosely allied with social elements based in the less industrialized areas of the nation.[14]

Accord did not result from the manipulative largess of the great magnates, though they certainly tried this strategy. I find, instead, the gradual emergence of compromise and cooperation between competing elites. Their factions were loosely united on the basis of economic, regional, ethnic, or national factors. All discovered the limitations of their powers. The system of checks and balances that emerged was somewhat analogous to the system that the authors of *The Federalist Papers* thought was essential in ordering the nation's political life.[15]

This new associational federalism did not result from predesign, as did the countervailing powers of the three branches of the federal government. Instead, the balance resulted from the inability of any single faction to concentrate sufficient power to dominate affairs in a country as vast and complex as America. The expansion of opportunity resulting from the rapid industrialization of the nation was so great that no single social group could control it. As a consequence, rival groups had an incentive to work together in trying to achieve their common objectives.

This study of the history of the AIA also casts some new light on the interpretations of the historians who view the most fundamental changes as being rooted in the formation of new business organizations. What are frequently overlooked by these organizational historians are the important connections between institutional development and social values. The organizational analysts want, I think, to correct the "misplaced" emphasis in U.S. historiography on intellectual constructs and values. They thus describe business leaders as dispassionate decision makers. In other words, the businessmen are searchers after new and objective methods for optimizing the efficient allocation of their firms' resources.

As indicated in this present study, questions of social value were key influences in shaping the outlook and decisions of the leaders of the new profession of public accountancy. Although they may have been ambiguous about political or social reform, they were not indifferent to certain salient aspects of the direction of social change in America. In designing a new structure for professionalism, they were trying to find a secure place in the changing economic order for their new and special knowledge; but as they sought the yellow brick road to wealth, income, and status, they were also seeking to preserve traditional values in a society threatened from within. The great achievement of their venture was not limited to securing new economic opportunities for the application of their expertise or to helping to solve the profession's technical, political, and ethical problems. They eventually came to accept social change and learned to be at ease with the social differences in their growing community of practitioners, and this too was a major accomplishment. In this and other regards, the public accountants had learned much about their new society and about themselves. They had forged new institutions suited to a world far different from the nineteenth-century society that had given rise to the drive for professional standing. In the years ahead the profession would build on the foundations constructed with cooperative effort in the years prior to the Second World War.

Notes

Abbreviations

AAA   American Accounting Association
AAPA   American Association of Public Accountants
AIA   American Institute of Accountants
DAB   *Dictionary of American Biography*
DNB   *Dictionary of National Biography*
FRB   Federal Reserve Board
FTC   Federal Trade Commission
ISCPA   Illinois Society of Certified Public Accountants
NCAB   *National Cyclopedia of American Biography*
NJSCPA New Jersey Society of Certified Public Accountants
NYIA   New York Institute of Accounts
NYSSCPA New York State Society of Certified Public Accountants
NYT   *New York Times*
SEC   Securities and Exchange Commission

Chapter 1

1. AIA, *Yearbook 1937*, pp. 1–62 passim; Montgomery, *Fifty Years of Accountancy*, pp. 73–75.

2. Montgomery, *Fifty Years of Accountancy*, pp. 72–73.

3. For a brief description of the backgrounds of these two associations, see Carey, *Rise of the Accounting Profession* 1:36–38 (for AIA), 330–32 (for ASCPA); Edwards, *History of Public Accounting*, pp. 52–57 (for AIA), 127–30 (for ASCPA); and Webster, *American Association of Public Accountants*. Montgomery also evidenced a deep concern for professional unity, as reflected in his article "Professional Standards," pp. 519–29.

4. For Montgomery's career, see his *Fifty Years of Accountancy*, chaps. 1, 2, 3, and 5 passim, and Roberts, "Robert H. Montgomery."

5. AIA, *Yearbook 1937*, p. 362; Carey, *Rise of the Accounting Profession* 1:348.

6. Montgomery, *Fifty Years of Accountancy*, pp. 322–23.

7. Berle and Means, *Modern Corporation and Private Property*; Ripley, *Main Street and Wall Street*.

8. See Parrish, *Securities Regulation and the New Deal*, pp. 201–8, for a discussion of the new responsibilities of public accountants under the Securities Acts of 1933 and 1934.

9. Montgomery, *Fifty Years of Accountancy*, p. 325.

10. Ibid., p. 327.

11. In this study I use the term "profession" in a broad sociological sense. This status is best defined in terms of a series of qualities differentiating it from other occupational categories; as such, the definition is scalar rather than binary. Inherent in this definition is the assumption that different occupations vary to the degree that they are "professional." Additionally, it also assumes that the degree of professionalization of particular professions may also vary over time.

Following Moore, *The Professions*, I deem the following six qualities as essential for professional status:

1. *Occupation*: A profession differs from mere amateur pursuit because it involves full-time employment that serves as the practitioner's primary source for acquiring income, status, and other scarce social resources.

2. *Calling*: The persistent application required of prospective practitioners implies that their commitment to a professional career will be long-term. It also implies that over the course of their professional lives, they willingly accept the norms and standards required of all practitioners.

3. *Organization*: A formal educational framework is necessary for ordering activities within the profession. At a minimum, organizations help to differentiate their members' expertise from other occupational pursuits, to define the boundaries of the community of competent practitioners, and to maintain minimal standards of professional performance.

4. *Education*: A profession requires a formal pattern for imparting the fundamental skills and knowledge required of competent practitioners. This usually involves completion of well-defined curricula provided by accredited institutions of higher education or other types of apprentice training.

5. *Service*: This quality has three elements relating to assurances practitioners provide to clients, colleagues, and society. First, practitioners warrant that they are competent in the performance of their function and that they will maintain and improve their basic skills. Second, they warrant that they will be conscientious in the application of their special skills. Third, they warrant that their service will be conducted with the best interests of clients and the public in mind.

6. *Autonomy*: A degree of independence is associated with a high degree of authority with respect to the profession's special knowledge and expertise. The greater the degree of technical skill required by the practitioner in the performance of his special task, the greater his autonomy in these matters.

12. See Carey, *CPA's Professional Heritage*; Carey, *Rise of the Accounting Profession*; Casler, *Evolution of CPA Ethics*; Davidson and Anderson, "Development of Accounting and Auditing Standards"; Edwards, *History of Public Accounting*; Edwards and Miranti, "AICPA," pp. 22–38; Mednick and Previts, "Scope of CPA Services," pp. 220–38; Previts and Merino, *Accounting in America*; and Webster, *American Association of Public Accountants*.

In addition to these published works, a substantial number of dissertations by doctoral candidates in accountancy have focused on narrower aspects of accounting history. See, for example, Bowen, "Social Responsibility of the Accounting Profession"; Boyd, "CPA Legislation in the United States"; C. D. Brown, "Balance Sheet to Income Statement"; Butler, "Certified Public Accounting Profession in Louisiana"; Coffey, "Government Regulations and Professional Pronouncements"; Cunningham, "Variables Influencing the Outcomes of Federal Court Cases Involving Anti-Trust Action"; J. W. Davis, "CPA Profession in Mississippi"; Dixon, "Certified Public Accounting Profession in Arkansas"; Frey, "Public Accounting Profession"; Hunthausen, "CPA Profession in Colorado"; Merino, "Professionalization of Public Accounting"; Miranti, "From Conflict to Consensus"; Previts, "Critical Evaluation of Comparative Financial Accounting Thought in America"; Walker, "CPA Profession in Tennessee"; and Zimmerman, "British Backgrounds of American Accountancy."

13. Beard, *Century of Progress*; Parrington, "Spirit of the Age," pp. 3–19. See also Hofstadter, *Age of Reform*, and Schlesinger, *Age of Roosevelt*, two outstanding examples of the culmination of this tradition. See also Hofstadter, *Progressive Historians*, for a critical analysis of this school.

14. See Block, *Origins of International Economic Disorder*; Carlisle, " 'American Century' Implemented," pp. 175–91; Kaufman, *Efficiency and Expansion*; Kaufman, "United States Economic Policy," pp. 342–63. See also Kolko, *Modern American History*; Kolko, *Triumph of Conservatism*; Lustig, *Corporate Liberalism*; and Smith, *United States and Revolutionary Nationalism in Mexico*.

15. Burrow, *Organized Medicine in the Progressive Era*; Gevitz, *The D.O.'s*; and Berlant, *Professions and Monopoly*.

16. Auerbach, *Unequal Justice*; Botein, "Professional History Reconsidered," pp. 60–79; Freidson, *Profession of Medicine*; and Freidson, *Professional Dominance*.

17. Layton, *The Revolt of the Engineers*; Leslie, *Boss Kettering*. See also the following articles: Leslie, "Kettering and the Copper-cooled Engine," pp. 752–76; Leslie, "Midgley and the Politics of Industrial Research," pp. 480–503; Reich, "Industrial Research and the Pursuit of Corporate Security," pp. 504–29; Reich, "Langmuir and the Pursuit of Science," pp. 199–221; Reich, "Patents and the Struggle to Control the Radio," pp. 504–29; and Servos, "Industrial Relations of Science," pp. 531–49.

18. Hays, "Upper Class Takes the Lead," pp. 79–83; Wiebe, *Search for Order*, chaps. 6–7 passim.

19. Kuhn, *Structure of Scientific Revolutions*.

20. Buck, *Social Sciences at Harvard*; Coats, "First Two Decades of the American Economic Association," pp. 555–72; Coats, "Political Economy Club," pp. 624–37; Grob, *Mental Institutions in America*; Grob, *Mental Illness and American Society*; Haskell, *Emergence of Professional Social Science*; Johnson and Kaplan, *Relevance Lost*; Kohlstedt, *Formation of the American Scientific Community*; Somit and Tanenhaus, *Development of Political Science*; and Stocking, "Franz Boas and the Founding of the American Anthropological Association," pp. 1–17.

21. See Aitken, *Syntony and Spark*; R. E. Kohler, *From Medical Chemistry to*

Biochemistry; R. E. Kohler, "Medical Reform and Biomedical Science," pp. 27–66; and Larson, *Rise of Professionalism*.

A recent extension of this approach is the innovative study of Abbott, *System of Professions*. In explaining professional development, Abbott shifts away from consideration of the role of organizations and, instead, emphasizes the importance of the skills and work of expert groups in securing for their practitioners jurisdiction over particular problems confronting society.

22. Chandler, *Strategy and Structure*; Chandler, *Visible Hand*; Haber, *Efficiency and Uplift*; Hays, *Conservation and the Gospel of Efficiency*; and Wiebe, *Search for Order*, pp. 151–55.

23. Galambos, "Technology, Political Economy, and Professionalization," pp. 471–93; Galambos, *America at Middle Age*, chaps. 4–5 passim.

24. Bledstein, *Culture of Professionalism*, chaps. 6–8 passim; Bryson, "Emergence of the Social Sciences from Moral Philosophy," pp. 304–22; and Daniels, "Process of Professionalization in American Science," pp. 151–66.

25. For examples of general works on the development of scholarly disciplines, see Crick, *American Science of Politics*; Furner, *Advocacy and Objectivity*, especially chaps. 2–4, 12, 13 passim; Haskell, *Emergence of Professional Social Science*, chaps. 7–9 passim; Higham, Krieger, and Gilbert, *History*; Storr, *Beginning of Graduate Education in America*; and Veysey, *Emergence of the American University*.

For specific studies of individual universities, see, for example: Curti and Carstensen, *University of Wisconsin*; Elliott, *Stanford University*; and Hawkins, *History of the Johns Hopkins University*. For studies of university-based professional training, see Hobson, "American Legal Profession," chaps. 3–4 passim; Calvert, *Mechanical Engineer in America*, chaps. 3–5; Sass, *Pragmatic Imagination*; and Stevens, *American Medicine and the Public Interest*, chaps. 2–3 passim.

26. Hays, *Response to Industrialism*; Higham, *Strangers in the Land*; and Wiebe, *Businessmen and Reform*.

27. Tocqueville, *Democracy in America*; Wiebe, *Segmented Society*.

28. *International Encyclopedia of the Social Sciences*, s.v.v. "Political Socialization," 14:551–55, and "Socialization: Anthropological Aspects," 14:545–51.

29. Ibid., s.v. "Concept of Consensus," 3:260–66.

30. Ibid., 3:266–70. For a discussion of self-interest as a factor motivating professional development, see Wilensky, "Professionalization of Everyone?" pp. 137–58.

31. By emphasizing the influence of economic, social, and political developments on professionalization, this model is close to the position taken by Larson in *Rise of Professionalism*. It is primarily based on the experience of four professions: law, accountancy, medicine, and, to a lesser extent, engineering. Although the nature of their work differed greatly, the dependence of these groups on state-granted licenses was a common condition that unified their experience and also differentiated it from that of other classes of experts. The analysis of the changing relationships between these licensed professions and the maturing American administrative state defines the central patterns that support my explanatory model. But, as Millerson reminds us in *The Qualifying*

Associations, attempts to extend such a model to too broad a spectrum of professions and differing historical contexts may be inappropriate.

32. Berlant, *Professions and Monopoly*, pp. 218–47; Burrow, *AMA*, chaps. 1–2; Edwards, *History of Public Accounting*, pp. 68–77; Hobson, "American Legal Profession," chap. 6; Shryock, *Medical Licensing in America*.

For the nature of American governmental institutions, see Keller, *Affairs of State*, and Skowronek, *Building a New American State*, Pts. 1, 2.

33. Berlant, *Professions and Monopoly*, chaps. 3–5; Carlin, *Lawyers' Ethics*; Johnson and Hopson, *Lawyers and Their Work*; Lepaulle, "Law Practice in France," pp. 945–58; Miranti, "Associationalism, Statism, and Professional Regulation," pp. 438–68; Moore, *The Professions*, pp. 118–20; and Schweinberg, *Law Training in Continental Europe*.

For a European view of the proper relationship between professions and government, see Durkheim, *Professional Ethics and Civic Morals*. For discussions of attitudes of the reformers who sought to augment power of government to counter private power, see Dorfman, *Relation of the State to Industrial Action*, pp. 3–55, and Rader, *Academic Mind and Reform*, especially chap. 2.

34. Abbott, "Status and Status Strain," pp. 819–25; Abbott, *System of Professions*, chap. 5 passim; Auerbach, *Unequal Justice*, chaps. 1, 2; Hartman, "Social Prestige of Representative Medical Specialties," pp. 659–63; Ladinsky, "Careers of Lawyers," pp. 47–54; Miranti, "Associationalism, Statism, and Professional Regulation," pp. 441–45; Ripley, *Trusts, Pools, and Corporations*, chaps. 1–4; and Stevens, *American Medicine and the Public Interest*, chaps. 2, 4, 5.

35. Abbott, *System of Professions*, chap. 5; Carlin, *Lawyers on Their Own*; Erlanger, "Allocation of Status within Occupations," pp. 882–903; Ladinsky, "Careers of Lawyers," pp. 47–54; Rosen, *Structure of American Medical Practice*, pp. 8, 19, 32–34; and Stevens, *American Medicine and the Public Interest*, pp. 49–52.

36. Burrow, *AMA*, pp. 8–10, 33–34; Calvert, *Mechanical Engineer in America*, chaps. 3–5 passim; and Stevens, *American Medicine and the Public Interest*, pp. 55–74, 117, 254.

37. See Abbott, *System of Professions*, chaps. 6–7, especially for discussion of the impact of the social environment on professional development; Auerbach, *Unequal Justice*, chap. 2; Bledstein, *Culture of Professionalism*, chap. 1; Miranti, "Associationalism, Statism, and Professional Regulation," pp. 442–44; Moore, *The Professions*, pp. 66–69; and Rosen, *Structure of American Medical Practice*, pp. 66–78.

For perceptions of the Middle West, see Cather, *O Pioneers!*; Twain, *Life on the Mississippi*; and Tarkington, *Penrod*.

38. Calvert, *Mechanical Engineer in America*, pp. 107–35; Haskell, *Emergence of Professional Social Science*, chaps. 8–9; Hobson, "American Legal Profession," chaps. 3, 6; Previts and Merino, *Accounting in America*, pp. 136–44; and Stevens, *American Medicine and the Public Interest*, pp. 34–54.

39. Burrow, *Organized Medicine*, chaps. 1, 2, 4, 6; Edwards, *History of Public Accounting*, pp. 86–90, 97, 101–3; Hobson, "American Legal Profession," chap. 7; and Previts and Merino, *Accounting in America*, pp. 136–44.

40. On the extension of federal governmental powers, see Skowronek, *Building a New American State*, pt. 3. On activities of professions, see Burrow, *AMA*, chaps. 2–3; Calvert, *Mechanical Engineer in America*, pp. 128–29, 131–34; Edwards, *History of Public Accounting*, pp. 87–90; Furner, *Advocacy and Objectivity*, pp. 260–65; Hobson, "American Legal Profession," pp. 290–313; and Previts and Merino, *Accounting in America*, pp. 138–44.

41. Burrow, *AMA*, pp. 33–36; Edwards, *History of Public Accounting*, pp. 68–83, 111; Hobson, "American Legal Profession," chap. 4; Shryock, *Medical Licensing in America*, pp. 77–80; and Stevens, *American Medicine and the Public Interest*, chap. 3.

42. Burrow, *AMA*, pp. 51–54, 54–66; Carey, *Rise of the Accounting Profession* 1:100–102; Hobson, "American Legal Profession," pp. 230–40; and Previts and Merino, *Accounting in America*, pp. 142–49.

43. Burrow, *AMA*, chaps. 4–7 passim; Carey, *Rise of the Accounting Profession* 1:53–73; Calvert, *Mechanical Engineer in America*, pp. 267–74; Edwards, *History of Public Accounting*, pp. 93–96, 101–3; Grossman, "Professors and Public Service"; Hobson, "American Legal Profession," pp. 242–55; Layton, *Revolt of the Engineers*, pp. 63–64; and Previts and Merino, *Accounting in America*, pp. 142–48. For connections to organized reform, see, for example, Furner, *Advocacy and Objectivity*, pp. 268–70; Stewart, *A Half Century of Municipal Reform*; and Potts, "Evolution of Municipal Accounting," pp. 518–36. For the extensive involvement of the legal profession, see Jessup, *Elihu Root*, and Harbaugh, *Lawyer's Lawyer*.

44. AAPA, "Report of Special Committee on Form of Organization," in *Yearbook 1916*, pp. 108–16; Auerbach, *Unequal Justice*, chaps. 3–4; Calvert, *Mechanical Engineer in America*, pp. 267–74; Miranti, "Associationalism, Statism, and Professional Regulation," pp. 441–48; Previts and Merino, *Accounting in America*, pp. 205–9; Rosen, *Structure of American Medical Practice*, pp. 19–26; and Shryock, *Medical Licensing in America*, chap. 2 and pp. 77–81.

45. Calvert, *Mechanical Engineer in America*, pp. 267–74; Furner, *Advocacy and Objectivity*, pp. 28–29, 260–65; Layton, *Revolt of the Engineers*, chap. 8; Miranti, "Associationalism, Statism, and Professional Regulation," pp. 453–56; Previts and Merino, *Accounting in America*, pp. 205–9; and Stevens, *American Medicine and the Public Interest*, pp. 44, 50–51.

46. Burrow, *AMA*, chap. 5; Carey, *Rise of the Accounting Profession* 1:139–45; Cuff, *War Industries Board*, chap. 1; Layton, *Revolt of the Engineers*, pp. 126–27; Miranti, "From Conflict to Consensus," p. 453; Stevens, *American Medicine and the Public Interest*, pp. 132–42; and Taylor, *Medical Profession and Social Reform*, chap. 6.

47. For a discussion of triocracy, see Galambos, *America at Middle Age*, chaps. 4–5 passim.

48. G. C. Davis, "Federal Trade Commission"; Hoogenboom and Hoogenboom, *History of the ICC*; Link, *Wilson: The New Freedom*, chaps. 7, 13; Mowry, *Era of Theodore Roosevelt*, pp. 123–25; Sharfman, *Interstate Commerce Commission*; and Willis, *Federal Reserve System*.

49. See Galambos, *America at Middle Age*, pp. 42–47; Hawley, *The Great War*, chap. 5; and Hawley, "Herbert Hoover, the Commerce Secretariat, and the

Vision of an Associative State," pp. 116–40. See also Gilb, *Hidden Hierarchies*, chap. 4, for a discussion of professional self-government.

50. Karl, *Uneasy State*, pp. 47–49.

51. Auerbach, *Unequal Justice*, chaps. 4–5; Berlant, *Professions and Monopoly*, pp. 97–127 passim; Burrow, *AMA*, chap. 8; Layton, *Revolt of the Engineers*, chaps. 8–9; Miranti, "From Conflict to Consensus," chaps. 8–9; Rosen, *Structure of American Medical Practice*, pp. 87–98 passim; Shryock, *Medical Licensing in America*, chap. 3; and Stevens, *American Medicine and the Public Interest*, pp. 75–122 passim.

52. Auerbach, *Unequal Justice*, chap. 3 passim; Carey, *Rise of the Accounting Profession* 1:132–38, 261–78, 304–6; and Rosen, *Structure of American Medical Practice*, pp. 47–48, 61–66, 81–94.

53. Auerbach, *Unequal Justice*, chap. 6; Burrow, *AMA*, pp. 178–84.

54. See Stevens, *American Medicine and the Public Interest*, chaps. 4–8 passim.

55. Layton, *Revolt of the Engineers*, pp. 122–26 and chap. 8 passim.

56. Auerbach, *Unequal Justice*, chap. 4 passim; Carey, *Rise of the Accounting Profession* 1:314–32; Miranti, "Associationalism, Statism, and Professional Regulation," pp. 453–60; and Previts and Merino, *Accounting in America*, pp. 205–9.

57. Hawley, *The Great War*, chaps. 12–13; Leuchtenberg, *Roosevelt and the New Deal*; Mitchell, *Depression Decade*; and Schlesinger, *Age of Roosevelt*.

58. Auerbach, *Unequal Justice*, chap. 7; Burrow, *AMA*, chaps. 11–13 passim; Layton, *Revolt of the Engineers*, chap. 10; Miranti, "Associationalism, Statism, and Professional Regulation," pp. 460–68; Previts and Merino, *Accounting in America*, pp. 249–65.

59. Auerbach, *Unequal Justice*, chap. 7; Miranti, "Associationalism, Statism, and Professional Regulation," pp. 460–63.

60. Auerbach, *Unequal Justice*, pp. 221–30; Burrow, *AMA*, chaps. 11–13 passim; and Previts and Merino, *Accounting in America*, pp. 254–72.

61. Burrow, *AMA*, chaps. 11–13 passim; McCraw, "With the Consent of the Governed," pp. 346–70; and Miranti, "Associationalism, Statism, and Professional Regulation," pp. 460–68. For a general discussion of the relationships between the state and the profession see also Gilb, *Hidden Hierarchies*, chap. 6.

62. Burrow, *AMA*, chaps. 13–14; Galambos, *America at Middle Age*, chap. 4; Karl, *Executive Reorganization and Reform*, chap. 6; Karl, *Uneasy State*, chap. 8; Keller, "Pluralist State," pp. 78–84; and McCraw, *Prophets of Regulation*.

Part 1

1. See Chandler, *Strategy and Structure* and *Visible Hand*, for the effects these developments had on business institutions and professional managers. See also Wiebe, *Search for Order*, for a discussion of the broader social impacts of these developments.

2. See Jones, *Accounting and the British Economy*, pp. 19–37 passim. See also Carey, *Rise of the Accounting Profession* 1:13–26; and Edwards, *History of Public Accounting*, pp. 5–18.

Chapter 2

1. Carey, *Rise of the Accounting Profession* 1:36–38; Edwards, *History of Public Accounting*, pp. 50–51, 52–57; Calvert, *Mechanical Engineer in America*, chap. 3 passim; and Previts and Merino, *Accounting in America*, pp. 93–96.

2. Carr-Saunders and Wilson, *The Professions*, pp. 208–27; Edwards, *History of Public Accounting*, pp. 15–24; Jones, *Accounting and the British Economy*, pp. 25–27, 48–52, 57–73 passim; and Walker, *Society of Accountants in Edinburgh*.

3. Bruchey, *Robert Oliver and Mercantile Bookkeeping*; Chatfield, *History of Accounting Thought*, pp. 113–15, 118; Jones, *Accounting and the British Economy*, pp. 34–38, 48–52, 98–100; Mepham, *Accounting in Eighteenth-Century Scotland*; and Previts and Merino, *Accounting in America*, pp. 6–16, 24–39.

4. Jones, *Accounting and the British Economy*, pp. 111–16; Littleton, *Accounting Evolution to 1900*, chaps. 16–18 passim; and Previts, *Scope of CPA Services*, chap. 1 passim.

5. Edwards, *History of Public Accounting*, pp. 5–9; Jones, *Accounting and the British Economy*, pp. 51–57.

6. Edwards, *History of Public Accounting*, pp. 15–29; Jones, *Accounting and the British Economy*, pp. 63–73 passim; and Previts, *Scope of CPA Services*, pp. 27–28.

7. Edwards, *History of Public Accounting*, pp. 15–29; Jones, *Accounting and the British Economy*, pp. 63–73 passim; and Walker, *Society of Accountants in Edinburgh*, chap. 3. See also the useful articles by Mary E. Murphy: "An Accountant in the Eighties," pp. 67–68, 85–86; "Accountancy in England: Public, Government, Profession," pp. 328–43; and "Rise of Accountancy in England," pp. 62–73.

8. On the acceptance of public accountants, see Chatfield, *History of Accounting Thought*, pp. 159–72 passim; Montgomery, *Fifty Years of Accountancy*, p. 33; and Previts and Merino, *Accounting in America*, pp. 89–99 passim. For a contemporary American view of the nature of practice, see Blacklock, "Profession of Accountancy Viewed from an American Standpoint," pp. 13, 143, 194, 253. For a somewhat earlier period, see Anyon, *Recollections of the Early Days of Accountancy*, which provides information about competition between British and American accountants in New York.

See *DAB*, s.v.v. "Adams, Henry Carter," and "Cooley, Thomas McIntyre." For Adams's role, see also Dorfman, *Relation of the State to Industrial Action*, p. 11. For a summary of their activities at the ICC, see Churchman, "Federal Regulation of Railroad Rates"; and Hoogenboom and Hoogenboom, *History of the ICC*, pp. 19–23, 25–32 passim.

9. The origins, objectives, and frustrations of the early ICC are succinctly analyzed in Skowronek, *Building a New American State*, chap. 5 passim.

10. For activities of James Thurber, see Benson, *Merchants, Farmers, and Railroads*, pp. 60–75 passim, 125–27, 164–77, 216–19. For connection with accountants, see Webster, *American Association of Public Accountants*, p. 189.

11. "United States Consular Reports and Chartered Accountants," p. 521; Webster, *American Association of Public Accountants*, p. 329.

12. For an excellent discussion of the extent of foreign investment in the

U.S., see Wilkins, *Foreign Investment in the United States*, especially pp. 536–45, for entry of British accounting firms. For local office openings, see also DeMond, *Price Waterhouse*, pp. 32–35, 59, 62; Edwards, *History of Public Accounting*, pp. 77–80; and Reckitt, *Reminiscences of the Accounting Profession*, p. 30.

13. DeMond, *Price Waterhouse*, pp. 11–12, 18, 32–35, 59, 62; Previts and Merino, *Accounting in America*, p. 91; and Reckitt, *Reminiscences of the Accounting Profession*, pp. 30–31.

14. For a synopsis of the professional career of each of these practitioners, see Webster, *American Association of Public Accountants*, pp. 328 (Allen), 336 (Broaker), 339 (Chapman), 377–78 (Stevens). See also obituary notice for Broaker in *NYT*, November 13, 1941, p. 27, col. 3. Letterhead of the Chapman and Broaker firm to Melvil Dewey, February 21, 1895, indicates the existence of correspondent relationships with several chartered accountants based in Britain (Box 75, Dewey Papers).

15. See Higham, *Strangers in the Land*, for a full discussion of nativist reaction to new immigration from eastern and southern Europe.

16. Webster, *American Association of Public Accountants*, pp. 9–17, 276–90.

17. See Edwards, *History of Public Accounting*, pp. 51–52; Previts and Merino, *Accounting in America*, pp. 93–94, 101–2, 109–10; and Webster, *American Association of Public Accountants*, pp. 276, 280–84.

18. *NCAB*, s.v. "Haskins, Charles W.," Jordan, *Charles Waldo Haskins*, pp. 1–41 passim; and Webster, *American Association of Public Accountants*, pp. 352–53.

19. Jordan, *Charles Waldo Haskins*, pp. 12–13.

20. Ibid., pp. 15–49; and Skowronek, *Building a New American State*, pp. 50–52, 83.

21. Jordan, *Charles Waldo Haskins*, pp. 53–57, 79.

22. Haskins's quotation is found in a letter to the Massachusetts Society of Public Accountants, reproduced in part in an unpublished manuscript entitled "Notes on Historical Material Compiled by Harvey S. Chase," November 6, 1946, in Webster Papers. For discussion of the social implications derived from contemporary statistical thinking, see Emerson's *Representative Men*, pp. 106–8, and his *Conduct of Life*, pp. 21–24. See Porter, *Rise of Statistical Thinking*, pp. 40–55, 100–111, 219–20, for Quetelet's contributions to social thinking. See also Previts and Merino, *Accounting in America*, pp. 162–63, for discussion of "scientific accountancy"; for discussion of "logismography," see Sprague, "Logismography I and Logismography II."

23. *DAB*, s.v. "Sprague, Charles Ezra."

24. Ibid., s.v. "Packard, Silas S."; Packard, *Manual of Theoretical Training in the Science of Accounts*.

25. See file entitled "Anson O. Kittredge" in Webster Papers and obituary notice in *NYT*, March 23, 1903, p. 7.

26. See Porter, *Rise of Statistical Thinking*, pp. 255–69, for implications of Edgeworth's work. For the views of some leading accountants, see Dickinson, *Accounting Practice and Procedure*, pp. 31–33; May, *Twenty-five Years of Accounting Responsibility* 2:305–18; and Previts and Merino, *Accounting in America*, pp. 163–64. For practitioners' backgrounds, see Webster, *American Association*

of Public Accountants, pp. 340 (Church), 348 (Fackler), 382 (Trenholm). See above, n. 14, for Broaker, Chapman, and Stevens.

27. Boyd, "CPA Legislation in the United States," pp. 22–24; Previts and Merino, *Accounting in America*, pp. 103–13.

28. *DAB*, s.v. "James, Edmund Jane"; Sass, *Pragmatic Imagination*, pp. 79–85.

29. DeMond, *Price Waterhouse*, p. 98; Montgomery, *Fifty Years of Accountancy*, p. 52.

30. These figures and the conclusions drawn from them are based on my analysis of association members' backgrounds as summarized in the biographical appendix in Webster, *American Association of Public Accountants*, pp. 325–99.

31. Jones, *Accounting and the British Economy*, pp. 71–72; for backgrounds, see Webster, *American Association of Public Accountants*, pp. 342 (Cook), 383 (Veysey), 387–88 (Yalden).

32. T. S. Smith, "Education of Accountants," pp. 201–4; Walker, *Society of Accountants in Edinburgh*, chap. 4 and pp. 182–84; and Webster, "Early Movements for Accountancy Education," pp. 411–50.

33. Jordan, *Charles Waldo Haskins*, pp. 63–73 passim. See also letter from Melbourne S. Moyer to N. E. Webster, February 13, 1953, on Haskins's guarantee in file, "NYU School of Commerce, Accounts, and Finance," in Webster Papers.

34. See Sass, *Pragmatic Imagination*, pp. 141–42, 182, 133n.

35. See above, n. 18.

36. See Higham, *Strangers in the Land*, particularly chap. 4, for discussion of nativist attitudes toward the new immigrant groups of the 1890s. See also Sons of the American Revolution, *United States*, and *National Register of the Society*, s.v.v. "Haskins, Charles W.," "Depew, Chauncey M.," and "Doane, William C."

37. See Higham, *Strangers in the Land*, p. 96, for discussion of some prominent Americans' ambivalent feelings toward Britain and its influence on their social and political outlooks.

38. Furer, "Career of William Henry Havemeyer," pp. 238–347 passim; Mullins, "Sugar Trust," pp. 113–48 passim.

39. See above, n. 23 for Sprague background; for Hopkins, see Webster, *American Association of Public Accountants*, p. 108.

40. C. S. Campbell, *Transformation of American Foreign Relations*, pp. 177–222 passim.

41. Webster, *American Association of Public Accountants*, p. 221.

42. Boyd, "CPA Legislation in the United States," pp. 3–4, 8–9, 15; Edwards, *History of Public Accounting*, pp. 51–52.

43. Letter from Richard M. Chapman, February 26, 1895, in Box 75, Dewey Papers.

44. Boyd, "CPA Legislation in the United States," pp. 8–9; Previts and Merino, *Accounting in America*, p. 102.

Chapter 3

1. See DeMond, *Price Waterhouse*, pp. 11–12, 18, 32–35, 59, 62; Previts and Merino, *Accounting in America*, p. 91; and Reckitt, *Reminiscences of the Accounting Profession*, pp. 30–31.

2. See DeMond, *Price Waterhouse*, pp. 10–12, for marketing securities. For branch office openings, see Edwards, *History of Public Accounting*, pp. 77–78; F. A. Ross, "Growth and Effect of Branch Offices," pp. 252–61; and Wilkins, *Foreign Investment in the United States*, pp. 536–45. For local legislative trends, see "Spread of Accountancy Legislation," p. 64.

3. For the development of state laws, see Boyd, "CPA Legislation in the United States," pp. 62, 70, and Edwards, *History of Public Accounting*, pp. 71–72. For state professional organizations, see Webster, *American Association of Public Accountants*, p. 271. See also New Jersey Society of Certified Public Accountants, *Fifty Years of Service*; NYSSCPA, *Ten Year Book*; Reckitt, "Accountancy in the State of Illinois," pp. 376–80; Rand, "Growth of the Profession," pp. 412–19; and Wilkinson, "Organization of the Profession in Pennsylvania," pp. 161–69.

4. See Webster, *American Association of Public Accountants*, pp. 291–96 passim, for activities of the federation of state societies. See Stevens, *American Medicine and the Public Interest*, pp. 55–73, for development of new modes for unifying the medical profession nationally.

5. For the College of Accounts, see Webster, *American Association of Public Accountants*, chaps. 35–37 passim. In the same volume, see background information for Bagot (p. 330); Briggs (pp. 335–36); Hunt (pp. 175, 198); and Mirick (p. 366). For backgrounds of other founders, see above, chap. 2, nn. 14, 26, 31. See also, "College of Accountants," p. 520; Webster, "Accountancy Education," pp. 441–50; and Wildman, "Early Instruction in Accounting," pp. 105–7.

6. See Webster, *American Association of Public Accountants*, pp. 177, 182–85, for description of curriculum; see also pp. 196–99 for Stevens's concerns about not affiliating with an established college or university.

7. Ibid., pp. 173, 182–85.

8. *DAB*, s.v. "Dewey, Melvil"; and Dawe, *Melvil Dewey*, pp. 196–98, 206–11.

9. Dawe, *Melvil Dewey*, pp. 174–76. For Sprague's and Dewey's mutual interest in simplified spelling, see Box 87 in Dewey Papers, which includes: a simplified spelling board notice (January 30, 1907) listing Sprague both as treasurer and executive board member; a list of members of the Spelling Reform Association for 1884 in which Sprague is listed as treasurer; a letter from Sprague (July 11, 1894) in which the banker communicated his resignation as treasurer of the Spelling Reform Association. See also *DAB* and *NCAB*, s.v.v. "Dewey, Melvil," and "Sprague, Charles Ezra."

10. Dawe, *Melvil Dewey*, pp. 174–76, 196–98, 206–11; see also letter from S. S. Packard, May 21, 1896, in Box 75, Dewey Papers.

11. Haskins, *Business Education and Accountancy*, p. 21; Furer, "Career of William Henry Havemeyer."

12. See *DAB*, s.v.v. "Depew, Chauncey Mitchell," "Reid, Whitelaw," and

"Doane, William Croswell." See also SAR, *National Register of the Society*, s.v.v. "Haskins, Charles W.," "Depew, Chauncey M.," and "Doane William C." See *DAB*, s.v. "Dewey, Melvil," and also file entitled "Birth Control" in Box 10, Dewey Papers, for his involvement in the International Eugenic Committee of the USA and the National Conference of Race Betterment.

Haskins's optimism about the positive potentials of contemporary immigration was most probably conditioned by the hopeful example of his uncle Emerson. For Emerson's views of the salutory effects of immigration, see Curti, *Growth of American Thought*, p. 306, and Gabriel, *Course of American Democratic Thought*, p. 46.

13. See McCormick, *From Realignment to Reform*, pp. 42–50, for an analysis of the split within the Democratic party during this period.

14. For a discussion of anti-Semitism among nativist patricians, see Higham, *Send These to Me*, pp. 130–31.

15. Horner, *Andrew Sloan Draper*, pp. 78–83, provides a description of some of the conflicts separating the Republican-led Department of Public Instruction and the Democratic regime of Governor David B. Hill.

16. See Dawe, *Melvil Dewey*, pp. 206–12, on tensions dividing Hill and the board of regents.

17. AAPA, *Minutes*, Members' Meeting (November 4, 1892), pp. 117–21; Webster, *American Association of Public Accountants*, pp. 174–76.

18. Webster, *American Association of Public Accountants*, pp. 117–200 passim.

19. Letter from R. M. Chapman, February 26, 1895, in Box 75, Dewey Papers.

20. Hein, *British Companies Acts*, pp. 26–27; Jones, *Accounting and the British Economy*, p. 72; and Webster, *American Association of Public Accountants*, pp. 218–19, 220–23. See also AAPA, *Minutes*, Members' Meeting (February 12, 1895), pp. 124–26.

21. See Webster, *American Association of Public Accountants*, pp. 214–17, for early legislative activities of the NYIA, and p. 218 for the AAPA's activities.

22. Ibid., pp. 219, 223.

23. Ibid., pp. 220–25.

24. Ibid., pp. 224–25; see also letter from E. G. Whitaker, February 21, 1895, in Box 75, Dewey Papers.

25. McCormick, *From Realignment to Reform*, pp. 61–68.

26. Ibid., pp. 88–92.

27. *NCAB*, s.v. "Haskins, Charles W."; Jordan, *Charles Waldo Haskins*, pp. 52–57, 79; and McCormick, *From Realignment to Reform*, pp. 111–14.

28. See *DAB*, s.v. "Choate, Joseph Hodges," and Webster, *American Association of Public Accountants*, p. 361, for connection between Choate and accountant John R. Loomis.

29. *DAB*, s.v. "Choate, Joseph Hodges."

30. Dawe, *Melvil Dewey*, pp. 214–16; *NYT*, August 23, 1895, p. 3; *NYT*, October 17, 1895, p. 7.

31. Webster, *American Association of Public Accountants*, pp. 227–28.

32. McCormick, *From Realignment to Reform*, pp. 114–23 passim.

33. Dawe, *Melvil Dewey*, pp. 215–16; *NYT*, April 25, 1896, p. 2; and Webster, *American Association of Public Accountants*, pp. 229–32.

34. Letter to C. E. Sprague, August 10, 1895, in Box 91, Dewey Papers; Dawe, *Melvil Dewey*, pp. 230–50 passim.

35. See letter to C. E. Sprague, April 24, 1896, in Box 91, Dewey Papers.

36. Webster, *American Association of Public Accountants*, pp. 234–35.

37. See letter from S. S. Packard, May 21, 1896, in Box 75, Dewey Papers, and correspondence cited above, n. 35.

38. Webster, *American Association of Public Accountants*, pp. 241–46.

39. See AAPA, *Minutes*, Members' Meeting (November 10, 1892), pp. 115–20; (December 12, 1892), pp. 137–38; (September 23, 1897), pp. 231–33. For Thurber connection see above, chap. 2, n. 10.

40. Webster, *American Association of Public Accountants*, pp. 241–43.

41. Ibid., pp. 243–46.

42. Edwards, *History of Public Accounting*, p. 352, indicates that 181 of the first 260 practitioners licensed in New York through 1903 were licensed under waiver. See also University of the State of New York, *Minutes of the Board of Certified Public Accountant Examiners* (December 17 and 22, 1897), p. 42, and (September 13, 1898), p. 50, which indicates that Birdseye represented at least seven candidates' licensure under waiver. See also "Accountancy in New York State," pp. 983–84.

43. DeMond, *Price Waterhouse*, pp. 58–64; University of the State of New York, *Minutes of the Board of Certified Public Accountant Examiners* (July 21, 1902), p. 116.

44. See discussion of examination fairness by a banker, James G. Cannon, in AAPA, *Yearbook 1908*, pp. 120–24; See also Edwards, *History of Public Accounting*, pp. 33–34; Merino, "Professionalization of Public Accounting," pp. 185–87, 209, nn. 89–90; and E. F. Suffern, "Are CPA Examinations Always Fair?" pp. 384–89.

45. AAPA, *Minutes*, Board of Trustees (November 26, 1897), p. 256; (February 24, 1898), p. 283; and (March 24, 1898), p. 288.

46. AAPA, *Minutes*, Members' Meeting (January 10, 1899), pp. 35–36; NYSSCPA, *Minutes*, Members' Meeting (March 30, 1897), pp. 5–8. See Webster, *American Association of Public Accountants*, p. 350, for Gottesberger's background, and pp. 90–91, for membership fees.

47. AAPA, *Minutes*, Board of Trustees (September 23, 1897), pp. 227–31.

48. AAPA, *Minutes*, Members' Meeting (October 12, 1897), pp. 234–36; and Webster, *American Association of Public Accountants*, pp. 286–90.

49. See Webster, *American Association of Public Accountants*, p. 341, for a synopsis of Conant's career.

50. See ibid., p. 246, for examining board membership and tenure and pp. 247–48 for proposal to appoint one representative from each association.

51. See ibid., p. 352, for dates of Haskins's membership in the AAPA. See also Haskins and Sells, *Our First Seventy-five Years*, pp. 18–19, for early partners in that firm.

52. See AAPA, *Minutes*, Members' Meeting (January 10, 1899), pp. 35–36;

and (October 10, 1899), p. 63, for passage of resolutions to cooperate with the NYSSCPA. See AAPA, *Minutes*, Board of Trustees (September 8, 1901), pp. 159–60, and *Minutes*, Members' Meeting (October, 5, 1901), p. 174 for admission of Haskins and Sells personnel and the AAPA's recognition of and scholarship for the NYU School of Commerce, Accounts, and Finance. For Bennett bill, see AAPA, *Minutes*, Members' Meeting (January 24, 1901), p. 133, and Meeting, Board of Trustees (July 28, 1901), p. 158. For synopsis of Sells's career, see Webster, *American Association of Public Accountants*, p. 375; and *NCAB*, s.v. "Sells, Elijah W."

53. AAPA, *Minutes*, Board of Trustees (February 27, 1902), pp. 196–99.

54. AAPA, *Minutes*, Members' Meeting (January 16, 1900), p. 83.

55. For Dickinson background, see DeMond, *Price Waterhouse*, pp. 47–49, 50–51; and Webster, *American Association of Public Accountants*, pp. 344–45.

56. Previts and Merino, *Accounting in America*, pp. 139–42. See Reckitt, *Reminiscences of the Accounting Profession*, pp. 136–38, for Price Waterhouse membership in ISCPA; see Webster, *American Association of Public Accountants*, pp. 344–45, for Dickinson's affiliation with ISCPA.

57. Reckitt, *Reminiscences of the Accounting Profession*, pp. 77–78; Boyd, "CPA Legislation in the United States," pp. 59, 193.

58. Wilkinson, "Genesis of the CPA Movement," pp. 261–66, 297–300. See also, by the same author, "Accounting Profession in the United States," pp. 339–47.

59. Webster, *American Association of Public Accountants*, pp. 292–94.

60. Edwards, *History of Public Accounting*, pp. 77–78.

61. Federation of State Societies of Public Accountants in the United States of America, *Executive Board Minutes* (October 28, 1903), pp. 1–2.

62. Ibid. (February 5, 1903), unnumbered.

63. See AAPA, *Minutes*, Board of Trustees (October 2, 1902), pp. 228–30; Webster, *American Association of Public Accountants*, pp. 309–10.

64. AAPA, *Minutes*, Members' Meeting (October 14, 1902), pp. 236–43, and (December 17, 1902), pp. 264–65. See also AAPA, *Minutes*, Board of Trustees (October 2, 1902), pp. 228–30, and (November 12, 1902), pp. 252–55.

65. Jordan, *Charles Waldo Haskins*, p. 79; see also AAPA, *Minutes*, Board of Trustees (January 22, 1903), pp. 284–85, for induction of Dickinson as trustee.

66. Chase, "Notes on Historical Material Compiled by Harvey S. Chase," pp. 20–21, in Webster Papers.

67. NYSSCPA, *Minutes*, Members' Meeting (November 9, 1903), p. 58, and (November 27, 1903), pp. 77–79. See also Wise, *Peat, Marwick, Mitchell, and Company*, pp. 8–12, for early competition with Haskins and Sells.

68. NYSSCPA, *Minutes*, Members' Meeting (April 11, 1904), pp. 70–74. For description of the congress and the Louisiana Purchase exposition, see: Carey, *Rise of the Accounting Profession* 1:49–52; Coats, "American Scholarship Comes of Age," pp. 404–17; DeMond, *Price Waterhouse*, p. 53; Edwards, *History of Public Accounting*, pp. 86–87; Previts and Merino, *Accounting in America*, pp. 143–47; Webster, *American Association of Public Accountants*, pp. 297–99. See also a contemporary article, "Congress of Accountants at St. Louis," pp. 704–

6, 761–64. For a brief description of earlier plans of Haskins and Kittredge, see Webster, *American Association of Public Accountants*, pp. 300–301.

69. NYSSCPA, *Minutes*, Members' Meeting (June 13, 1904), pp. 85–89.

70. See *DAB* and *NCAB*, s.v. "Draper, Andrew Sloan." See also Horner, *Andrew Sloan Draper*, pp. 54, 58–66, and 176–84; McCormick, *From Realignment to Reform*, pp. 172–73; and Mowry, *Era of Theodore Roosevelt*, p. 175.

71. Dawe, *Melvil Dewey*, pp. 220–22; Horner, *Andrew Sloan Draper*, pp. 180–84.

72. University of the State of New York, *Minutes of the Board of Certified Public Accountant Examiners* (October 15, 1904), p. 147. See also Webster, *American Association of Public Accountants*, pp. 248–50.

73. NYSSCPA, *Minutes*, Members' Meeting (February 18, 1904), pp. 71–74.

74. Dawe, *Melvil Dewey*, pp. 224–29; Horner, *Andrew Sloan Draper*, p. 128; and *DAB*, s.v. "Dewey, Melvil." See also *NYT*, January 21, 1905, p. 5; *NYT*, January 24, 1905, p. 5; *NYT*, February 3, 1905, p. 3; *NYT*, February 16, 1905, p. 1.

75. NYSSCPA, *Minutes*, Members' Meeting (February 20, 1905), pp. 256–57. See also Buley, *Equitable Life Assurance Society* 1:539–696 passim; and Keller, *Life Insurance Enterprise*, pp. 245–64 passim.

76. Haskins and Sells, *Our First Seventy-five Years*, p. 31.

77. See Webster, *American Association of Public Accountants*, pp. 308–17.

Chapter 4

1. For synopses of the lives of Dickinson and Sterrett, see Burns and Coffman, *Accounting Hall of Fame*, pp. 18–19, 76–77, respectively. For the views of these leaders on accounting professionalism, see Dickinson, "Profession of the Public Accountant," pp. 650–58; Sterrett, "Professional Ethics," pp. 407–23; Sterrett, "Progress in the Accounting Profession," pp. 11–16, and Sterrett, "Development of Accountancy as a Profession," pp. 265–73.

2. See *DNB*, s.v. "Dickinson, Lowes"; DeMond, *Price Waterhouse*, pp. 46–48; and Webster, *American Association of Public Accountants*, pp. 344–45.

3. DeMond, *Price Waterhouse*, pp. 10, 58–62.

4. See ibid., after p. 62, for photograph. See also Carey, *Rise of the Accounting Profession* 1:207, for another.

5. *DNB*, s.v. "Dickinson, Goldsworthy Lowes." See also Forster, *Goldsworthy Lowes Dickinson*, and above, n. 2, for family background.

6. Carey, *Rise of the Accounting Profession* 1:97, 100–101; Webster, *American Association of Public Accountants*, pp. 109, 161–62.

7. Carey, *Rise of the Accounting Profession* 1:97, 100–101; see Merino, "Professionalization of Public Accounting," pp. 115, 379–80, 140 nn. 180–82, for Sterrett's involvement with the *Journal of Accountancy*.

8. AAPA, *Yearbook 1908*, pp. 84–85.

9. See, for example, the following articles in the *Journal of Accountancy*: Belser, "Cost Accounting for Fertilizer Manufacturers," p. 165; Castenholz, "Ac-

counting Procedures for State Universities," pp. 81–92, 167–75; H. S. Chase, "Municipal Industries and Public Service Corporations," pp. 647–54; Grundman, "Brewery Accounting," pp. 285–93; Hardt, "Railway Maintenance of Way," pp. 438–48; Hunter, "Accounting Systems for Retail Merchants," pp. 100–104; Joplin, "Interest Does Not Enter the Cost of Production," pp. 334–35; May, "Proper Treatment of Premiums and Discounts on Bonds," pp. 32–37; and Walton, "Inventories," pp. 338–39.

10. Niven, "Income Tax Department," pp. 384–407; "New Department," pp. 373–74.

11. See, for example, the following articles in the *Journal of Accountancy*: Brandeis, "New Conception of Industrial Efficiency," pp. 35–43; Bryan, "Government Should Issue Notes and Guarantee Bank Deposits," pp. 366–79; Carnegie, "Worst Banking System in the World," pp. 357–61; Gage, "Difficulties Lie in the Reformer's Path," pp. 361–65; Mixter, "Measures of Banking Reform," pp. 463–76, 123–32, 194–203; Seligman, "Underwriting the Sale of Corporate Securities," pp. 321–30; and Taylor, "Principles of Scientific Management," pp. 117–24, 181–84.

12. Jones, *Accounting and the British Economy*, pp. 50–54, 70–71. May contributed twenty-one articles to the journal during the period 1906–40 (Grady, *Memoirs of George O. May*, pp. 299–300).

13. See the following articles in the *Journal of Accountancy*: Cooper, "Professional Ethics," pp. 81–94; Forbes, "Some Phases of Professional Ethics," pp. 271–75; Joplin, "Ethics of Accountancy," pp. 187–96; Montgomery, "Professional Ethics," pp. 94–96; Sterrett, "Professional Ethics," pp. 407–31; and E. L. Suffern, "Responsibility of the Accountant," pp. 197–202. See also Abbott, "Professional Ethics," pp. 855–85, for a contemporary sociological view.

14. See Sterrett's comments on touting in AAPA, *Yearbook 1907*, pp. 122–29.

15. On unethical fee arrangements, see ibid., pp. 119–24.

16. See ibid., pp. 130–33, for comments on audit companies. See also Haskins and Sells, *Our First Seventy-five Years*, pp. 28–30.

17. AAPA, *Yearbook 1915*, pp. 81–85.

18. An exception to the pattern prevalent in England was found in Scotland, where candidates were required to pass university courses in commercial law. See Jones, *Accounting and the British Economy*, p. 84, and, for English training, pp. 118–19. See also Walker, *Society of Accountants in Edinburgh*, chaps. 4–5 passim; "Education of English and American Accountants," pp. 764–65.

19. AAPA, *Yearbook 1910*, pp. 132–34. But concerns about the status of accounting education within academia would continue. In 1923, Henry Rand Hatfield addressed this in his speech entitled "An Historical Defense of Bookkeeping," pp. 3–13.

20. AAPA, *Yearbook 1911*, pp. 108–14.

21. AAPA, *Yearbook 1907*, pp. 36–40; AAPA, *Yearbook 1908*, pp. 96–98; AAPA, *Yearbook 1911*, pp. 108–14; and AAPA, *Yearbook 1916*, pp. 74–94 passim. See also Carey, *Rise of the Accounting Profession* 1:96–100; Sass, *Pragmatic Imagination*, pp. 79–85, 133n., 141–42, 157–58, 182.

22. Grady, *Memoirs of George O. May*, p. 32.

23. AAPA, *Yearbook 1911*, pp. 108–14.

24. "Student's Department," pp. 70–79.

25. AAPA, *Yearbook 1913*, pp. 77–78, 81–101. See also Montgomery, "Accountancy Laboratory," pp. 405–11.

26. Carey, *Rise of the Accounting Profession* 1:49–52; Webster, *American Association of Public Accountants*, pp. 297–307. See also the following AAPA yearbooks for business and government leaders who participated in annual meetings: H. C. Adams, in *Yearbook 1908*, pp. 146–58; J. G. Cannon, in *Yearbook 1908*, pp. 120–24; J. F. Fitzgerald, in *Yearbook 1913*, pp. 47–51; D. R. Forgam, in *Yearbook 1912*, pp. 215–17; E. F. Gay, in *Yearbook 1913*, pp. 81–101; E. J. James, in *Yearbook 1912*, pp. 100–102; J. P. Mitchell, in *Yearbook 1910*, p. 41; P. Morton, in *Yearbook 1905*, pp. 47–52; W. C. Redfield, in *Yearbook 1914*, pp. 67–76; J. H. Schiff, in *Yearbook 1905*, p. 45; and A. Smith, in *Yearbook 1912*, pp. 169–79. For participation of foreign professional associations, see, for example, AAPA, *Yearbook 1908*: J. B. Bell of Institute of Chartered Accountants (pp. 124–25); H. L. Price of the Society of Incorporated Accountants and Auditors (pp. 125–28); R. Brown of the Society of Accountants in Edinburgh (pp. 129–30); and A. F. C. Ross of the Dominion Association of Chartered Accountants (pp. 130–32). See also various communiqués listed from other associations in the same number at pp. 61–81.

27. E. W. Sells to Leon O. Fisher, September 30, 1904, in Haskins and Sells Library.

28. Miranti, "Professionalism and Nativism," pp. 374–77.

Chapter 5

1. Buley, *Equitable Life Assurance Society*, pp. 609–95 passim; Carosso, *Investment Banking*, pp. 117–19, 125–27, Carosso, *The Morgans*, pp. 530–34; Garraty, *Right Hand Man*, pp. 163–86; and Keller, *Life Insurance Enterprise*, pp. 675–705 passim.

2. Buley, *Equitable Life Assurance Society*, pp. 691–95; Keller, *Life Insurance Enterprise*, pp. 200–215 passim.

3. Buley, *Equitable Life Assurance Society*, pp. 667, 669, 708–9; DeMond, *Price Waterhouse*, pp. 77–80; Haskins and Sells, *Our First Seventy-five Years*, p. 31; and Swaine, *Cravath Firm and Its Predecessors* 1:750–66.

4. Carey, *Rise of the Accounting Profession* 1:29–30, 57–58.

5. Buley, *Equitable Life Assurance Society*, pp. 705–13; Keller, *Life Insurance Enterprise*, pp. 254–59.

6. See Churchman, "Federal Regulation of Railroad Rates," chap. 5 passim; Hoogenboom and Hoogenboom, *History of the ICC*, pp. 25–31; McFarland, *Judicial Control*, pp. 100–113 passim; Sharfman, *Interstate Commerce Commission* 1:19–34, 71–103 passim; and Skowronek, *Building a New American State*, pp. 150–60.

7. For an overview of the basic objectives of railway accounting, see Adams, *American Railway Accounting*, chap. 1. For a general discussion of the inadequacies of capital cost accounting among nineteenth-century railroads, see Brief, "Nineteenth-Century Accounting Error," p. 21, Brief, "Evolution of

Asset Accounting," pp. 1–23. See Dusenbury, "Effect of ICC Regulation on Accounting Practices," for a criticism of this accounting model for managerial purposes. The extensive deficiencies of railroad accounting from the perspective of contemporary regulators are outlined in the following sections of the ICC's *Annual Reports:* 1888, pp. 58–68; 1890, p. 68; 1891, p. 68; 1893, pp. 71–77; 1894, pp. 63–64; 1895, pp. 60–64; 1896, p. 116; 1897, pp. 80–83, and pp. 146–47; 1898, 78–79; 1899, pp. 63–64; and 1903, pp. 17–22. See also Smykay, "National Association of Railroad and Utility Commissioners," chaps. 3–4, for the role of the state regulatory agencies in advancing railroad accounting.

8. For Adams's ideas about accounting and regulation, see his "Bureau of Railway Statistics and Accounts," pp. 1384–85, and his "Decade of Federal Railway Regulation," pp. 437–38. For insight into the chief statistician's character and beliefs about the connections among economics, religion, and ethics, see Furner, *Advocacy and Objectivity*, pp. 49–53, 127–28, 130–32, 146.

9. Letter to W. G. Veazey, March 23, 1893, in *ICC Letterbook, 1891–1893*, p. 403, in Adams Papers.

10. Ibid., pp. 404–5. On the problem of joint costing, see ICC, *Statistics of Railways, 1893*, p. 83; and Ripley, *Railroads: Rates and Regulation*, pp. 67–70. For discussion of cost-of-service versus value-of-service pricing, see Dusenbury, "Effect of ICC Regulation on Accounting Practices"; Sharfman, *Interstate Commerce Commission* 3:425–63; and Smykay, "National Association of Railroad and Utility Commissioners," pp. 85–88.

11. U.S. Congress, Senate, *Regulation of Railway Rates.*

12. AAPA, *Minutes*, Members' Meeting (October 16, 1906), pp. 110–11; AAPA, *Yearbook 1907*, p. 12. See also Adams's expectations after the Hepburn Act was passed in Adams, "Administrative Supervision of Railways," pp. 375–76.

13. DeMond, *Price Waterhouse*, pp. 83–84; see letter to Mary E. Murphy from Herbert M. Temple, April 4, 1941, both in May Papers.

14. AAPA, *Yearbook 1908*, pp. 146–58. See also Brief, "Nineteenth-Century Accounting Error," p. 23, for a discussion of the problem of railroad capital asset accounting, and Dickinson, "Maintenance and Depreciation Accounts." For some of the connections of some leading firms to the railroad industry, see DeMond, *Price Waterhouse*, pp. 29, 32–33; and Haskins and Sells, *Our First Seventy-five Years*, p. 19.

15. See AAPA, *Yearbook 1908*, pp. 166–67 for the comments of H. A. Dunn, a partner in Haskins and Sells, about status concerns, and pp. 147–52, 156–57, for Adams's perspective on the new law.

16. Undated newspaper clipping entitled "Federal Auditors Scorned," attached to a letter from Lupkin, October 19, 1908, in Box 9, Adams Papers.

17. Undated poem attached to news clipping noted above, n. 16.

18. See Martin, *Enterprise Denied*, chap. 12 passim; Neal, "Investment Behaviour of American Railroads," pp. 126–35.

19. Mowry, *Era of Theodore Roosevelt*, pp. 171–72.

20. Memorandum by N. E. Webster, "AAPA Committee on Department Methods of Government (Keep Commission)," n.d., Webster Papers.

21. Ibid., pp. 3–4; Carey, *Rise of the Accounting Profession* 1:58–59. For a more

general evaluation of the activities of the Keep Commission, see Skowronek, *Building a New American State*, pp. 177, 182–85, 203.

22. AAPA, *Yearbook 1907*, pp. 29–31; AAPA, *Yearbook 1908*, pp. 90–91.

23. DeMond, *Price Waterhouse*, pp. 80–82; Wise, *Peat, Marwick, Mitchell, and Company*, p. 70.

24. AAPA, *Yearbook 1907*, p. 31.

25. Carey, *Rise of the Accounting Profession* 1:64–71; Pringle, *Life and Times of William Howard Taft* 2:444–57; and Ratner, *Taxation and Democracy in America*, chaps. 14–15.

26. AAPA, *Yearbook 1909*, pp. 44–48; AAPA, *Yearbook 1910*, p. 83.

27. AAPA, *Yearbook 1909*, p. 14; AAPA, *Yearbook 1910*, p. 14. See Merino, "Professionalization of Public Accounting," pp. 383–84.

28. DeMond, *Price Waterhouse*, pp. 85–86; "Accounting Errors in Corporation Tax Bill," pp. 212–13. See also facsimile letters of accountants' committee to Attorney General Wickersham (July 8 and 21, 1909), a facsimile copy of a letter from Wickersham to Deloitte, Plender, Griffiths and Company (July 12, 1909), and a facsimile letter from the AAPA, Committee on Federal Legislation, to the membership and facsimile copy of attached form letter (August 24, 1911), all in Webster Papers.

29. Carey, *Rise of the Accounting Profession* 1:63–66. Efforts were also made to introduce uniform accounting for municipalities, see H. S. Chase, "Movement toward Uniform Municipal Reports and Accounts," p. 375; H. S. Chase, "Municipal Industries and Public Service Corporations," pp. 647–54; and Hartwell, "Financial Reports of Municipalities," pp. 124–25.

30. Carey, *Rise of the Accounting Profession* 1:63–66, 222–27; Edwards, *History of Public Accounting*, pp. 93–97, 101–4.

Chapter 6

1. See Link, *Wilson: The Road to the White House*, pp. 479–85; see Kolko, *Railroads and Regulation*, pp. 160–61, for Lodge's belief about the impetus for Brandeis's work; see also Roosevelt's reply to Lodge, May 28, 1908, in *Letters of Theodore Roosevelt* 6:1040; and see letter of Frank A. Vanderlip to James Stillman, December 29, 1911, concerning sponsorship of "money trust" investigation in Series 1, Box B–1–4, Vanderlip Papers. See also Brandeis, *Other People's Money and How the Bankers Use It*; and *DAB*, s.v.v. "Brandeis, Louis Dembitz" and "Untermyer, Samuel."

For a full discussion of the emergence of banking regulation, see the recent studies by Livingston, *Origins of the Federal Reserve System*, and White, *Regulation and Reform of the American Banking System*.

2. See McCraw, *Prophets of Regulation*, pp. 109–22, for an analysis of original intentions and options available to the FTC's founders. See also chap. 13 passim in Link, *Wilson: The New Freedom*.

3. See McCraw, *Prophets of Regulation*, pp. 122–35, for later modification of the FTC's role, and pp. 135–42 for sensitivity of Brandeis to small business concerns in giving shape to this agency's objectives.

4. Miranti, "From Conflict to Consensus," pp. 165–67.

5. See Carosso, *Investment Banking*, p. 150, for J. P. Morgan's feelings about the importance of "character" in lending; see Bledstein, *Culture of Professionalism*, chap. 4 passim, for a more general discussion of the importance of this quality in America's changing social setting.

6. See the following contemporary articles published in the *Journal of Accountancy* and relating to the FRB's proposals: "Certificates of Borrower Statements," pp. 128–29; "Borrowers Certified Statements," pp. 418–26; Hamlin, "Federal Reserve Act," pp. 329–37; Peple, "Statements of Borrowers," pp. 410–23, Peple, "Registration of Accountants," pp. 185–89. See Willis, *Federal Reserve System*, pp. 905–11, 936–37, for background and objectives of "Circular Thirteen" and the abandonment of the "zone expert" plan. See also *NCAB*, s.v.v. "Davies, Joseph E." and "Hurley, Edwin N."

7. Link, *Wilson: The New Freedom*, pp. 202, 209; and McCraw, *Prophets of Regulation*, pp. 112–18.

8. AAPA, *Minutes*, Board of Trustees (September 18, 1916), pp. 108–30.

9. U.S. FTC, *Annual Report 1916*, pp. 14–18; and Willis, *Federal Reserve System*, pp. 909–19.

10. Link, *Wilson: The New Freedom*, chaps. 13–14 passim.

11. McCraw, *Prophets of Regulation*, pp. 118–35.

12. AAPA, *Yearbook 1916*, pp. 107–8; G. C. Davis, "Federal Trade Commission," chaps. 6–8 passim; FTC, *Annual Report 1916*, pp. 14–18; FTC, *Annual Report 1917*, pp. 21–23; Grady, *Memoirs of George O. May*, pp. 36–37; and Hurley, *Awakening of American Business*, especially pt. 2, chaps. 3–4 passim. For other activities of Davies and Hurley in promoting American foreign trade, see Becker, *Dynamics of Business Government Relations*, pp. 149–52.

13. See Carey, *Rise of the Accounting Profession* 1:141, and Cuff, *War Industries Board*, chaps. 1–3 passim, for associational involvement in mobilization.

14. For credit men see AAPA, *Yearbook 1914*, pp. 234–35; AAPA, *Yearbook 1915*, pp. 211–12; AAPA, *Yearbook 1916*, pp. 107–8. See also Carey, *Rise of the Accounting Profession* 1:135–36; Grady, *Memoirs of George O. May*, p. 36; and Previts and Merino, *Accounting in America*, pp. 187–90.

15. AAPA, *Yearbook 1915*, pp. 147–50; AAPA, *Yearbook 1916*, pp. 41–43, 108–16; and Carey, *Rise of the Accounting Profession* 1:122–26.

16. See AAPA, *Yearbook 1908*, pp. 353–55 for example of model laws. See also Boyd, "CPA Legislation in the United States," pp. 77–80, 192–200; *Minutes*, Board of Trustees (April 10, 1916), pp. 1–63 passim; and AAPA, *Yearbook 1916*, pp. 110–11.

17. AAPA, *Minutes*, Executive Committee (October 23, and November 9, 1911) pp. 62–63; AAPA, *Yearbook 1911*, pp. 102–3, 106–7; Carey, *Rise of the Accounting Profession* 1:100, 110–11; DeMond, *Price Waterhouse*, pp. 97, 99–104; and Merino, "Professionalization of Public Accounting," pp. 107–16.

18. AAPA, *Yearbook 1911*, pp. 65–68; AAPA, *Yearbook 1915*, p. 65. See also Carey, *Rise of the Accounting Profession* 1:113–14. For names of new entrants to the profession in New York, see Merritt, *Accountants' Directory and Who's Who*, pp. 765–70 passim.

19. AAPA, *Minutes* Board of Trustees (April 10, 1916), pp. 1–13; AAPA,

Yearbook 1916, pp. 108–16. See also Previts and Merino, *Accounting in America*, pp. 205–7.

20. DeMond, *Price Waterhouse*, pp. 135–42, 224–32; Previts and Merino, *Accounting in America*, pp. 177, 305–10; and Arthur Young and Company, *Arthur Young and the Company He Founded*, pp. 31–34. See also Forbes, *Stettinius, Sr.*, pp. 43–64 passim, Forbes, *J. P. Morgan, Jr.*, pp. 87–103 passim; Carosso, *Investment Banking*, pp. 211–13; and Jones, *Accounting and the British Economy*, pp. 122–26, 136–37. For May's brother's war injuries, see Grady, *Memoirs of George O. May*, p. 6. See Swaine, *Cravath Firm and Its Predecessors* 2:247, 643 (for connections to AIA), 1:488, 642, 705, 736, 2:247, 631–32 (for connections with Price Waterhouse), and 1:14, 17, 21, 43, 149, 245, 274–81, 367, 2:440 (for connections to Bank of England).

21. Carey, *Rise of the Accounting Profession* 1:139–41.

22. See Lamont, *Across World Frontiers*, pp. 56–57, for apathy in the Middle West. See also war discussion in Luebke, *Bonds of Loyalty*, and Peterson and Fite, *Opponents of War*. For connection to Schiff, see Link, *Wilson: The Road to the White House*, pp. 338, 435, 479. For von Papen's activities, see Landau, *Enemy Within*, pp. 77–85. For the attack on Morgan, see Forbes, *J. P. Morgan, Jr.*, pp. 93–94.

23. For role of Gilbert Parker, see H. C. Peterson, *Propaganda for War*, chaps. 1–2 passim.

24. See Sells, "Plan for International Peace," pp. 85–96, and an editorial in the same issue, "Practical Plan for Peace," p. 139.

25. Ernst and Ernst, *History of the Firm*, pp. 25–28, 47. See Carey, *Rise of the Accounting Profession* 1:330–32 for Springer background.

26. AAPA, *Yearbook 1915*, pp. 15, 147–50.

27. AAPA, *Minutes*, Board of Trustees (April 10, 1916), pp. 1–66, and (September 18, 1916), pp. 7–139 passim; and AAPA, *Yearbook 1916*, pp. 41–43, 108–16.

28. For Niven's comments, see AAPA, *Minutes*, Board of Trustees (April 10, 1916), pp. 40–41; and, for the position of Niven and Forbes, see AAPA, *Minutes*, Board of Trustees (September 19, 1916), pp. 117–20.

29. AIA, *Yearbook 1917*, p. 28. See also the following articles appearing in the *Accountant*: "American Institute of Accountants," pp. 419, 454–56; and "Institute of Accountants in the United States," pp. 438–42, 444–45.

30. AIA, *Yearbook 1917*, pp. 76, 231; AIA, *Yearbook 1918*, pp. 82–83, 92–93, 112–13; and AIA, *Yearbook 1919*, pp. 115–17. See also Carey, *Rise of the Accounting Profession* 1:139–44; and Grady, *Memoirs of George O. May*, pp. 36–37. The earliest contact with the preparedness movement involved the agreement of the AAPA's Executive Committee to support Howard E. Coffin's Industrial Preparedness Committee (AAPA, *Minutes*, Executive Committee [August 8, 1916]), p. 141. For Coffin's prewar organizing activities, see Cuff, *War Industries Board*, chaps. 1–3 passim.

31. Bledstein, "Professions, Professionals, Professionalism," pp. 1–4; Hughes, *Men and Their Work*, pp. 133–37; and Wilensky, "Professionalization of Everyone?" pp. 137–40.

32. See Abbott, "Professional Ethics," pp. 855–79; and Carey, *Rise of the*

Accounting Profession 1:230–34, 325–27. For concerns about ethical practice building see "Branch Office Ethics," pp. 212–16.

33. AIA, *Yearbook 1918*, pp. 100–101; AIA, *Yearbook 1919*, pp. 75, 102; and Merino, "Professionalization of Public Accounting," pp. 71–77.

34. See Merritt, *Accountants' Directory and Who's Who*, p. 567, for Nau's background.

35. Edwards, *History of Public Accounting*, pp. 138, 197; and Ernst and Ernst, *History of the Firm*, pp. 3–6, 13–17, 20–23, 36–40, 57–58, 82.

36. AIA, *Yearbook 1920*, p. 127; *DAB*, s.v.v. "Gilbert, Seymour Parker," and "Adams, Thomas Sewall"; "Income Tax Experts," pp. 134–36; and "Preparation of Tax Returns," pp. 447–51. See letter to S. G. Parker, May 15, 1923, in file, "Taxation, 1923," in May Papers.

37. AIA, *Yearbook 1921*, pp. 70–71.

38. AIA, *Minutes*, Members' Meeting (September 20, 1921), pp. 35–85.

39. Ibid., p. 49.

40. AIA, *Yearbook 1921*, pp. 75–77.

41. AIA, *Yearbook 1923*, pp. 92–93; Carey, *Rise of the Accounting Profession* 1:230–34; and Ernst and Ernst, *History of the Firm*, p. 138.

42. Carey, *Rise of the Accounting Profession* 1:330–32; Edwards, *History of Public Accounting*, pp. 127–30; and Previts and Merino, *Accounting in America*, pp. 205–12.

43. Carey, *Rise of the Accounting Profession* 1:370. See also "American Society and the American Institute," pp. 242–47; "Constitution and By-Laws," pp. 213–15; and Miller, "American Society and American Institute," pp. 157–62

44. AIA, *Yearbook 1924*, pp. 96–97, and 189–95; AIA, *Yearbook 1925*, pp. 140–45, 182.

45. Carey, *Rise of the Accounting Profession* 1:297–301.

46. AIA, *Yearbook 1917*, pp. 151–56. See also Boyd, "CPA Legislation in the United States," pp. 110–11; "American Institute of Accountants Board of Examiners," pp. 1–20; and "Institute Examinations," pp. 132–33.

47. Boyd, "CPA Legislation in the United States," pp. 110–11.

48. AIA, *Yearbook 1917*, pp. 111–17.

49. AIA, *Yearbook 1921*, p. 81; AIA, *Yearbook 1922*, pp. 162–63. See also Edwards, *History of Public Accounting*, pp. 120–23.

50. AIA, *Yearbook 1922*, pp. 102, 135. See also Carey, *Rise of the Accounting Profession* 1:281–82; Edwards, *History of Public Accounting*, pp. 118–20; and Previts and Merino, *Accounting in America*, pp. 205–6. See also *Certified Public Accountant*, February 1922, p. 10; and March 1922, p. 16.

51. AIA, *Yearbook 1922*, p. 128; AIA, *Yearbook 1923*, pp. 97, 133, 165. AIA, *Minutes*, Council (September 18, 1921); *NCAB*, s.v. "Covington, J. Harry"; *DAB*, s.v. "Rublee, George," See also "Injunction against National Association of Certified Public Accountants," pp. 30–31.

52. AIA, *Yearbook 1922*, pp. 105, 135; and AIA, *Yearbook 1923*, pp. 119, 162–63. AIA, *Minutes*, Council (September 19, 1921), pp. 15–37, and *Minutes*, Council (April 10, 1922), p. 11, for ultimate abandonment of incorporation plan. See also Carey, *Rise of the Accounting Profession* 1:328–29; "Federal In-

corporation of the Institute," pp. 286–88; and "For Federal Incorporation," pp. 37–39.

53. AIA, *Yearbook 1917*, pp. 151–52; AIA, *Yearbook 1922*, pp. 98–99, 103–4; AIA, *Yearbook 1923*, p. 110. See also Carey, *Rise of the Accounting Profession* 1:318–21.

54. This analysis of members not certified is based on information provided in AIA, *Yearbook 1926*, pp. 12–92 passim. See also Carey, *Rise of the Accounting Profession* 1:324.

55. Carey, *Rise of the Accounting Profession* 1:336–37; Grady, *Memoirs of George O. May*, pp. 35, 48–49.

56. See names of new members accepted into the ASCPA in *Certified Public Accountant*: July 1922, pp. 71–72; March, September, November 1923, pp. 96, 224, 228; January 1925, pp. 47–48. See also p. 5 of January 1925 issue for list of top recruiters.

57. Carey, *Rise of the Accounting Profession* 1:263–71; and Previts and Merino, *Accounting in America*, pp. 213–16. On establishment of accounting educators' association, see Zeff, *American Accounting Association*; and an editorial entitled "American Association of University Instructors in Accounting," pp. 155–56.

58. Carey, *Rise of the Accounting Profession* 1:263–68. For contemporary developments in accounting education and their relationship to practice, see Allen, "Growth of Accounting Instruction," pp. 150–66; W. A. Chase, "University Education of Accounting Students," pp. 179–80; and McCrea and Kester, "A School of Professional Accountancy," pp. 106–17.

59. AIA, *Yearbook 1929*, pp. 115, 129. See also Merritt, *Accountants' Directory and Who's Who*, p. 628, for Quigley's background.

60. Carey, *Rise of the Accounting Profession* 1:301–2.

61. Ibid., 2:212–14.

62. AIA, *Yearbook 1926*, pp. 184–87. See letter to F. R. Fairchild, May 28, 1937, in file "Accountants, Education, and Training, 1937 (1)," in May Papers. See also Carey, *Rise of the Accounting Profession* 1:348; Higgins, *Thomas G. Higgins, CPA*, pp. 164–65, 185–86; and Roberts, "Robert H. Montgomery," p. 64.

63. AIA, *Yearbook 1927*, p. 174.

64. Ibid., pp. 172–74; and AIA, *Yearbook 1930*, pp. 176–77. See also Fitzgerald, *Last Tycoon*.

Chapter 7

1. AIA, *Yearbook 1920*, p. 75. See also Carey, *Rise of the Accounting Profession* 1:206.

2. See *DAB*, s.v.v. "Adams, Thomas Sewall," "Leffingwell, Russell Cornell," and "Parker, Seymour Gilbert." See also Carey, *Rise of the Accounting Profession* 1:70; DeMond, *Price Waterhouse*, pp. 133–34; and Grady, *Memoirs of George O. May*, pp. 36–44 passim, 47.

3. AIA, *Yearbook 1919*, p. 109; AIA, *Yearbook 1924*, pp. 184–85.

4. AIA, *Yearbook 1920*, pp. 125–27; and AIA, *Yearbook 1924*, pp. 90–91. See

also Carey, *Rise of the Accounting Profession* 1:221–24; and the editorial "Board of Tax Appeals," p. 205.

5. AIA, *Yearbook 1919*, p. 82.

6. AIA, *Yearbook 1928*, pp. 179–81. See also Ripley, *Main Street and Wall Street*, pp. 174–75.

7. See Ripley, *Main Street and Wall Street*, pp. 194–207, for problems of surplus accounting during this period.

8. AIA, *Yearbook 1921*, pp. 137–38; AIA, *Yearbook 1922*, pp. 164–67.

9. AIA, *Yearbook 1927*, pp. 169–71. See also Carey, *Rise of the Accounting Profession* 1:158–59; DeMond, *Price Waterhouse*, pp. 94–95; and Edwards, *History of Public Accounting*, p. 138.

10. Carey, *Rise of the Accounting Profession* 1:162–63; DeMond, *Price Waterhouse*, p. 183.

11. Zeff, *American Accounting Association*, pp. 4–7; Carey, *Rise of the Accounting Profession* 1:311–13.

12. Zeff, *American Accounting Association*, pp. 14–19, 24–29. Concerns about the lack of standardization are reflected, for example, in contemporary articles by leading educators: see Canning, "Some Divergences of Accounting Theory from Economic Theory," pp. 84–94, and Paton, "Postulates of Accounting," pp. 64–83. For a general overview of the contributions of educators during this period, see Previts and Merino, *Accounting in America*, pp. 220–31.

13. See above, Chap. 2, n. 26, for reference to May's thinking about the nature of accounting knowledge.

14. Mautz and Previts, "Eric Kohler," pp. 20–25; Wagner, *Eric Louis Kohler*, pp. 24–33 passim.

15. Zeff, *American Accounting Association*, pp. 30–35; Wagner, *Eric Louis Kohler*, chaps. 4, 5, and 7 passim.

16. E. L. Kohler, "Nervous Profession," p. 4.

17. *DAB*, s.v. "Ripley, William Zebina."

18. Ibid.; Higham, *Strangers in the Land*, pp. 154–56.

19. See also Ripley, *Main Street and Wall Street*, and *Railway Problems*.

20. Ripley, *Main Street and Wall Street*, pp. 222–28, 229–55 passim. More recent studies of the accounting problems of the 1920s include Dillon, *Role of Accounting in the Stock Market Crash of 1929*, and Previts and Merino, *Accounting in America*, pp. 231–37.

21. May, *Twenty-five Years of Accounting Responsibility* 1:49–52, 53–59.

22. AIA, *Yearbook 1917*, pp. 68, 132, 147; AIA, *Yearbook 1920*, pp. 67–69, 112; and AIA, *Yearbook 1926*, pp. 129, 156, 159, 187. See also Carey, *Rise of the Accounting Profession* 1:298–301.

23. AIA, *Yearbook 1923*, pp. 167–70. See also Carey, *Rise of the Accounting Profession* 1:237–39. Rose, "Responsibility of Auditors," p. 335; and "Significance of an Accountant's Certificate," pp. 33–34.

24. Carey, *Rise of the Accounting Profession* 1:291–96.

25. AIA, *Yearbook 1923*, pp. 167–70. See also Carey, *Rise of the Accounting Profession* 1:265–66, 291–96; and DeMond, *Price Waterhouse*, pp. 131–32, 171, 183, 185–88.

26. DeMond, *Price Waterhouse*, pp. 180–81.

27. Edwards, *History of Public Accounting*, p. 146; Previts and Merino, *Accounting in America*, p. 204.

28. Carey, *Rise of the Accounting Profession* 1:254–58; Edwards, *History of Public Accounting*, pp. 141–45; and Previts and Merino, *Accounting in America*, p. 204. See also "Liability in Question," pp. 81–85.

29. Grady, *Memoirs of George O. May*, pp. 47–50, 54–74 passim.

30. Ibid.

31. *DAB*, s.v. "Gay, Edmund F."; and Heaton, *Scholar in Action*.

32. Berle and Jacobs, *Navigating the Rapids*, pp. 20–21.

33. Schlesinger, *Age of Roosevelt* 1:190–93.

34. *NCAB*, s.v. "Sharfman, Isaiah L." Sharfman worked for H. C. Adams after he left the ICC to organize the Chinese railroads. See also *Who's Who in America*, s.v. "Bonbright, James C." Vol. 21. Bonbright was a protégé of Felix Frankfurter and was appointed a member of the Power Authority of New York in 1931 by Franklin Roosevelt: see Freidel, *Franklin D. Roosevelt*, pp. 102–17.

35. *Who's Who in America*, s.v.v. "Catchings, Waddill," Vol. 15; "Dalton, Henry G.," Vol. 18; and "Kelley, Nicholas," Vol. 24. See also Grady, *Memoirs of George O. May*, pp. 37–38, 44 for Kelley.

36. Berle and Means, *Modern Corporation and Private Property*, pp. 264–68.

37. Ibid., pp. 271–77. On the limitations of blue-sky laws, see Parrish, *Securities Regulation and the New Deal*, pp. 5–36 passim; and Seligman, *Transformation of Wall Street*, pp. 39–48.

38. Carey, *Rise of the Accounting Profession* 1:163–66; Previts and Merino, *Accounting in America*, p. 238; and Seligman, *Transformation of Wall Street*, pp. 35–41.

39. Carey, *Rise of the Accounting Profession* 1:171–80; Edwards, *History of Public Accounting*, pp. 148–53; and Seligman, *Transformation of Wall Street*, pp. 48–49. See also: "Accountants and the New York Stock Exchange," pp. 241–42; "Chicago Stock Exchange Requires Certified Statements," pp. 321–22; and "Stock Exchange Demands Audits of Listed Companies," pp. 81–82.

Chapter 8

1. Carey, *Rise of the Accounting Profession* 1:182.

2. U.S. Congress, Senate, Committee on Banking and Currency, *Hearings on Stock Exchange Practices*, pts. 1–3 (April–June, 1932), pts. 4–6 (January–May, 1933). For May testimony see pt. 4, pp. 1259–74.

3. See ibid., pp. 875–92, pt. 3, for Ripley testimony. See also Flesher and Flesher, "Ivar Krueger's Contribution," pp. 421–34; and Seligman, *Transformation of Wall Street*, p. 47.

4. Parrish, *Securities Regulation and the New Deal*, pp. 44, 48–51; Seligman, *Transformation of Wall Street*, pp. 51–57.

5. Parrish, *Securities Regulation and the New Deal*, pp. 48–51; and Seligman, *Transformation of Wall Street*, pp. 53–57.

6. Parrish, *Securities Regulation and the New Deal*, pp. 48–51.

7. Carey, *Rise of the Accounting Profession* 1:183–84; and *NCAB*, s.v. "Covington, J. Harry."

8. See letter to H. R. Hatfield, September 28, 1934, in file "Securities and Exchange Commission (2)," in May Papers. See also Carey, *Rise of the Accounting Profession* 1:182–90.

9. Carey, *Rise of the Accounting Profession* 1:182–90.

10. Parrish, *Securities Regulation and the New Deal*, pp. 52–57.

11. Ibid., p. 57; Seligman, *Transformation of Wall Street*, pp. 56–61 passim.

12. Parrish, *Securities Regulation and the New Deal*, pp. 62–64; Seligman, *Transformation of Wall Street*, pp. 62–72 passim.

13. Edwards, *History of Public Accounting*, pp. 155–57.

14. Ibid.

15. May, *Twenty-five Years of Accounting Responsibility* 2:69.

16. Edwards, *History of Public Accounting*, pp. 158–59; Parrish, *Securities Regulation and the New Deal*, pp. 202–3.

17. Parrish, *Securities Regulation and the New Deal*, pp. 200–205.

18. Ibid., p. 206.

19. See letters from R. D. White, April 13, 1936, and April 20, 1936, in file "Securities and Exchange Commission, 1936 (2)," in May Papers.

20. Carey, *Rise of the Accounting Profession* 1:197–98. See also "Administration of the Federal Securities Acts," p. 7; Gordon, "Accountants and the Securities Acts," pp. 438–51; Gordon, "Liability of Public Accountants," pp. 251–57; "Great Responsibility and Great Opportunity," pp. 82–83; "Greatest Opportunity of All," pp. 326–27; May, "Influence of the Depression," pp. 336–50, May, "Position of Accountants under the Securities Acts," pp. 9–23; Sanders, "Corporate Information," pp. 9–22; C. A. Smith, "Accounting Practice," pp. 325–32; Starkey, "Practice under the Securities Act," pp. 431–47; Stempf, "Securities and Exchange Commission and the Accountant," pp. 12–16; Watson, "Practice under the Securities Act," p. 445; and Weidenhammer, "Accountant and the Securities Acts," pp. 272–78.

21. Carey, *Rise of the Accounting Profession* 1:199; Parrish, *Securities Regulation and the New Deal*, pp. 202–5. See also minutes of meeting (July 18, 1934) between representatives of the accounting profession and the Securities and Exchange Commission in Washington, D.C. in file, "Securities and Exchange Commission, 1934 (9)," in May Papers.

22. See letter to Hatfield, September 28, 1934, cited above, n. 8.

23. Letter from R. F. Starkey, June 28, 1935, in file "Securities and Exchange Commission, 1935," in May Papers.

24. Carey, *Rise of the Accounting Profession* 1:20–22. See also "Memorandum of Luncheon Meeting at the Broad Street Club (May 28, 1935)," in file "Auditing Certificates and Reports, 1935," in May Papers.

25. Carey, *Rise of the Accounting Profession* 1:354–55.

26. Ibid., 1:355–58.

27. Ibid.

28. Ibid., 1:349, 362.

29. Ibid., 1:351–52.

30. Zeff, *American Accounting Association*, pp. 30–34, 38–41.

31. See letter from H. R. Hatfield, September 21, 1935, and letter to H. R. Hatfield, September 28, 1935, both in file "Securities and Exchange Commission, 1934 (2)," in May Papers. See also Carey, *Rise of the Accounting Profession* 2:12–14; Heaton, *Scholar in Action*, pp. 125–26; and Zeff, *American Accounting Association*, pp. 38–41, n. 47.

32. Zeff, *American Accounting Association*, pp. 40–41.

33. Ibid., pp. 42–49.

34. Carey, *Rise of the Accounting Profession* 1:199–202; and Parrish, *Securities Regulation and the New Deal*, pp. 206–8.

35. Quoted in Carey, *Rise of the Accounting Profession* 1:201. For accounts of Landis's career as a regulator, see McCraw, *Prophets of Regulation*, chap. 5, and Ritchie, *James M. Landis*, chap. 5.

36. Carey, *Rise of the Accounting Profession* 2:8–12.

37. Quoted in ibid. 2:10–11.

38. Ibid., 1:201–2, 2:8.

Chapter 9

1. See Schlesinger, *The Age of Roosevelt* 2:179–94, 486, 3:385–408. See also Leuchtenburg, *Roosevelt and the New Deal*, chaps. 10–11 passim; and Moley, *First New Deal*.

See *NCAB, DAB*, s.v.v. "Peek, George," and "Johnson, Hugh Lawrence." See also Schwarz, *Speculator*, pp. 183–84, 321, 386.

See also Galbraith, *American Capitalism*, chap. 9, for a discussion of "countervailing power" in a purely economic context.

2. Schlesinger, *The Age of Roosevelt* 3:287–90, 325–44, 487–90, 635–36; Schwarz, *Speculator*, pp. 314–22.

3. See Blum, *From the Morgenthau Diaries* 1:324–26, for tax avoidance techniques.

4. Ibid., 1:306–7; Schlesinger, *The Age of Roosevelt* 3:505–7.

5. Blum, *From the Morgenthau Diaries* 1:305–7.

6. Schwarz, *Speculator*, pp. 17–18, 314–22.

7. See May's articles on tax reform in *Twenty-five Years of Accounting Responsibility* 2:127–43, 159–66, 167–68; 172–75, 187–200.

8. Ibid., 2:201–28.

9. Letter to E. F. Gay, October 18, 1934, in file "Securities Act of 1933 (1)," in May Papers.

10. Letter from E. F. Gay, October 24, 1934, in file "Securities Act of 1933 (1)," in May Papers.

11. See letter from D. C. Roper, November 20, 1934, in file "Taxation, 1934," in May Papers. See also *NCAB*, s.v. "Weinberg, Sidney J."; and DeMond, *Price Waterhouse*, pp. 257–66, 281.

12. Schwarz, *Speculator*, pp. 329–88 passim.

13. See letter to Joseph S. Davis, April 28, 1936, in file "Taxation, 1936 (3)," in May Papers.

14. See letter from L. G. Sutherland, April 30, 1936, and copy of a letter from V. H. Stempf to D. Arthur, May 5, 1936, both in file "Taxation, 1936 (3)," in May Papers.

15. Letter to P. G. Gerry, May 7, 1936, in file "Taxation, 1936 (3)," in May Papers.

16. See Blum, *From the Morgenthau Diaries* 1:311–13. See also letter to H. Morgenthau, Jr., May 27, 1936, in file "Taxation, 1936 (3)," in May Papers.

17. Blum, *From the Morgenthau Diaries* 1:315–19.

18. Cuff, *War Industries Board*, chaps. 1–2; and Schwarz, *Speculator*, pp. 79–88.

19. See letters from S. J. Weinberg, February 4, 1935, from W. P. Gifford, February 8, 1935, and to S. J. Weinberg, February 11, 1935, all in file "Securities and Exchange Commission, 1935 (3)," in May Papers.

20. Schwarz, *Speculator*, pp. 50–108 passim.

21. Ibid., pp. 79–80, 284–86.

22. Carey, *Rise of the Accounting Profession* 1:365–67.

23. Ibid., 1:361–64.

24. AIA, *Minutes*, Council (April 8, 1935), pp. 8–58.

25. Ibid., pp. 30–54.

26. Ibid., pp. 28–29.

27. Ibid., p. 58.

28. Ibid., pp. 12–13.

29. Carey, *Rise of the Accounting Profession* 1:362–63.

30. Ibid.

31. See letter from C. B. Couchman, January 21, 1935, in file "Auditing, Certificates and Reports, 1935 (1)," in May Papers.

32. See letter to A. H. Carter, February 25, 1935, in file "Auditing, Certificates, and Reports, 1935 (1)," in May Papers.

33. Letter from L. Ashman, December 19, 1934, in file "AIA Special Committee on Development of Accounting Principles, 1934 (1)," in May Papers. See also Kohler, "A Nervous Profession," p. 4.

34. See Zeff, *American Accounting Association*, pp. 35–41; and Mautz and Previts, "Eric L. Kohler," pp. 21–23.

35. Letter to T. H. Sanders, December 20, 1934, in file "AIA Special Committee on the Development of Accounting Principles, 1934 (1)," in May Papers.

36. Letter to T. H. Sanders, December 29, 1934, in file "AIA Special Committee on the Development of Accounting Principles," in May Papers.

37. Carey, *Rise of the Accounting Profession* 2:8–16; Zeff, *American Accounting Association*, pp. 47–49.

38. Carey, *Rise of the Accounting Profession* 1:365–66; Montgomery, *Fifty Years of Accountancy*, pp. 72–73. See also: "Amalgamation in America," p. 37; "Consolidation," pp. 516–17; "Institute's Annual Meeting," p. 164; "Institute's Dallas Meeting," pp. 626–28; Jay, "Consolidation—Now What?" pp. 569–79; and Springer, "Institute-Society-Institute," pp. 743–51.

39. Carey, *Rise of the Accounting Profession* 1:170–80.

40. Ibid., 2:8–12; Previts and Merino, *Accounting in America*, pp. 260–75; and Montgomery, *Fifty Years of Accountancy*, pp. 72–73. See also Berle, "Accounting

and the Law," pp. 116–24; Blough, "Relation of the Securities and Exchange Commission to the Accountant," pp. 23–29; and Sanders, "Recent Accounting Developments," pp. 535–44. See also Walsh, *Identifying Accounting Principles*, pp. 14–16.

41. Carey, *Rise of the Accounting Profession* 2:12–16.

42. Ibid., 2:14–15; and AIA, *Yearbook 1937*, p. 5.

43. Carey, *Rise of the Accounting Profession* 2:15–16, 60–65; U.S. SEC, *Annual Report 1939*, pp. 174–75.

44. Carey, *Rise of the Accounting Profession* 2:20–22.

45. Ibid., 2:22–23; and DeMond, *Price Waterhouse*, pp. 257–66, 269–79. See also *NCAB*, s.v. "Weinberg, Sidney J."

46. Shaplen, "Annals of Crime," pp. 49–50, 39–40. See also Edwards, *History of Public Accounting*, pp. 163–70; Previts and Merino, *Accounting in America*, pp. 257–60. U.S. SEC, *Annual Report 1939*, pp. 117–21; and U.S. SEC, *Annual Report 1940*, pp. 164–69.

47. Carey, *Rise of the Accounting Profession* 1:33–35, 37–38; Edwards, *History of Public Accounting*, p. 170; and Previts and Merino, *Accounting in America*, pp. 259–60.

48. Carey, *Rise of the Accounting Profession* 2:176–78; and Edwards, *History of Public Accounting*, pp. 161–63.

49. Carey, *Rise of the Accounting Profession* 2:35–38.

50. Ibid., 2:175–80.

51. Ibid., 2:37.

Chapter 10

1. Baum, *Wizard of Oz*; *New York Tribune*, January 10, 1903, p. 5. See also Henry M. Littlefield, "Wizard of Oz," for a fuller discussion of the allegorical symbolism.

2. For business, see Chandler, *Strategy and Structure*; for professions, see Burrow, *AMA*; and for government, see Winter, *State and Local Government in a Decentralized Republic*.

3. Higham, *Strangers in the Land*, pp. 165–75.

4. Ibid., pp. 132–49, 150–57, 164–75, 317–23.

5. Hidy, *House of Baring*. See also Thistlewaite, *Anglo-American Connection in the Early Nineteenth Century*, and Perkins, *Financing Anglo-American Trade*.

6. Abbott, "Status and Status Strain," pp. 819–35; Burnham, "Medical Specialists and Movements toward Social Control," pp. 19–30; Calhoun, *American Civil Engineer*; Calvert, *Mechanical Engineer in America*; Faber and McIntosh, *History of the American Pediatric Society*; Guthrie, *History of Medicine*; Hartmen, "Social Prestige of Representative Medical Specialties," pp. 659–63; and Spence, *Mining Engineers and the American West*.

7. Hobson, "American Legal Profession," pp. 88–103.

8. Ibid., pp. 237–48, Stevens, *American Medicine and the Public Interest*, pp. 42–43, 59–62.

9. Hobson, "American Legal Profession," pp. 237–48.

10. Ibid., pp. 249–52; Stevens, *American Medicine and the Public Interest*, pp. 42–43, 59–62.

11. *DAB*, s.v. "Adams, Henry Carter," and Hoogenboom and Hoogenboom, *History of the ICC*, chaps. 3–5 passim.

12. Figures on certified public accountants estimated from tables in Edwards, *History of Public Accounting*, pp. 362–63.

13. See Hawley, *The New Deal and the Problem of Monopoly*, especially chaps. 4–7, for the NRA.

14. See Schlesinger, *The Age of Roosevelt*.

15. See Hamilton, Jay, and Madison, *Federalist Papers*.

Bibliography

Manuscript Collections

Albany, New York
  New York State Library
    William C. Doane Papers
Ann Arbor, Michigan
  University of Michigan
    Henry Carter Adams Papers
Cambridge, Massachusetts
  Harvard University
    William Z. Ripley Papers
New Haven, Connecticut
  Yale University
    Chauncey M. Depew Papers
New York, New York
  American Institute of Public Accountants
    Norman E. Webster Papers
  Columbia University
    Melvil Dewey Papers
    George W. Perkins Papers
    Frank A. Vanderlip Papers
  Deloitte, Haskins, and Sells
    Elijah W. Sells Papers
  New York Public Library
    Levi P. Morton Papers
  Price Waterhouse and Company
    George O. May Papers
Palo Alto, California
  Hoover Institution
    Edwin F. Gay Papers
Princeton, New Jersey
  Princeton University
    Bernard M. Baruch Papers

Books

Abbott, Andrew. *The System of Professions: An Essay on the Division of Expert Knowledge*. Chicago: University of Chicago Press, 1988.

Abernathy, William J. *The Productivity Dilemma: Roadblock to Innovation in the Automobile Industry*. Baltimore: Johns Hopkins University Press, 1978.

Adams, Henry Carter. *American Railway Accounting: A Commentary*. New York: Henry Holt, 1918.

————. *Public Debts: An Essay in the Science of Finance*. New York: D. Appleton and Company, 1890.

Aitken, Hugh G. J. *Syntony and Spark: The Origins of Radio*. New York: John Wiley, 1976.

American Association of Public Accountants. *Minutes of Board of Trustees, 1903–1916*. New York: Author, 1903–16.

————. *Minutes of Executive Committee, 1905–1916*. New York: Author, 1905–16.

————. *Minutes of Member Meetings, Executive Committee, and Board of Trustees, 1886–1905*. New York: Author, 1886–1905.

————. *Yearbooks of Annual Meetings*. 11 vols. Various publishers: 1906–16.

American Institute of Accountants. *Minutes of Annual Meetings, 1917–1940*. Bound annually. New York: Author, 1917–40.

————. *Minutes of Council Meetings*. Bound semiannually. New York: Author, 1917–40.

————. *Yearbooks of Annual Meetings, 1917–1940*. New York: Author, 1917–40.

Anyon, James T. *Recollections of the Early Days of Accountancy, 1883–1893*. New York: Privately printed, 1925.

Apter, David E. *The Politics of Modernization*. Chicago: University of Chicago Press, 1965.

Arthur Young and Company. *Arthur Young and the Company He Founded*. New York: Author, 1948.

Auerbach, Jerold A. *Unequal Justice: Lawyers and Social Change in Modern America*. New York: Oxford University Press, 1976.

Batelle, L. G. *Story of Ohio Accountancy*. Columbus, Ohio: Ohio Society of Certified Public Accountants, 1954.

Baum, L. Frank. *The Wizard of Oz*. Chicago: G. M. Hall, 1900. Reprint. New York: Random House, 1960.

Beard, Charles A., ed. *A Century of Progress*. New York: Harper Brothers, 1932. Reprint. Freeport, N.Y.: Books for Libraries Press, 1960.

Becker, William H. *The Dynamics of Business Government Relations: Industry and Exports, 1893–1921*. Chicago: University of Chicago Press, 1982.

Bell, Hermon F. *Reminiscences of a Certified Public Accountant*. New York: Privately printed, 1959.

Benjamin, Jules Robert. *The United States and Cuba: Hegemony and Dependent Development*. Pittsburgh: University of Pittsburgh Press, 1977.

Benson, Lee. *Merchants, Farmers and Railroads: Railroad Regulation and New York Politics, 1855–1887*. Cambridge: Harvard University Press, 1955.

Berger, Peter, and Brigitte Berger. *The Homeless Mind: Modernization and Consciousness*. New York: Random House, 1973.

Berlant, J. *Professions and Monopoly: A Study of Medicine in the United States and Great Britain*. Berkeley and Los Angeles: University of California Press, 1975.

Berle, Adolf A. *The Twentieth-Century Capitalist Revolt*. New York: Harcourt Brace, 1954.

Berle, Adolf A., and Gardiner C. Means. *The Modern Corporation and Private Property*. New York: Commerce Clearing House, 1932.

Berle, Beatrice B., and Travis B. Jacobs, eds. *Navigating the Rapids, 1918–1971: From the Papers of Adolf A. Berle*. New York: Harcourt Brace Jovanovich, 1973.

Black, Cyril E. *The Dynamics of Modernization*. New York: Harpers, 1962.

Blau, Peter M., and W. Richard Scott. *The American Organizational Structure*. New York: John Wiley, 1967.

Bledstein, Burton J. *The Culture of Professionalism: The Middle Class and the Development of Higher Education in America*. New York: Norton, 1976.

Block, Fred L. *The Origins of International Economic Disorder: A Study of United States International Monetary Policy from World War II to Present*. Berkeley and Los Angeles: University of California Press, 1977.

Blum, John M. *From the Morgenthau Diaries, 1928–1945*. 3 vols. Boston: Houghton Mifflin, 1959.

———. *The Republican Roosevelt*. Cambridge: Harvard University Press, 1954.

Bonner, Thomas Neville. *American Doctors and German Universities: A Chapter in International Intellectual Relations*. Lincoln: University of Nebraska Press, 1963.

Brand, J. L. *Doctors and the State*. Baltimore: Johns Hopkins University Press, 1965.

Brandeis, Louis D. *Other People's Money and How the Bankers Use It*. New York: Harpers, 1913–14. Reprint. New York: Harper Torchbooks, 1967.

Brown, E. Richard. *Rockefeller Medicine Men: Medicine and Capitalism in America*. Berkeley and Los Angeles: University of California Press, 1979.

Bruchey, Stuart W. *Robert Oliver and Mercantile Bookkeeping in the Early Nineteenth Century*. New York: Arno Press, 1976.

Buck, Paul, ed. *The Social Sciences at Harvard: From Inculcation to the Open Mind*. Cambridge: Harvard University Press, 1965.

Buley, R. Carlyle. *The Equitable Life Assurance Society of the United States, 1859–1964*. 2 vols. New York: Appleton-Century-Crofts, 1967.

Burns, Thomas J., and Edward N. Coffman. *The Accounting Hall of Fame: Profile of Forty-one Members*. Columbus: Ohio State University Press, 1982.

Burrow, James Gordon. *AMA: Voice of American Medicine*. Baltimore: Johns Hopkins University Press, 1963.

———. *Organized Medicine in the Progressive Era: The Move toward Monopoly*. Baltimore: Johns Hopkins University Press, 1977.

Calhoun, David H. *The American Civil Engineer: Origins and Conflict*. Cambridge: Harvard University Press, 1960.

———. *Professional Lives in America: Structure and Aspiration, 1750–1850*. Cambridge: Harvard University Press, 1965.

Calvert, Monte A. *The Mechanical Engineer in America, 1830–1910: Professional Cultures in Conflict*. Baltimore: Johns Hopkins University Press, 1967.

Campbell, Charles S. *The Transformation of American Foreign Relations, 1865–1900*. New York: Harper and Row, 1976.

Campbell, E. G. *The Reorganization of the American Railroad System, 1893–1900*. New York: Columbia University Press, 1938.

Carey, John L. *The CPA's Professional Heritage*. Working Papers nos. 1 and 5. Tuscaloosa, Ala.: Academy of Accounting Historians, 1974.

––––––. *The Rise of the Accounting Profession*. 2 vols. New York: American Institute of Certified Public Accountants, 1969–70.

Carlin, J. *Lawyers' Ethics*. New York: Russell Sage Foundation, 1966.

––––––. *Lawyers on Their Own: A Study of Individual Practitioners in Chicago*. New Brunswick, N.J.: Rutgers University Press, 1962.

Carosso, Vincent P. *Investment Banking in America: A History*. Cambridge: Harvard University Press, 1970.

––––––. *More Than a Century of Investment Banking: The Kidder, Peabody, and Company Story*. New York: McGraw-Hill, 1978.

––––––. *The Morgans: Private Investment Bankers, 1854–1913*. Cambridge: Harvard University Press, 1987.

Carr-Saunders, A. P., and P. A. Wilson. *The Professions*. Oxford: Oxford University Press, 1933.

Casler, Darwin J. *The Evolution of CPA Ethics: A Profile of Professionalization*. Occasional Paper no. 12. East Lansing: Bureau of Business and Economic Research, Michigan State University, 1964.

Cather, Willa. *O Pioneers!* New York: Houghton Mifflin, 1913.

Chalk, R., M. S. Frankel, and S. B. Chafer. *Professional Ethics in the Scientific and Engineering Societies*. Washington, D.C.: American Association for the Advancement of Science, 1980.

Chandler, Alfred D., Jr. *Henry Varnum Poor: Business Editor, Analyst, and Reformer*. Cambridge: Harvard University Press, 1956.

––––––. *Strategy and Structure: Chapters in the History of the Industrial Enterprise*. Cambridge: MIT Press, 1963.

––––––. *The Visible Hand: The Managerial Revolution in American Business*. Cambridge: Harvard University Press, 1977.

––––––, ed. *The Railroads: The Nation's First Big Business*. New York: Harcourt, Brace, and World, 1965.

Chatfield, Michael. *A History of Accounting Thought*. Hinsdale, Ill.: Dryden Press, 1974.

Christian, P. *Ethics in Business Conduct*. Detroit: Gale Research, 1970.

Cochran, Thomas C. *American Business in the Twentieth Century*. Cambridge: Harvard University Press, 1972.

––––––. *The American Business System: A Historical Perspective*. Cambridge: Harvard University Press, 1957.

Cole, Arthur Morse. *The Fundamentals of Accounting*. Boston: Houghton Mifflin, 1921.

Cooper, William W., and Yuji Ijiri, eds. *Eric Louis Kohler: Accounting's Man of Principles*. Reston, Va.: Reston Publishing, 1979.

Crick, Bernard. *The American Science of Politics: Its Origins and Conditions*. Berkeley and Los Angeles: University of California Press, 1962.

Cuff, Robert D. *The War Industries Board: Business Government Relations during World War I*. Baltimore: Johns Hopkins University Press, 1973.

Curti, Merle. *The Growth of American Thought*. 3d ed. New York: Harper and Row, 1964.

Curti, Merle, and Vernon Carstensen. *The University of Wisconsin: A History, 1848–1925*. 2 vols. Madison: University of Wisconsin Press, 1949.

Dawe, Grosvenor. *Melvil Dewey: Seer, Inspirer, Doer, 1851–1931*. Lake Placid, N.Y.: Lake Placid Club, 1932.

DeMond, C. W. *Price Waterhouse and Company in America: A History of a Public Accounting Firm*. New York: Comet Press, 1951.

Dickinson, Arthur Lowes. *Accounting Practice and Procedure*. New York: Ronald Press, 1913. Reprint. New York: Ronald Press, 1917.

――――, ed. *Official Record of the Proceedings of the Congress of Accountants Held at the World's Fair at St. Louis*. New York: Federation of Societies of Public Accountants, 1904.

Dictionary of American Biography. New York: Scribner's, various.

Dictionary of National Biography. London: Oxford University Press, various.

Dillon, Gadis J. *The Role of Accounting in the Stock Market Crash of 1929*. Research Monograph no. 96. Atlanta: Georgia State University, Business Publishing Division, 1984.

Dorfman, Joseph, ed. *Relation of the State to Industrial Action and Economics and Jurisprudence*. New York: Columbia University Press, 1954.

Douglas, William O. *Democracy and Finance*. New Haven: Yale University Press, 1940.

Durkheim, E. *Professional Ethics and Civic Morals*. Glencoe, Ill.: Free Press, 1958.

Edwards, James Don. *History of Public Accounting in the United States*. East Lansing: Bureau of Business and Economic Research, Michigan State University, 1965.

Elliott, Orrin L. *Stanford University: The First Twenty-five Years*. Palo Alto, Calif.: Stanford University Press, 1937.

Ely, Owen. *Railway Rates and Cost of Service*. Boston: Houghton Mifflin, 1924.

Ely, Richard T. *Ground under Our Feet: An Autobiography*. New York: Macmillan, 1938.

Emerson, Ralph Waldo. *The Conduct of Life*. Cambridge, Mass.: Ticknor and Fields, 1860. Reprint. Cambridge, Mass.: Riverside Press, 1885.

――――. *Representative Men*. Cambridge, Mass.: Philips, Sampson, and Company, 1850. Reprint. Cambridge, Mass.: Riverside Press, 1885.

Ernst and Ernst. *Ernst and Ernst: A History of the Firm*. Cleveland: Privately printed, 1960.

Etzione, Amitai. *A Comparative Analysis of Complex Organizations: On Power, Involvement, and Their Correlates*. New York: Free Press, 1975.

_____. *Political Unification: A Comparative Study of Leaders and Forces*. New York: Holt, Rinehart, and Winston, 1965.

_____, ed. *The Semi-Professions and Their Organization*. New York: Free Press, 1969.

Faber, Harold Kniest, and Robert McIntosh. *History of the American Pediatric Society, 1887–1965*. New York: McGraw-Hill, 1966.

Faulkner, Harold U. *The Decline of Laissez Faire, 1897–1947*. New York: Rinehart, 1951.

Federation of State Societies of Public Accountants in the United States of America. *Executive Board Minutes, 1902–1905*. New York: Author, 1902–5.

Finnegan, John Patrick. *Against the Specter of a Dragon: The Campaign of American Military Preparedness, 1914–1917*. Westport, Conn.: Greenwood, 1974.

Fishbein, Morris. *A History of the American Medical Association, 1847–1947*. Philadelphia: Saunders, 1947.

Fitzgerald, F. Scott. *The Last Tycoon: An Unfinished Novel*. New York: Scribner's, 1941.

Flegm, Eugene H. *Accounting: How to Meet the Challenges of Relevance and Regulation*. New York: John Wiley, 1984.

Forbes, John Douglas. *J. P. Morgan, Jr., 1867–1943*. Charlottesville: University Press of Virginia, 1981.

_____. *Stettinius, Sr.: Portrait of a Morgan Partner*. Charlottesville: University Press of Virginia, 1974.

Forster, E. M. *Goldsworthy Lowes Dickinson*. New York: Harcourt, Brace, 1934.

Freidel, Frank. *Franklin D. Roosevelt: The Triumph*. Boston: Little, Brown, 1956.

Freidson, Eliot. *Professional Dominance: The Social Structure of Medical Care*. New York: Aldine, 1970.

_____. *Profession of Medicine*. New York: Dodd, Mead, 1970.

Friedman, L. M. *A History of American Law*. New York: Simon and Schuster, 1973.

Furner, Mary O. *Advocacy and Objectivity: A Crisis in the Professionalization of American Social Science, 1865–1905*. Lexington: University of Kentucky Press, 1973.

Gabriel, Ralph H., with Robert H. Walker. *The Course of American Democratic Thought: An Intellectual History since 1815*. 3d ed. Westport, Conn.: Greenwood Press, 1986.

Galambos, Louis. *America at Middle Age: A New History of the United States in the Twentieth Century*. New York: McGraw-Hill, 1982.

_____. *American Business History*. Washington, D.C.: Service Center for Teachers of History, 1967.

_____. *Competition and Cooperation: The Emergence of a National Trade Association*. Baltimore: Johns Hopkins University Press, 1966.

_____. *The Public Image of Big Business in America, 1880–1940: A Quantitative Study in Social Change*. Baltimore: Johns Hopkins University Press, 1975.

Galambos, Louis, and Joseph Pratt. *The Rise of the Corporate Commonwealth: U.S. Business and Public Policy in the Twentieth Century*. New York: Basic Books, 1987.

Galbraith, John K. *American Capitalism: The Concept of Countervailing Power*. Boston: Houghton Mifflin, 1952.

_____. *The Great Crash*. Boston: Houghton Mifflin, 1955.

Garnier, S. Paul. *The Evolution of Cost Accounting*. Tuscaloosa: University of Alabama Press, 1954.

Garraty, John A. *Right Hand Man: The Life of George W. Perkins*. New York: Harper and Brothers, 1957.

Gevitz, Norman. *The D.O.'s: Osteopathic Medicine in America*. Baltimore: Johns Hopkins University Press, 1982.

Gilb, Corinne Lathrop. *Hidden Hierarchies: The Professions and Government*. New York: Harper and Row, 1966.

Grady, Paul, ed. *Memoirs and Accounting Thought of George O. May*. New York: Ronald Press, 1962.

Graebner, William. *Coal-mining Safety in the Progressive Period: The Political Economy of Reform*. Lexington: University of Kentucky Press, 1976.

Green, Wilmer. *History and Survey of Accountancy*. Brooklyn: Standard Books, 1930.

Grob, Gerald N. *Mental Illness and American Society, 1875–1940*. Princeton: Princeton University Press, 1983.

_____. *Mental Institutions in America: Social Policy to 1875*. New York: Free Press, 1973.

Guthrie, Douglas. *A History of Medicine*. Philadelphia: J. B. Lippincott, 1946.

Haber, Samuel. *Efficiency and Uplift: Scientific Management in the Progressive Era, 1890–1920*. Chicago: University of Chicago Press, 1964.

Hamilton, Alexander, John Jay, and James Madison. *The Federalist Papers*. Edited by Willmore Kendall and George W. Carey. New Rochelle, N.Y.: Arlington House, 1966.

Harbaugh, William H. *Lawyer's Lawyer: The Life of John W. Davis*. New York: Oxford University Press, 1973.

Haskell, Thomas L. *The Emergence of Professional Social Science: The American Social Science Association and the Nineteenth-Century Crisis of Authority*. Urbana: University of Illinois Press, 1977.

Haskins, Charles W. *Business Education and Accountancy*. Edited by Frederick A. Cleveland. New York: Harper and Brothers, 1904.

_____. *The Growing Need of Higher Accountancy*. New York: Haskins and Sells, 1901.

Haskins and Sells. *The First Fifty Years*. New York: Author, 1947.

_____. *Haskins and Sells, Certified Public Accountants: A History of the Origin and Growth of the Firm, 1895–1935*. New York: Author, 1935.

_____. *Our First Seventy-five Years*. New York: Author, 1970.

Hawkins, Hugh. *Pioneer: A History of the Johns Hopkins University, 1874–1889*. Ithaca: Cornell University Press, 1960.

Hawley, Ellis W. *The Great War and the Search for a Modern Order: A History of the American People and Their Institutions, 1917–1933*. New York: St. Martin's Press, 1978.

_____. *Herbert Hoover as Secretary of Commerce: Studies in New Era Thought and*

Practice. Iowa City: University of Iowa Press, 1981.

———. *The New Deal and the Problem of Monopoly*. Princeton: Princeton University Press, 1966.

Hays, Samuel P. *Conservation and the Gospel of Efficiency*. Cambridge: Harvard University Press, 1959.

———. *The Response to Industrialism, 1885–1914*. Chicago: University of Chicago Press, 1957.

Heaton, Herbert. *A Scholar in Action: Edwin F. Gay*. Cambridge: Harvard University Press, 1952.

Hein, Leonard W. *The British Companies Acts and the Practice of Accountancy, 1844–1962*. New York: Arno Press, 1978.

Hessen, Robert. *Steel Titan: The Life of Charles M. Schwab*. New York: Oxford University Press, 1975.

Hidy, Ralph W. *The House of Baring in American Trade and Finance, 1763–1861*. Cambridge: Harvard University Press, 1949.

Higgins, Thomas G. *Thomas G. Higgins, CPA: An Autobiography*. New York: Comet Press, 1965.

Higham, John. *Send These to Me: Jews and Other Immigrants In Urban America*. New York: Atheneum, 1975.

———. *Strangers in the Land: Patterns of American Nativism, 1860–1925*. New Brunswick, N.J.: Rutgers University Press, 1956. Reprint. New York: Atheneum, 1963.

———. *Writing American History: Essays on Modern Scholarship*. Bloomington: University of Indiana Press, 1970.

———, ed. *Ethnic Leadership in America*. Baltimore: Johns Hopkins University Press, 1977.

Higham, John, Leonard Krieger, and Felix Gilbert. *History: The Development of Humanistic Studies in the United States*. Englewood Cliffs, N.J.: Prentice-Hall, 1965.

Hofstadter, Richard. *The Age of Reform: From Bryan to FDR*. New York: Vintage, 1955.

———. *The Progressive Historians: Turner, Beard, and Parrington*. Chicago: University of Chicago Press, 1979.

Hoogenboom, Ari, and Olive Hoogenboom. *A History of the ICC: From Panacea to Palliative*. New York: Norton, 1976.

Horner, Harlan Hoyt. *The Life and Work of Andrew Sloan Draper*. Urbana: University of Illinois Press, 1934.

Horrigan, James O. *Financial Statement Analysis: An Historical Perspective*. New York: Arno Press, 1978.

Hughes, E. C. *Men and Their Work*. Glencoe, Ill.: Free Press, 1958.

Hughes, Thomas Parke. *Elmer Sperry: Inventor and Engineer*. Baltimore: Johns Hopkins University Press, 1971.

———. *Networks of Power: Electrification in Western Society, 1880–1930*. Baltimore: Johns Hopkins University Press, 1983.

Hurley, Edwin N. *Awakening of American Business*. New York: Doubleday, Page, and Company, 1917.

Institute of Accountants in the United States of America. *1916 Yearbook of the*

Institute of Accountants in the United States of America. New York: Author, 1916.

International Encyclopedia of the Social Sciences. Edited by David L. Sills. New York: Macmillan and Free Press, 1968.

Israel, Jerry, ed. *Building the Organizational Society.* New York: Free Press, 1972.

Jenkins, Reese V. *Images and Enterprise: Technology and the American Photographic Industry, 1839–1929.* Baltimore: Johns Hopkins University Press, 1975.

Jessup, Philip C. *Elihu Root.* 2 vols. New York: Dodd, Mead, 1938.

Johnson, H. Thomas, and Robert S. Kaplan. *Relevance Lost: The Rise and Fall of Management Accounting.* Boston: Harvard Business School Press, 1987.

Johnson, James P. *The Politics of Soft Coal: The Bituminous Industry from World War I through the New Deal.* Urbana: University of Illinois Press, 1979.

Johnson, Quintin, and Dan Hopson, Jr. *Lawyers and Their Work: An Analysis of the Legal Profession in the United States and England.* Indianapolis: Bobbs-Merrill, 1967.

Johnson, T. J. *Profession and Power.* London: Macmillan, 1967.

Jones, Edgar. *Accounting and the British Economy, 1840–1940: The Evolution of Ernst and Whinney.* London: B. T. Batsford, 1981.

Jordan, William. *Charles Waldo Haskins.* New York: Prentice-Hall, 1923.

Josephson, Mathew. *The Robber Barons: The Great American Capitalists, 1861–1901.* New York: Harcourt, Brace, 1934.

Karl, Barry D. *Executive Reorganization and Reform in the New Deal: The Genesis of Administrative Management, 1900–1939.* Cambridge: Harvard University Press, 1963.

————. *The Uneasy State: The United States from 1915 to 1945.* Chicago: University of Chicago Press, 1983.

Kaufman, Burton I. *Efficiency and Expansion: Foreign Trade Organization in the Wilson Administration, 1913–1921.* Westport, Conn.: Greenwood Press, 1974.

Keller, Morton. *Affairs of State: Public Life in Late-Nineteenth-Century America.* Cambridge: Harvard University Press, 1977.

————. *The Life Insurance Enterprise, 1885–1910: A Study in the Limits of Corporate Power.* Cambridge: Harvard University Press, 1963.

Kennan, George. *The Chicago and Alton Case: A Misunderstood Transaction.* Garden City, N.Y.: Country Life Press, 1916.

————. *E. H. Harriman: A Biography.* 2 vols. Boston: Houghton Mifflin, 1922.

————. *Misrepresentation in Railroad Affairs.* Garden City, N.Y.: Country Life Press, 1916.

Kerr, K. Austin. *American Railroad Politics, 1914–1920: Rates, Wages, and Efficiency.* Pittsburgh: University of Pittsburgh Press, 1968.

Kirkendall, Richard S. *Social Scientists and Farm Politics in the Age of Roosevelt.* Columbia: University of Missouri Press, 1967.

Knight, C. L., G. J. Previts, and T. A. Ratcliffe. *A Reference Chronology of Events Significant to the Development of Accountancy in the United States.* Augusta, Ga.: Academy of Accounting Historians, 1976.

Kohler, Robert E. *From Medical Chemistry to Biochemistry: The Making of a Biochemical Discipline.* New York: Cambridge University Press, 1982.

Kohlstedt, Sally Gregory. *The Formation of the American Scientific Community:*

The American Association for the Advancement of Science, 1848–1860. Urbana: University of Illinois, 1975.

Kolko, Gabriel. *Main Currents in Modern American History.* New York: Harper and Row, 1976.

―――. *Railroads and Regulation, 1877–1916.* Princeton: Princeton University Press, 1965.

―――. *The Triumph of Conservatism: A Reinterpretation of American History, 1900–1916.* New York: Free Press, 1963.

Kuhn, Thomas L. *The Structure of Scientific Revolutions.* Chicago: University of Chicago Press, 1968.

Lamont, Thomas W. *Across World Frontiers.* New York: Harcourt, Brace, 1951.

―――. *Henry P. Davison: The Record of a Useful Life.* New York: Harper Brothers, 1933.

Landau, Henry. *The Enemy Within: The Inside Story of German Sabotage in America.* New York: Putnam's, 1937.

Landis, James M. *The Administrative Process.* New Haven: Yale University Press, 1938.

Larson, M. S. *The Rise of Professionalism.* Berkeley and Los Angeles: University of California Press, 1977.

Layton, Edwin T. *The Revolt of the Engineers: Social Responsibility and the American Engineering Profession.* Cleveland: Case Western Reserve University Press, 1971.

Lee, Thomas A., ed. *Transactions of the Chartered Accountants Students' Societies of Edinburgh and Glasgow: A Selection of Writings, 1886–1958.* New York: Garland Publishing, 1984.

Leonard, William Norris. *Railroad Consolidation under the Transportation Act of 1920.* New York: Columbia University Press, 1946.

Lerner, Daniel. *The Passing of Traditional Society: Modernizing the Middle East.* Glencoe, Ill.: Free Press, 1958.

Leslie, Stuart W. *Boss Kettering.* New York: Columbia University Press, 1983.

Leuchtenberg, W. E. *Franklin D. Roosevelt and the New Deal, 1932–1940.* New York: Harper and Row, 1963.

Link, Arthur S. *The American Epoch: A History of the United States since the 1890s.* 2d ed. New York: Knopf, 1967.

―――. *Wilson: The New Freedom.* Princeton: Princeton University Press, 1956.

―――. *Wilson: The Road to the White House.* Princeton: Princeton University Press, 1947.

Lipset, Seymour Martin. *The First New Nation: The United States in Historical and Comparative Perspective.* New York: Basic Books, 1973. Reprint. New York: Norton, 1979.

―――. *Political Man: The Social Bases of Politics.* Garden City, N.Y.: Doubleday, 1960.

Littleton, A. C. *Accounting Evolution to 1900.* New York: American Institute Publishing Company, 1933.

―――. *Directory of Early American Public Accountants.* University of Illinois Bulletin, vol. 40, no. 8. Bureau of Business and Economic Research Bulletin Series, no. 62. Urbana: University of Illinois, 1942.

Livingston, James. *Origins of the Federal Reserve System: Money, Class, and Corporate Capitalism, 1890–1913*. Ithaca, N.Y.: Cornell University Press, 1986.

Lubove, Roy. *The Professional Altruist: The Emergence of Social Work as a Career, 1880–1930*. Cambridge: Harvard University Press, 1965.

Luebke, Frederick C. *Bonds of Loyalty: German-Americans and World War I*. De Kalb: Northern Illinois University Press, 1974.

Lurie, Jonathan. *The Chicago Board of Trade, 1895–1905: The Dynamics of Self-Regulation*. Urbana: University of Illinois Press, 1979.

Lustig, R. Jeffrey. *Corporate Liberalism: The Origins of Modern American Political Theory, 1890–1920*. Berkeley and Los Angeles: University of California Press, 1982.

Lybrand, Ross Brothers, and Montgomery. *Fiftieth Anniversary, 1898–1948*. New York: Author, 1948.

McCormick, Richard L. *From Realignment to Reform: Political Change in New York State, 1893–1910*. Ithaca, N.Y.: Cornell University Press, 1979.

McCraw, Thomas K. *Prophets of Regulation: Charles Francis Adams, Louis D. Brandeis, James M. Landis, Alfred E. Kahn*. Cambridge: Harvard University Press, 1984.

_____, et al., eds. *Regulation in Perspective: Historical Essays*. Cambridge: Harvard University Press, 1981.

McFarland, Carl. *Judicial Control of the Federal Trade Commission and the Interstate Commerce Commission, 1920–1930: A Comparative Study in the Relations of Courts to Administrative Commissions*. Cambridge: Harvard University Press, 1933.

McQuaid, Kim. *Big Business and Presidential Power: From FDR to Reagan*. New York: Morrow, 1981.

Margulies, H., and L. S. Block. *Foreign Medical Graduates in the United States*. Cambridge: Harvard University Press, 1969.

Martin, Albro. *Enterprise Denied: Origin of the Decline of American Railroads, 1897–1917*. New York: Columbia University Press, 1971.

_____. *James J. Hill and the Opening of the Northwest*. New York: Oxford University Press, 1976.

May, George O. *Twenty-five Years of Accounting Responsibility, 1911–1936*. Edited by Bishop Carlton Hunt. 2 vols. New York: American Institute Publishing Company, 1936.

Mepham, Michael J. *Accounting in Eighteenth-Century Scotland*. New York: Garland, 1988.

Merrill, Horace S., and Norma G. Merrill. *The Republican Command, 1897–1913*. Lexington: University of Kentucky Press, 1971.

Merritt, Rita Perrine. *The Accountants' Directory and Who's Who, 1925*. New York: Prentice-Hall, 1925.

Merton, Robert K. *Some Thoughts on the Professions in American Society*. Brown University Paper no. 37. Providence, R.I.: Brown University Press, 1960.

Meyer, Balthasar H. *History of the Northern Securities Case*. Madison: University of Wisconsin Press, 1906.

Miller, George H. *Railroads and the Grainger Laws*. Madison: University of Wisconsin Press, 1971.

Millerson, G. *The Qualifying Associations*. London: Routledge and Kegan Paul, 1964.

Mitchell, Broadus. *Depression Decade: From New Era through New Deal, 1929–1941*. New York: Rinehart, 1947.

———. *The First New Deal*. New York: Harcourt, 1966.

Moley, Raymond. *After Seven Years*. New York: Harper, 1939.

Montgomery, Robert H. *Fifty Years of Accountancy*. New York: Ronald Press, 1939. Reprint. New York: Arno Press, 1978.

Moonitz, Maurice, and A. C. Littleton, eds. *Significant Accounting Essays*. Englewood Cliffs, N.J.: Prentice-Hall, 1965.

Moore, W. E. *The Professions: Roles and Rules*. New York: Russell Sage Foundation, 1970.

Morison, Elting E. *Turmoil and Tradition: A Study of the Life and Times of Henry L. Stimson*. Boston: Atheneum, 1964.

Morris, Edmund. *The Rise of Theodore Roosevelt*. New York: Coward, McCann, and Geoghan, 1979.

Mowry, George E. *The California Progressives*. Berkeley and Los Angeles: University of California Press, 1951. Reprint. Chicago: Quadrangle Books, 1963.

———. *The Era of Theodore Roosevelt, 1900–1912*. New York: Harper and Row, 1958.

———. *The Progressive Era, 1900–1918: Recent Literature and New Ideas*. Washington, D.C.: Service Center for Teachers of History, 1958.

———. *Theodore Roosevelt and the Progressive Movement*. Madison: University of Wisconsin Press, 1946.

———. *The Urban Nation, 1920–1960*. New York: Hill and Wang, 1965.

Murphy, Mary. *Accounting: A Social Force in the Community*. Melbourne: Melbourne University Press, 1956.

Myers, Gustavus. *History of the Great American Fortunes*. Chicago: C. H. Kerr, 1909.

Myers, Margaret G. *A Financial History of the United States*. New York: Columbia University Press, 1970.

National Cyclopedia of American Biography. Clifton, N.J.: J. T. White, various.

New Jersey Society of Certified Public Accountants. *Fifty Years of Service, 1898–1948*. Trenton, N.J.: Author, 1948.

New York State Society of Certified Public Accountants. *Fiftieth Anniversary of the Founding of the New York State Society of Certified Public Accountants*. New York: Author, 1947.

———. *Minutes Books*. New York: Author, various.

———. *Ten Year Book, 1897–1906*. New York: Author, 1906.

———. *Thirty Year Book, 1897–1927*. New York: Author, 1927.

Noble, David W. *The Progressive Mind, 1890–1917*. Minneapolis: Burgess Publishing, 1981.

Packard, Silas S. *Manual of Theoretical Training in the Science of Accounts*. New York: Privately printed, 1882.

Parrish, Michael E. *Securities Regulation and the New Deal*. Yale Historical Publication Miscellany, no. 93. New Haven: Yale University Press, 1970.

Parsons, Talcott. *Structure and Process in Modern Society*. Glencoe, Ill.: Free Press, 1960.

Pennsylvania Institute of Certified Public Accountants. *Fifth Annual Banquet*. Philadelphia: George H. Buchanan, 1905.

_____. *Records of the Twenty-fifth Anniversary Proceedings*. Philadelphia: Author, 1922.

Perkins, Edwin J. *Financing Anglo-American Trade: The House of Brown, 1800–1880*. Cambridge: Harvard University Press, 1975.

Perrine, Rita. *The Accountants' Directory and Who's Who, 1920*. New York: Fifty-fifth Street Press, 1920.

Peterson, Horace C. *Propaganda for War: The Campaign against American Neutrality*. Norman: University of Oklahoma Press, 1939.

Peterson, Horace C., and Gilbert C. Fite. *Opponents of War, 1917–1918*. Madison: University of Wisconsin Press, 1957.

Peterson, M. J. *The Medical Profession in Mid-Victorian London*. Berkeley and Los Angeles: University of California Press, 1978.

Polenberg, Richard. *Reorganizing Roosevelt's Government, 1936–1939: The Controversy over Executive Reorganization*. Cambridge: Harvard University Press, 1966.

Pollock, John C. *Wilberforce*. New York: St. Martin's Press, 1977.

Porter, Thomas M. *The Rise of Statistical Thinking, 1820–1900*. Princeton: Princeton University Press, 1986.

Previts, Gary John. *Early Twentieth-Century Developments in American Accounting Thought: A Preclassical School*. New York: Arno Press, 1978.

_____. *The Scope of CPA Services: A Study of the Development of Independence and the Profession's Role in Society*. New York: John Wiley, 1985.

Previts, Gary John, and Barbara Dubis Merino. *A History of Accounting in America: An Historical Interpretation of the Historical Significance of Accounting*. New York: John Wiley, 1979.

Pringle, Henry F. *The Life and Times of William Howard Taft: A Biography*. 2 vols. New York: Farrar and Rinehart, 1939.

_____. *Theodore Roosevelt: A Biography*. Rev. ed. New York: Harcourt Brace and World, 1956.

Rader, Benjamin G. *The Academic Mind and Reform: The Influence of Richard T. Ely in American Life*. Louisville: University of Kentucky Press, 1966.

Ratner, Sidney. *Taxation and Democracy in America*. Rev. ed. New York: John Wiley, 1967.

Reader, W. J. *Professional Men*. New York: Basic Books, 1966.

Reckitt, Ernest. *Reminiscences of Early Days of the Accounting Profession*. Chicago: Illinois Society of Certified Public Accountants, 1953.

Ripley, William Z. *Main Street and Wall Street*. Boston: Little, Brown, 1926.

_____. *The Races of Europe: A Sociological Study*. New York: Appleton, 1899.

_____. *Railroads: Finance and Organization*. New York: Longmans, Green, 1915.

_____. *Railroads: Rates and Regulation*. New York: Longmans, Green, 1912.

_____. *Trusts, Pools, and Corporations*. New York: Ginn and Company, 1905.

————, ed. *Railway Problems*. New York: Ginn and Company, 1913.

Ritchie, Donald A. *James M. Landis: Dean of Regulators*. Cambridge: Harvard University Press, 1980.

Romasco, Albert. *The Poverty of Abundance: Hoover, the Nation, and the Depression*. New York: Oxford University Press, 1965.

Roosevelt, Theodore. *The Letters of Theodore Roosevelt*. Edited by Elting E. Morison and John M. Blum. 8 vols. Cambridge: Harvard University Press, 1951–54.

————. *The Winning of the West*. 4 vols. New York: Putnam's Sons, 1889–96.

Rosen, George. *The Structure of American Medical Practice, 1875–1941*. Philadelphia: University of Pennsylvania Press, 1983.

Ross, T. Edward. *Joseph Edmund Sterrett*. Philadelphia: Pennsylvania Institute of Certified Public Accountants, 1934.

————. *Pioneers of Public Accountancy in the United States*. Philadelphia: Edward Stern, 1940.

Roy, Robert A., and James H. McNeil, *Horizons for a Profession*. New York: American Institute of Certified Public Accountants, 1967.

Rueschemeyer, D. *Lawyers and Their Society*. Cambridge: Harvard University Press, 1973.

Sass, Steven A. *The Pragmatic Imagination: A History of the Wharton School, 1881–1981*. Philadelphia: University of Pennsylvania Press, 1981.

Schlesinger, Arthur M., Jr., *The Age of Roosevelt*. 3 vols. Boston: Houghton Mifflin, 1957–60.

Schwarz, Jordan A. *The Speculator: Bernard M. Baruch in Washington, 1917–1965*. Chapel Hill: University of North Carolina Press, 1981.

Schweinberg, Eric. *Law Training in Continental Europe: Its Principles and Public Function*. New York: Russell Sage Foundation, 1945.

Scott, D. R. *The Cultural Significance of Accounts*. New York: Holt, 1931. Reprint. Lawrence, Kans.: Scholars Book Company, 1973.

Seligman, Joel. *The Transformation of Wall Street: A History of the Securities and Exchange Commission and Modern Corporate Finance*. Boston: Houghton Mifflin, 1982.

Sharfman, I. L. *The Interstate Commerce Commission: A Study in Administrative Law and Procedure*. 5 vols. New York: Commonwealth Fund, 1931–37.

Shryock, R. H. *Medical Licensing in America, 1650–1965*. Baltimore: Johns Hopkins University Press, 1967.

Skowronek, Stephen. *Building a New American State: The Expansion of National Administrative Capacities, 1877–1920*. Cambridge: Cambridge University Press, 1982.

Smith, Robert Freeman. *The United States and Revolutionary Nationalism in Mexico, 1916–1932*. Chicago: University of Chicago Press, 1972.

Sobel, Robert. *The Big Board: A History of the New York Stock Exchange*. New York: Free Press, 1965.

————. *The Great Bull Market: Wall Street in the 1920s*. New York: Norton, 1968.

Somit, Albert, and Joseph Tanenhaus. *The Development of Political Science: From Burgess to Behaviouralism*. Boston: Allyn and Bacon, 1967.

Sons of the American Revolution. *A National Register of the Society*. New York: Author, 1902.

_____. *The United States: Information for Immigrants*. New York: Author, n.d.

Soule, George. *Prosperity Decade: From War to Depression, 1917–1929*. New York: Harper Torchbooks, 1968.

Spence, Clark C. *Mining Engineers and the American West: The Lace Boot Brigade, 1849–1933*. New Haven: Yale University Press, 1970.

Sprague, Charles E. *The Philosophy of Accounts*. New York: Privately printed, 1908. Reprint. New York: Ronald Press, 1917.

Staub, Walter. *Auditing Developments during the Present Century*. Cambridge: Harvard University Press, 1942.

Stevens, R. *American Medicine and the Public Interest*. New Haven: Yale University Press, 1971.

_____. *Medical Practice in Modern England*. New Haven: Yale University Press, 1966.

Stevens, R., L. W. Goodman, and S. S. Mick. *The Alien Doctors*. New York: John Wiley, 1978.

Stewart, Frank M. *A Half Century of Municipal Reform: The History of the National Municipal Reform League*. Berkeley and Los Angeles: University of California Press, 1950.

Storr, Richard J. *The Beginning of Graduate Education in America*. Chicago: University of Chicago Press, 1953.

Swaine, Robert T. *The Cravath Firm and Its Predecessors, 1819–1948*. 2 vols. New York: Privately printed, 1946.

Tarkington, Booth. *Penrod*. New York: Grosset and Dunlop, 1914.

Taylor, Lloyd C., Jr. *The Medical Profession and Social Reform, 1885–1945*. New York: St. Martin's Press, 1974.

Thistlewaite, Frank. *The Anglo-American Connection in the Early Nineteenth Century*. Philadelphia: University of Pennsylvania Press, 1959.

Tocqueville, Alexis de. *Democracy in America*. New York: Knopf, 1966.

Towle, J. N., ed. *Ethics and Standards in American Business*. Boston: Houghton Mifflin, 1964.

Tumulty, James P. *Woodrow Wilson as I Know Him*. Garden City, N.Y.: Garden City Publishing, 1925.

Twain, Mark. *Life on the Mississippi*. Boston: Osgood, 1887.

U.S. Congress. Senate. Committee on Banking and Currency. *Hearings on Stock Exchange Practices, April–June 1932 and January–May 1933*. 2 vols. Washington, D.C.: Government Printing Office, 1933.

_____. Committee on Interstate Commerce. *Hearings on Bills to Amend the Interstate Commerce Act, December 16, 1904, to May 23, 1905: Regulation of Railway Rates*. 5 vols. Washington, D.C.: Government Printing Office, 1905.

U.S. Federal Trade Commission. *Annual Reports, 1916–1917*. Washington, D.C.: Government Printing Office, various dates.

U.S. Interstate Commerce Commission. *Annual Reports, 1888–1911*. Washington, D.C.: Government Printing Office, various dates.

_____. *Statistics of Railways in the United States, 1888–1911*. Washington, D.C.:

Government Printing Office, various dates.

University of the State of New York. *Minutes of the Board of Certified Public Accountant Examiners, October 28, 1896–March 3, 1911*. Albany: Author, 1896–1911.

Veysey, Laurence. *The Emergence of the American University*. Chicago: University of Chicago Press, 1965.

Wagner, Nancy A. *Eric Louis Kohler in the Accounting Profession*. Research Monograph no. 100. Atlanta: Georgia State University, Business Publishing Division, 1987.

Walker, Stephen P. *The Society of Accountants in Edinburgh, 1854–1914: A Study of Recruitment to a New Profession*. New York: Garland, 1988.

Walsh, Francis J., Jr. *Identifying Accounting Principles: The Process of Developing Financial Reporting Standards and Rules in the United States*. New York: Conference Board, 1979.

Weber, Max. *The Theory of Social and Economic Organization*. Translated by A. M. Henderson and T. Parsons. New York: Free Press, 1964.

Webster, Norman E., comp. *The American Association of Public Accountants: Its First Twenty Years, 1886–1906*. New York: American Institute of Accountants, 1954.

White, Eugene Nelson. *The Regulation and Reform of the American Banking System, 1900–1929*. Princeton: Princeton University Press, 1983.

Who's Who in America. Edited by Albert N. Marquis. Chicago: A. N. Marquis and Company, various dates.

Wiebe, Robert H. *Businessmen and Reform: A Study of the Progressive Movement*. Cambridge: Harvard University Press, 1962.

––––––. *The Search for Order, 1877–1920*. New York: Hill and Wang, 1967.

––––––. *The Segmented Society: An Introduction to the Meaning of America*. New York: Oxford University Press, 1975.

Wilkins, Mira. *The History of Foreign Investment in the United States to 1914*. Cambridge: Harvard University Press, 1989.

Wilkinson, George. *The CPA Movement*. New York: Wilkinson, Reckitt, Williams, and Company, 1903.

Willis, Henry P. *The Federal Reserve System: Legislation, Organization, and Operation*. New York: Ronald Press, 1923.

Winter, William Orville. *State and Local Government in a Decentralized Republic*. New York: Macmillan, 1981.

Wise, T.A. *Peat, Marwick, Mitchell, and Company*. New York: Privately printed, 1982.

Zeff, Stephen A. *American Accounting Association: Its First Fifty Years*. Evanston, Ill.: Author, 1966.

––––––. *Forging Accounting Principles in Five Countries: A History and Analysis of Trends*. Champaign: University of Illinois Press, 1972.

Zeff, Stephen A., and Maurice Moonitz, eds. *Source Book on Accounting Principles and Auditing Procedures, 1917–1953*. 2 vols. New York: Garland Publishing, 1984.

Articles

Abbott, Andrew. "Professional Ethics." *American Journal of Sociology* 88 (May 1983): 855–85.

———. "Status and Status Strain in the Professions." *American Journal of Sociology* 86 (April 1981): 819–35.

"Accountancy in New York State." *Accountant* 27 (September 1901): 983–84.

"Accountancy in the States." *Accountant* 22 (June, September, November 1896): 504, 744–45, 951–52; 23 (January, September 1897): 52–55, 99, 857–58; 24 (April 1898): 349–50, 376–77; 25 (April, August 1899): 367–69, 889; 29 (November 1903): 1392; 38 (June 1908): 824–25.

"Accountants and the New York Stock Exchange." *Journal of Accountancy* 55 (April 1933): 241–42.

"Accountants in England from the Nineteenth Century." *Accountant* 46 (January 1912): 259–61.

"Accountants Necessary in Tax Practice." *Journal of Accountancy* 41 (March 1926): 202.

"Accounting and the Securities and Exchange Commission." *Journal of Accountancy* 63 (May 1937): 323–24.

"Accounting Errors in Corporation Tax Bill." *Journal of Accountancy* 8 (July 1909): 212–13.

Adams, Henry Carter. "The Administrative Supervision of Railways under the Twentieth Section of the Act to Regulate Commerce." *Quarterly Journal of Economics* 22 (May 1908): 375–76.

———. "A Bureau of Railway Statistics and Accounts." *Independent* 44 (October 6, 1892): 1384–85.

———. "A Decade of Federal Railway Regulation." *Atlantic Monthly* 81 (1898): 437–38.

"Administration of the Federal Securities Acts." *Journal of Accountancy* 56 (July 1933): 7.

Allen, C. E. "The Growth of Accounting Instruction since 1900." *Accounting Review* 2 (June 1927): 150–66.

"Amalgamation in America." *Accountant* 96 (March 1937): 372.

"Amalgamation of American Societies of Accountants." *Accountant* 25 (June 1899): 660.

"American Accountants." *Accountant* 17 (May 1891): 329.

"American Accountants and the New York Stock Exchange." *Accountant* 88 (May 1933): 627–28.

"American Accountants and the War." *Accountant* 56 (May 1917): 429–30.

"American Association of University Instructors in Accounting." *Journal of Accountancy* 25 (February 1918): 155–56.

"The American Institute and Audit Procedure." *Accountant* 100 (February 1939): 263–67.

"American Institute of Accountants." *Accountant* 56 (April, December 1917): 419, 454–56; 90 (February 1934): 197–202.

"American Institute of Accountants Board of Examiners." *Journal of Accountancy* 24 (July 1917): 1–20.

"The American Institute's Fiftieth Anniversary." *Accountant* 96 (March 1937): 372.

"The American Society and the American Institute." *Certified Public Accountant* 3 (October 1924): 242–47.

Andersen, Arthur. "Thirtieth Anniversary Report." *Arthur Andersen Chronicle* 4 (December 1943): 1–130.

"Another Chapter of the History." *Journal of Accountancy* 47 (May 1929): 359–60.

Anyon, James T. "Early Days of American Accountancy." *Journal of Accountancy* 39 (January, February, March 1925): 1–8, 81–92, 161–69.

Banks, Alexander S. "Problems Now Confronting the Public Accounting Profession." *Certified Public Accountant* 3 (January 1924): 17–20.

Belser, F. C. "Cost Accounting for Fertilizer Manufacturers." *Journal of Accountancy* 19 (March 1915): 165.

———. "How the Universities Can Aid the Accounting Profession." *Accounting Review* 2 (March 1927): 37–42.

Berle, A. A., Jr. "Accounting and the Law." In *Significant Accounting Essays*, edited by Maurice Moonitz and A. C. Littleton, pp. 116–24. Englewood Cliffs, N.J.: Prentice-Hall, 1965.

Blacklock, Frank. "The Profession of Accountancy Viewed from an American Standpoint." *Accountant* 26 (January, February, March 1900): 13, 143, 194, 253.

Bledstein, Burton J. "Professions, Professionals, Professionalism." Paper presented at the meeting of the Organization of American Historians, April 1984.

Blough, Carman G. "The Relationship of the Securities and Exchange Commission to the Accountant." *Journal of Accountancy* 63 (January 1937): 23–39.

Blum, John M. "Theodore Roosevelt and the Hepburn Act: Toward an Orderly System of Control." In *The Letters of Theodore Roosevelt*, edited by Elting E. Morison and John M. Blum, 6:1558–71. Cambridge: Harvard University Press, 1952.

"Board of Tax Appeals." *Journal of Accountancy* 38 (November 1924): 205.

"Borrowers Certified Statements as a Basis for a National Currency." *Journal of Accountancy* 18 (December 1914): 418–26.

Botein, Stephen. "Professional History Reconsidered." *American Journal of Legal History* 21 (January 1977): 60–79.

"Branch Office Ethics." *Journal of Accountancy* 28 (September 1919): 212–16.

Brandeis, Louis D. "New Conception of Industrial Efficiency." *Journal of Accountancy* 12 (May 1911): 35–43.

Brief, Richard. "The Evolution of Asset Accounting." *Business History Review* 40 (Spring 1966): 1–23.

———. "Nineteenth-Century Accounting Error." *Journal of Accounting Research* 3 (Spring 1968): 21.

"Bright Prospects of Accountancy." *Journal of Accountancy* 16 (December 1913): 459–60.

Bryan, William Jennings. "The Government Should Issue Notes and Guarantee Bank Deposits." *Journal of Accountancy* 5 (March 1908): 366–69.

Bryson, Gladys. "The Emergence of the Social Sciences from Moral Philosophy." *International Journal of Ethics* 42 (April 1932): 304–22.

"A Bureau of Research." *Journal of Accountancy* 41 (May 1926): 354.

Burnham, John C. "Medical Specialists and Movements toward Social Control in the Progressive Era: Three Examples." In *Building the Organizational Society: Essays on Associational Activities in Modern America*, edited by Jerry Israel, pp. 19–30. New York: Free Press, 1972.

Byrne, Gilbert R. "To What Extent Can the Practice of Accounting Be Reduced to Rules and Standards?" In *Significant Accounting Essays*, edited by Maurice Moonitz and A. C. Littleton, pp. 103–15. Englewood Cliffs, N.J.: Prentice-Hall, 1965.

Canning, John B. "Some Divergences of Accounting Theory from Economic Theory." In *Significant Accounting Essays*, edited by Maurice Moonitz and A. C. Littleton, pp. 84–94. Englewood Cliffs, N.J.: Prentice-Hall, 1965.

Carey, John L. "The Place of the CPA in Contemporary Society." *Journal of Accountancy* 106 (September 1958): 27–32.

Carlisle, Rodney. " 'The American Century' Implemented: Stettinius and the Liberian Flag of Convenience." *Business History Review* 54 (Summer 1980): 175–91.

Carnegie, Andrew. "The Worst Banking System in the World." *Journal of Accountancy* 5 (March 1908): 357–61.

Castenholz, William B. "Accounting Procedures for State Universities." *Journal of Accountancy* 21 (February, March 1916): 81–92, 167–75.

"Certificates of Borrower Statements." *Journal of Accountancy* 18 (August 1914): 124–29.

Chase, Harvey S. "A Brief History of the Movement toward Uniform Municipal Reports and Accounts in the United States." *Accountant* (October 1904): 375.

———. "Report of Committee on Standard Schedules for Uniform Reports upon Municipal Industries and Public Service Corporations." *Journal of Accountancy* 8 (May 1909): 647–54.

Chase, W. Arthur. "University Education of Accounting Students in the United States." *Accountant* 57 (September 1917): 179–80.

"Chicago Stock Exchange Requires Certified Statements." *Journal of Accountancy* 55 (May 1933): 321–22.

Coats, Alfred W. "American Scholarship Comes of Age: The Louisiana Purchase Exposition 1904." *Journal of the History of Ideas* 22 (July 1961): 404–17.

———. "The First Two Decades of the American Economic Association." *American Economic Review* 50 (September 1960): 555–72.

———. "The Political Economy Club: A Neglected Episode in American Economic Thought." *American Economic Review* 51 (September 1961): 624–37.

"College Degree as CPA Prerequisite." *Journal of Accountancy* 63 (May 1937): 321–23.

"A College of Accountants: Petition for It Sent to the University Regents." *Accountant* 18 (June 1892): 520.

Collins, Robert M. "Positive Business Responses to the New Deal: The Roots of the Committee for Economic Development, 1933–1942." *Business History Review* 52 (Autumn 1978): 369–91.

"The Congress of Accountants at St. Louis." *Accountant* 31 (December 1904): 704–6, 761–64.

"The Consolidation." *Certified Public Accountant* 16 (September 1936): 516–17.

"Constitution and By-Laws of the American Society of Certified Public Accountants." *Certified Public Accountant* 2 (August 1923): 213–15.

Cooper, John A. "Professional Ethics." *Journal of Accountancy* 5 (December 1907): 81–94.

"The Corporation Tax Correspondence." *Journal of Accountancy* 8 (August 1909): 300–303.

Daniels, George. "The Process of Professionalization in American Science." *Isis* 58 (Summer 1967): 151–66.

Davidson, Sidney, and George D. Anderson. "The Development of Accounting and Auditing Standards." *Journal of Accountancy* 163 (May 1987): 130–35.

Davies, W. Sanders. "Genesis, Growth, and Aims of the Institute." *Journal of Accountancy* 42 (August 1926): 105–11.

Dickinson, Arthur Lowes. "Business Ideals." In *Early Twentieth-Century Developments in American Accounting Thought: A Preclassical School*, edited by Gary John Previts, unnumbered pages. New York: Arno Press, 1978.

———. "The Profession of the Public Accountant." *Accountant* 32 (May 1905): 650–58.

———. "Treatment of Maintenance and Depreciation Accounts in the New Classification of Accounts by Interstate Commerce Commission." In *Early Twentieth-Century Developments in American Accounting Thought: A Preclassical School*, edited by Gary John Previts, unnumbered pages. New York: Arno Press, 1978.

Dorfman, Joseph. "Henry Carter Adams: The Harmonizer of Liberty and Reform." In *Relation of the State to Industrial Action and Economics and Jurisprudence*, edited by Joseph Dorfman, pp. 1–55. New York: Columbia University Press, 1954.

Dusenbury, Richard. "The Effect of ICC Regulation on the Accounting Practices of Railroads since 1887." Academy of Accounting Historians Working Paper no. 62 (June 1985).

"Early Days of Accountancy." *Journal of Accountancy* 16 (October 1913): 310–11.

"The Education of English and American Accountants." *Accountant* 26 (April 1907): 764–65.

Edwards, James D., and Paul J. Miranti. "The AICPA: A Professional Institution in a Dynamic Society." *Journal of Accountancy* 163 (May 1987): 22–38.

"Enforcement of Rules of Conduct." *Journal of Accountancy* 38 (September 1924): 204.

Erlanger, Howard S. "The Allocation of Status within Occupations: The Case of the Legal Profession." *Social Forces* 58 (March 1980): 882–903.

"Federal Incorporation of the Institute." *Journal of Accountancy* 33 (April 1922): 286–88.

"Fifty Years of Progress." *Journal of Accountancy* 63 (March 1937): 175–76.

"Financial Statements for Stock Exchange." *Journal of Accountancy* 42 (July 1926): 37.

Flesher, Dale L., and Tonya A. R. Flesher. "Ivar Krueger's Contribution to U.S. Financial Reporting." *Accounting Review* 61 (July 1986): 421–34.

Forbes, John F. "Some Phases of Professional Ethics." *Journal of Accountancy* 20 (October 1915): 271–75.

"For Federal Incorporation." *Journal of Accountancy* 33 (January 1922): 37–39.

Gage, Lyman J. "Difficulties Lie in the Reformer's Path." *Journal of Accountancy* 5 (March 1908): 361–65.

Galambos, Louis. "The Emerging Organizational Synthesis in Modern American History." *Business History Review* 44 (Autumn 1970): 279–90.

———. "Technology, Political Economy, and Professionalization: Central Themes of the Organizational Synthesis." *Business History Review* 57 (Winter 1983): 471–93.

Goode, William J. "Encroachment, Charlatanism, and the Emerging Profession: Psychology, Sociology, and Medicine." *American Sociological Review* 25 (December 1960): 905–13.

Gordon, Spencer. "Accountants and the Securities Acts." *Journal of Accountancy* 56 (December 1933): 438–51.

———. "Liability of Public Accountants under Securities Act of 1934." *Journal of Accountancy* 58 (October 1934): 251–57.

"The Greatest Opportunity of All." *Journal of Accountancy* 55 (May 1933): 326–27.

"Great Responsibility and Great Opportunity." *Journal of Accountancy* 55 (February 1933): 82–83.

"Growth in Accountancy." *Journal of Accountancy* 23 (April 1917): 283–86.

"Growth of Accountancy." *Accountant* 57 (August 1917): 134–35.

Grundman, Otto A. "Brewery Accounting." *Journal of Accountancy* 3 (February 1907): 285–93.

Hamlin, Charles S. "The Federal Reserve Act." *Journal of Accountancy* 22 (November 1916): 329–37.

Harbeson, Robert W. "Railroads and Regulation, 1877–1916: Conspiracy or Public Interest?" *Journal of Economic History* 27 (1967): 230–42.

Hardt, Walter K. "Railway Maintenance of Way." *Journal of Accountancy* 3 (April 1907): 438–48.

Hartman, George W. "The Relative Social Prestige of Representative Medical Specialties." *Journal of Applied Psychology* (December 1936): 659–63.

Hartwell, Edward M. "The Financial Reports of Municipalities with Special Reference to the Requirement of Uniformity." In *Proceedings of the National Municipal League*, pp. 124–25. Philadelphia: National Municipal League, 1899.

Haskins, Charles W. "History of Accountancy." *Accountant* 27 (June 1901): 699–705.

Hatfield, H. R. "An Historical Defense of Bookkeeping." In *Significant Accounting Essays*, edited by Maurice Moonitz and A. C. Littleton, pp. 3–13. Englewood Cliffs, N.J.: Prentice-Hall, 1965.

Hawley, Ellis W. "Herbert Hoover, the Commerce Secretariat, and the Vision

of the Associative State." *Journal of American History* 61 (June 1974): 116–40.
————. "Three Facets of Hooverian Associationalism: Lumber, Aviation, and Movies, 1921–1930." In *Regulation in Perspective: Historical Essays*, edited by Thomas K. McCraw, pp. 95–123. Cambridge: Harvard University Press, 1981.

Hays, Samuel P. "The Upper Class Takes the Lead." In *The Progressive Era: Major Issues of Interpretation*, edited by Arthur Mann, pp. 79–83. Hinsdale, Ill.: Dryden, 1975.

"History of Accountants and Accountancy." *Accountant* 45 (July 1911): 560–62, 597–600, 640–42, 670–71, 712–14, 748–50, 780–82, 823–24, 855–57, and 901–3; 46 (January 1912): 6–8, 44–46, 80–82, 124–26, 200–201, 259–61, 308–11, 340–42, 379–82.

"A History of the Accountancy Profession." *Accountant* 21 (April 1895): 375–76.

"Holding the Accountant Responsible." *Journal of Accountancy* 28 (July 1919): 39–42.

Hunter, Joel. "Accounting Systems for Retail Merchants." *Journal of Accountancy* 24 (August 1917): 100–104.

"The Income Tax." *Journal of Accountancy* 15–16 (March, October 1913): 185–87, 307–9.

"Income Tax Amendment." *Journal of Accountancy* 19 (April 1915): 292–94.

"Income Tax Experts." *Journal of Accountancy* 27 (February 1919): 134–36.

"Injunction against National Association of Certified Public Accountants." *Journal of Accountancy* 36 (July 1923): 30–31.

"Institute Examinations." *Journal of Accountancy* 23 (February 1917): 132–33.

"The Institute of Accountants in the United States." *Accountant* 55 (November 1916): 438–42, 444–45.

"The Institute Rejects an Amendment." *Journal of Accountancy* 40 (November 1925): 355.

"Institute's Annual Meeting." *Journal of Accountancy* 62 (September 1936): 164.

"Institute's Dallas Meeting." *Certified Public Accountant* 16 (October 1936): 626–28.

Jackson, J. Hugh. "Accounting as a Profession." *Journal of Accountancy* 40 (September 1925): 161–72.

Jay, Harry M. "Consolidation—Now What?" *Certified Public Accountant* 16 (October 1936): 569–70.

Jeal, E. F. "Some Reflections on the Evolution of the Professional Practice in Great Britain." *Accountant* 96 (April 1937): 521–29.

Johnson, Harlan. "New York Stock Exchange Questionnaire." *Journal of Accountancy* 48 (July 1929): 18–26.

Jones, Charles W. "A Chronological Outline of the Development of the Firm." *Arthur Andersen Chronicle* 4 (December 1943): 9–16.

Joplin, J. Porter. "The Ethics of Accountancy." *Journal of Accountancy* 17 (March 1914): 187–96.

————. "Growing Responsibilities of the Public Accountant." *Journal of Accountancy* 28 (July 1919): 9–15.

————. "Interest Does Not Enter the Cost of Production." *Journal of Accountancy* 15 (May 1913): 334–35.

Kaufman, Burton I. "The Organizational Dimension of United States Economic Policy, 1900–1920." *Business History Review* 46 (Spring 1972): 17–44.

———. "United States Foreign Economic Policy: The Wilson Years." *Journal of American History* 57 (September 1971): 342–63.

Keller, Morton. "The Pluralist State: American Economic Regulation in Comparative Perspective." In *Regulation in Perspective: Historical Essays*, edited by Thomas K. McCraw, et al., pp. 78–85, Cambridge: Harvard University Press, 1981.

Ker, Charles. "Depreciation." In *Transactions of the Chartered Accountants Students' Societies of Edinburgh and Glasgow: A Selection of Writings, 1886–1958*, edited by Thomas A. Lee, pp. 87–112. New York: Garland Publishing, 1984.

Kester, Roy B. "Principle of Valuation as Related to the Function of the Balance Sheet." In *Early Twentieth-Century Developments in American Accounting Thought: A Preclassical School*, edited by Gary John Previts, unnumbered pages. New York: Arno Press, 1978.

———. "Standardization of the Balance Sheet." In *Early Twentieth-Century Developments in American Accounting Thought: A Preclassical School*, edited by Gary John Previts, unnumbered pages. New York: Arno Press, 1978.

Kohler, Eric L. "A Nervous Profession." *Accounting Review* 9 (December 1934): 4.

Kohler, Robert E. "Medical Reform and Biomedical Science: Biochemistry—A Case Study." In *The Therapeutic Revolution*, edited by Morris J. Vogel and Charles E. Rosenberg, pp. 27–66. Philadelphia: University of Pennsylvania Press, 1979.

Ladinsky, Jack. "Careers of Lawyers, Law Practice, and Legal Institutions." *American Sociological Review* 28 (February 1961): 47–54.

Lane, Chester T. "Cooperation with the Securities and Exchange Commission." *New York Certified Public Accountant* 8 (April 1938): 5–11.

Lee, G. A. "The Concept of Profit in British Accounting, 1760–1900." *Business History Review* 49 (Spring 1975): 6–36.

"Legislation for Accountants in the States." *Accountant* 22 (May 1896): 427, 504, 763.

Lepaulle, Pierre G. "Law Practice in France." *Columbia Law Review* 50 (November 1950): 945–58.

Leslie, Stuart W. "Charles F. Kettering and the Copper-cooled Engine." *Technology and Culture* 20 (October 1979): 752–76.

———. "Thomas Midgley and the Politics of Industrial Research." *Business History Review* 54 (Winter 1980): 480–503.

"Liability in Question." *Journal of Accountancy* 50 (August 1930): 81–85.

Lipset, Seymour Martin. "Political Cleavages in 'Developed' and 'Emerging' Politics." In *Cleavages, Ideologies, and Party Systems: Contributions to Comparative Sociology*, edited by Eric Allardt and Yrgo Littunen, pp. 21–55. Helsinki: Westermarck Society, 1964.

Littlefield, Henry M. "The Wizard of Oz: Parable on Populism." *American Quarterly* 16 (Spring 1964): 47–58.

Littleton, A. C. "Auditor Independence." *Journal of Accountancy* 59 (April 1935): 283–91.

_____. "The Development of Accounting Literature." *Publication of the American Association of University Instructors in Accounting* 9 (April 1925): 7–17.

_____. "Social Origins of Modern Accountancy." *Journal of Accountancy* 56 (October 1933): 261–70.

Lockwood, Jeremiah. "Early University Education in Accounting." *Accounting Review* 13 (June 1938): 131–44.

McCraw, Thomas K. "With the Consent of the Governed: The SEC's Formative Years." *Journal of Policy Analysis and Management* 1, no. 3 (1982): 346–70.

McCrea, Roswell C., and Roy B. Kester, "A School of Professional Accountancy." *Journal of Accountancy* 61 (February 1936): 106–17.

McLaren, Norman L. "The Influence of Federal Taxation upon Accountancy." *Journal of Accountancy* 64 (December 1937): 426–39.

McQuaid, Kim. "Corporate Liberalism in the American Business Community, 1920–1940." *Business History Review* 52 (Autumn 1978): 342–68.

Martin, Albro. "The Troubled Subject of Railroad Regulation in the Gilded Age: A Reappraisal." *Journal of American History* 61 (1974): 339–71.

Marx, Thomas G. "Technological Change and the Theory of the Firm: The American Locomotive Industry, 1900–1955." *Business History Review* 50 (Spring 1976): 1–24.

Masters, J. E. "The Accounting Profession in the United States." *Journal of Accountancy* 19 (January 1915): 349–55; 20 (November 1915): 349–55.

_____. "The Accounting Profession in the United States." *Accountant* 53 (December 1915): 724–26.

Mautz, Robert K., and Gary John Previts. "Eric Kohler: An Accounting Original." In *Eric Louis Kohler: Accounting's Man of Principles*, edited by William W. Cooper and Yuji Ijiri, pp. 20–30. Reston, Va.: Reston Publishing, 1979.

May, George O. "Accounting and Regulation." *Journal of Accountancy* 76 (October 1943): 295–301.

_____. "Influence of the Depression on the Practice of Accountancy." *Journal of Accountancy* 54 (November 1932): 336–50.

_____. "The Position of Accountants under the Securities Acts." *Journal of Accountancy* 57 (January 1934): 9–23.

_____. "Proper Treatment of Premiums and Discounts on Bonds." *Journal of Accountancy* 2 (July 1906): 32–37.

Mead, Edward S. "Established Preliminary Examinations in Law and Economics." *Journal of Accountancy* 3 (January 1907): 193–95.

Mednick, Robert, and Gary J. Previts. "The Scope of CPA Services: A View from the Perspective of a Century of Progress." *Journal of Accountancy* 163 (May 1987): 220–38.

Meyer, Balthasar H. "The Administration of Prussian Railroads." In *Annals of the American Academy of Political and Social Sciences* 10, no. 3 (Publication no. 215) (Philadelphia: American Academy of Political and Social Sciences, 1897), pp. 389–423.

Miller, Henry J. "The American Society and the American Institute." *Certified Public Accountant* 5 (December 1925): 157–62.

Miranti, Paul J. "Associationalism, Statism, and Professional Regulation: Public Accountants and the Reform of the Financial Markets, 1896–1940." *Business History Review* 60 (Autumn 1986): 438–68.

———. "Professionalism and Nativism: The Competition for Professional Licensing Legislation in New York during the 1890s." *Social Science Quarterly* 69 (June 1988): 361–80.

———. "Robert H. Montgomery: A Leader of the Profession." *CPA Journal* 56 (August 1986): 106–8.

Mixter, Charles W. "Measures of Banking Reform." *Journal of Accountancy* 5 (April 1908): 463–76; 6 (June, July 1908): 123–32, 194–203.

"A Momentous Decision." *Journal of Accountancy* 48 (August 1929): 125–27.

Montgomery, Robert H. "Accountancy Laboratory: The Connecting Link between Theory and Practice." *Journal of Accountancy* 17 (June 1914): 405–11.

———. "Professional Ethics." *Journal of Accountancy* 5 (December 1907): 94–96.

———. "Professional Standards: A Plea for Co-operation among Accountants." In *Significant Accounting Essays*, edited by Maurice Moonitz and A. C. Littleton, pp. 519–29. Englewood Cliffs, N.J.: Prentice-Hall, 1965.

———. "The Value and Recent Development of Theoretical Training for the Public Accountant." In *Early Twentieth-Century Developments in American Accounting Thought: A Preclassical School*, edited by Gary John Previts, unnumbered pages. New York: Arno Press, 1978.

Murphy, Mary E. "An Accountant in the Eighties." *Accountant* 117 (July, August 1947): 53–54, 67–68, 85–86.

———. "Notes on Accounting History." *Accounting Research* 1 (January 1950): 275–80.

———. "The Profession of Accountancy in England: The Client and the Investor." *Accounting Review* 15 (June 1940): 241–60.

———. "The Profession of Accountancy in England: The Public, the Government, the Profession." *Accounting Review* 15 (September 1940): 328–43.

———. "The Rise of Accountancy in England." *Accounting Review* 15 (March 1940): 62–73.

Musaus, William P. "What Is a CPA?" *Journal of Accountancy* 20 (December 1915): 438–50.

"National Aspects of Public Accounting." *Journal of Accountancy* 19 (January 1914): 46–50.

Nau, Carl H. "The Aims of the Institute." *Journal of Accountancy* 31 (May 1921): 321–28.

———. "The American Institute of Accountants." *Journal of Accountancy* 31 (February 1921): 103–9.

Neal, Larry. "Investment Behaviour of American Railroads." *Review of Economics and Statistics* 51 (May 1969): 126–35.

"A New Department." *Journal of Accountancy* 16 (November 1913): 373–74.

Niven, John B. "Income Tax Department." *Journal of Accountancy* 16 (November 1913): 384–407.

Parrington, Vernon Louis. "Vernon Louis Parrington Recalls the Spirit of the Age." In *The Progressives*, edited by Carl Resek, pp. 3–19. New York: Bobbs-Merrill, 1960.

Paton, William A. "The Postulates of Accounting." In *Significant Accounting Essays*, edited by Maurice Moonitz and A. C. Littleton, pp. 64–83. Englewood Cliffs, N.J.: Prentice-Hall, 1965.

Payne, Robert E. "The Effect of Recent Laws on Accountancy." *Accounting Review* 10 (March 1935): 84–95.

Peloubet, Maurice E. "Professional Societies and Professional Men." *Journal of Accountancy* 72 (October 1941): 323.

Peple, Charles H. "Registration of Accountants." *Journal of Accountancy* 23 (August 1917): 185–89.

———. "Statements of Borrowers from the Viewpoint of the Federal Reserve Bank." *Journal of Accountancy* 21 (June 1916): 410–23.

Potts, James H. "The Evolution of Municipal Accounting in the United States, 1900–1935." *Business History Review* 52 (Winter 1978): 518–36.

"A Practical Plan for Peace." *Journal of Accountancy* 19 (February 1915): 139.

"Practice before the Tax Board." *Journal of Accountancy* 38 (November 1924): 205–6.

"Preparation of Tax Returns." *Journal of Accountancy* 25 (June 1918): 447–51.

"Present Status of the Profession." *Journal of Accountancy* 1 (November 1905): 1.

"Proposed Amendments to By-Laws." *Certified Public Accountant* 17 (February 1937): 10.

"The Public Accountant in Chicago." *Accountant* 25 (April 1899): 349–50, 395.

"Public Accountant's Work." *Accountant* 17 (June 1891): 430.

Purcell, Edward A., Jr. "Ideas and Interests: Businessmen and the Interstate Commerce Act." *Journal of American History* 54 (1967): 561–78.

"Purposes of Accounting." *Journal of Accountancy* 32 (August 1938): 74–76.

"Questions of Constitutionality." *Journal of Accountancy* 41 (June 1926): 444–45.

Rand, Waldron H. "Growth of the Profession." *Journal of Accountancy* 27 (June 1919): 412–19.

Reckitt, Ernest. "History of Accountancy in the State of Illinois." *Journal of Accountancy* 69 (May 1940): 376–80.

"The Record of the American Institute of Accountants." *Accountant* 57 (December 1917): 453–54.

Reich, Leonard S. "Industrial Research and the Pursuit of Corporate Security: The Early Years of Bell Labs." *Business History Review* 54 (Winter 1980): 504–29.

———. "Irving Langmuir and the Pursuit of Science and Technology in the Corporate Environment." *Technology and Culture* 24 (April 1983): 199–221.

———. "Patents and the Struggle to Control the Radio: A Study of Big Business and the Uses of Industrial Research." *Business History Review* 51 (Summer 1971): 208–35.

Reimerth, C. H. "Historical Review of Accounting." *Certified Public Accountant* 6 (May 1926): 138–40.

"Report of the Committee on Uniform Municipal Accounting and Statistics." In *Proceedings of the National Municipal League*, p. 249. Philadelphia: National Municipal League, 1903.

Rintoul, Peter. "The Treatment in the Accounts of Joint-Stock Companies of

Depreciation in the Value of Assets and to the Duties of an Auditor Relating Thereto." In *Transactions of the Chartered Accountants Students' Societies of Edinburgh and Glasgow: A Selection of Writings, 1886–1958*, edited by Thomas A. Lee, pp. 147–68. New York: Garland Publishing, 1984.

Rose, Bernard. "Responsibility of Auditors." *Journal of Accountancy* 35 (May 1923): 335.

Rosenberry, Marvin A. "Henry Carter Adams." In *Michigan and the Cleveland Era*, edited by Earl D. Babst and Lewis Vander Velder, pp. 23–25. Ann Arbor: University of Michigan Press, 1948.

Ross, F. A. "Growth and Effect of Branch Offices." *Journal of Accountancy* 30 (October 1920): 252–61.

Ross, T. Edward. "Random Recollections of an Eventful Half Century." *Journal of Accountancy* 64 (October 1937): 256–78.

Rowe, L. S. "Public Accounting under the Proposed Municipal Program." In *Proceedings of the National Municipal League*, pp. 105–23. Philadelphia: National Municipal League, 1899.

Sanders, T. H. "Corporate Information Required by Federal Security Legislation." *New York Certified Public Accountant* 5 (April 1935): 9–22.

_____. "Recent Accounting Developments in the United States." *Accountant* 100 (April 1939): 535–44.

"Securities and Exchange Commission." *New York Certified Public Accountant* 11 (January 1941): 274–77.

"Securities and Exchange Commission Release on Independence of Public Accountants." *Journal of Accountancy* 77 (March 1944): 179–81.

Seligman, Isaac N. "Underwriting the Sale of Corporate Securities." *Journal of Accountancy* 2 (September 1906): 321–30.

Sells, E. W. "The Accountant of 1917." *Journal of Accountancy* 3 (February 1907): 297–99.

_____. "The Accounting Profession: Its Demands and Its Future." *Journal of Accountancy* 20 (November 1915): 325–33.

_____. "A Plan for International Peace." *Journal of Accountancy* 19 (February 1915): 85–96.

Servos, John W. "The Industrial Relations of Science: Chemical Engineering at MIT, 1900–1939." *Isis* 71 (December 1980): 531–49.

Shaplen, Robert. "Annals of Crime: The Metamorphosis of Philip Musica." Parts 1, 2. *New Yorker*, October 22, 29, 1955, pp. 49–50, 39–40.

"Significance of an Accountant's Certificate." *Journal of Accountancy* 41 (January 1926): 33–34.

"A Single National Organization." *Certified Public Accountant* 15 (October 1935): 604–10.

Smith, C. Aubrey. "Accounting Practice under the Securities and Exchange Commission." *Accounting Review* 10 (December 1935): 325–32.

Smith, Frank P. "Accounting Requirements of Stock Exchanges." *Accounting Review* 12 (June 1937): 145–53.

Smith, T. Savage. "The Education of Accountants: What They Ought to Learn, and How They Are to Learn It." *Accountant* 21 (December 1894): 201–4.

Sprague, Charles E. "Logismography I and Logismography II." In *Early Twen-*

tieth-Century Developments in American Accounting Thought: A Preclassical School, edited by Gary John Previts, unnumbered pages. New York: Arno Press, 1978.

"The Spread of Accountancy Legislation." *Journal of Accountancy* 16 (July 1913): 64.

Springer, D. W. "Institute-Society-Institute." *Certified Public Accountant* 16 (December 1936): 743–51.

────. "Regulatory Legislation." *Certified Public Accountant* 16 (September 1936): 522–31.

Starkey, Rodney F. "Practice under the Securities Act of 1933 and the Securities Exchange Act of 1934." *Journal of Accountancy* 58 (December 1934): 431–47.

Stempf, Victor H. "The Securities and Exchange Commission and the Accountant." *New York Certified Public Accountant* 8 (April 1938): 12–16.

Sterrett, Joseph E. "The Development of Accountancy as a Profession." *Journal of Accountancy* 7 (February 1909): 265–73.

────. "Professional Ethics." *Journal of Accountancy* 4 (October 1907): 407–31.

────. "Progress in the Accounting Profession." *Journal of Accountancy* 8 (November 1909): 11–16.

Stewart, Andrew. "Accountancy and the Regulation Bodies in the United States." *Journal of Accountancy* 65 (January 1938): 33–60.

"Stock Exchange Demands Audits of Listed Companies." *Journal of Accountancy* 55 (February 1933): 81–82.

Stocking, George W. "Franz Boas and the Founding of the American Anthropological Association." *American Anthropologist* 62 (February 1960): 1–17.

"Student's Department." *Journal of Accountancy* 17 (January 1914): 70–79.

Suffern, Edward L. "Responsibility of the Accountant." *Journal of Accountancy* 17 (March 1917): 197–202.

────. "Twenty-five Years of Accountancy." *Journal of Accountancy* 34 (September 1922): 174–81.

Suffern, Ernest F. "Are CPA Examinations Always Fair?" *Journal of Accountancy* 7 (March 1909): 384–89.

Taylor, Frederick W. "Principles of Scientific Management." *Journal of Accountancy* 12 (June, July 1911): 117–24, 181–84.

"Trend of Modern Accountancy." *Journal of Accountancy* 41 (January 1926): 1–8.

"United States Consular Reports and Chartered Accountants." *Accountant* 2 (November 1884): 521.

"United States Income Tax." *Accountant* 49 (August 1913): 152.

"University Education of Accountant Students in the United States." *Accountant* 57 (September 1917): 179–80.

"Verification of Financial Statements." *Accountant* 81 (July 1929): 115–24.

Walton, Seymour. "Inventories." *Journal of Accountancy* 17 (May 1914): 338–89.

────. "Relation of Commercial Lawyer to the CPA." *Journal of Accountancy* 7 (January 1909): 205–13.

Watson, Albert J. "Practice under the Securities Act." *Journal of Accountancy* 59 (June 1935): 434–45.

Webster, Norman E. "Congress of Accountants." *Journal of Accountancy* 78 (December 1944): 513–14.

————. "Early Movements for Accountancy Education." *Journal of Accountancy* 71 (May 1941): 441–50.

————. "The Meaning of Public Accountant." *Accounting Review* 19 (October 1944): 366–76.

Weidenhammer, Robert. "The Accountant and the Securities Acts." *Accounting Review* 8 (December 1933): 272–78.

Wildman, John R. "Appreciation from the Point of View of the Certified Public Accountant." In *Early Twentieth-Century Developments in American Accounting Thought: A Preclassical School*, edited by Gary John Previts, unnumbered pages. New York: Arno Press, 1978.

————. "Depreciation and Obsolescence As Affected by Appraisals." In *Early Twentieth-Century Developments in American Accounting Thought: A Preclassical School*, edited by Gary John Previts, unnumbered pages. New York: Arno Press, 1978.

————. "Early Instruction in Accounting." *Accounting Review* 1 (March 1926): 105–7.

Wilensky, H. L. "The Professionalization of Everyone?" *American Journal of Sociology* 70 (September 1964): 137–58.

Wilkinson, George. "The Accounting Profession in the United States." *Journal of Accountancy* 10 (September 1910): 339–47.

————. "The Genesis of the CPA Movement." *Certified Public Accountant* 8 (September, October 1928): 261–66, 297–300.

————. "Organization of the Profession in Pennsylvania." *Journal of Accountancy* 44 (September 1927): 161–69.

Dissertations

Antler, Joyce. "The Educated Woman and Professionalization: The Struggle for a New Feminine Identity, 1890–1920." Ph.D. diss., State University of New York at Stony Brook, 1977.

Ballew, Van Bennett. "Organization, Size, Technology, and Formalization in Professional Accountancy Organizations." Ph.D. diss., University of Houston, 1977.

Beardsley, Edward Henry. "Portrait of a Scientist: The Professional Career of Harry Lumen Russell." Ph.D. diss., University of Wisconsin, 1966.

Beekman, Emma E. "Life and Letters of Johns Martin Vincent, Pioneer American Professional Historian." Ph.D. diss., University of Southern California, 1954.

Bowen, Linda Carolyn Polston. "A Study of the Social Responsibility of the Accounting Profession." Ph.D. diss., Georgia State University, 1972.

Boyd, Ralph Lester. "A Study of CPA Legislation in the United States, 1896–1940." Ph.D. diss., University of Illinois, 1941.

Brown, Clifford Dean. "The Balance Sheet to Income Statement: A Study in the History of Accounting Thought." Ph.D. diss., Michigan State University, 1968.

Brown, Isadore. "The Historical Development of the Use of Ratios in Financial Statement Analysis to 1933." Ph.D. diss., Catholic University of America, 1955.

Burns, Helen Marie. "The American Banking Community and New Deal Banking Reform, 1933–1935." Ph.D. diss., New York University, 1965.

Butler, Daniel Louie. "A History of the Certified Public Accounting Profession in Louisiana." Ph.D. diss., Louisiana State University and Agricultural and Mechanical College, 1976.

Cambell, Terry Lee. "The Certified Public Accounting Profession: An Exploratory Industry Survey." Ph.D. diss., Indiana University, 1980.

Cary, Lorin Lee. "Adolph Berner: From Labor Agitator to Labor Professional." Ph.D. diss., University of Wisconsin, 1968.

Church, Robert L. "The Development of the Social Sciences as Academic Disciplines at Harvard University, 1869–1900." Ph.D. diss., Harvard University, 1965.

Churchman, John H. "Federal Regulation of Railroad Rates, 1880–1898." Ph.D. diss., University of Wisconsin, 1976.

Coffey, William James. "Government Regulations and Professional Pronouncements: A Study of the Securities and Exchange Commission and the American Institute of CPAs, 1934 through 1974." Ph.D. diss., New York University, 1976.

Cravens, Hamilton. "American Scientists and the Heredity-Environment Controversy, 1883–1940." Ph.D. diss., University of Iowa, 1969.

Cunningham, Billie Marie. "An Analysis of Variables Influencing the Outcomes of Federal Court Cases Involving Anti-Trust Action against Accountancy and Other Professions Brought under the Sherman Act." Ph.D. diss., North Texas State University, 1981.

Davis, G. C. "The Federal Trade Commission: Promise and Practice, 1900–1929." Ph.D. diss., University of Illinois, 1969.

Davis, James Wilbur. "The Development of the CPA Profession in Mississippi." Ph.D. diss., University of Mississippi, 1972.

Dickens, Marion Rachel. "The Influence of the Position of Women in Society on the Development of Nursing as a Profession In America." Ph.D. diss., University of New Mexico, 1977.

Dixon, Hollis Austen. "A Study of the Certified Public Accounting Profession in Arkansas." Ph.D. diss., University of Arkansas, 1964.

Douthit, Nathan Cranmer. "Police Professionalism 1890s–1960s: A Study of Ideas in American Policing." Ph.D. diss., University of California, Berkeley, 1974.

Esworthy, Raymond W. "A Historical View of Accounting Aspects of the Securities and Exchange Legislation of 1933 and 1934." Ph.D. diss., University of Illinois, 1944.

Frey, Ralph Wylie, III. "The Public Accounting Profession: The Impact of External Environmental Factors from 1900 [to] 1971." D.B.A. diss., University of Maryland, 1972.

Furer, Howard B. "The Public Career of William Henry Havemeyer." Ph.D. diss., New York University, 1963.

Gawalt, Gerard Wilfred. "Massachusetts Lawyers: A Historical Analysis of the Process of Professionalization, 1760–1840." Ph.D. diss., Clark University, 1969.

Geiger, Roger Lewis. "The Development of French Sociology, 1871–1905." Ph.D. diss., University of Michigan, 1972.

Gilb, Corinne L. "Self-Regulating Professions and the Public Welfare: A Case Study of the California State Bar." Ph.D. diss., Radcliffe College, 1957.

Gould, David Asher. "Policy and Pedagogues: School Reform and Teacher Professionalization in Massachusetts, 1840–1920." Ph.D. diss., Brandeis University, 1977.

Greenberg, Estelle Filker. "Pioneers of Professional Social Work: A Case Study of Professionalization, 1908–1919." Ph.D. diss., New York University, 1969.

Griess, Thomas Everett. "Dennis Hart Mahan: West Point Professor and Advocate of Military Professionalism, 1830–1871." Ph.D. diss., Duke University, 1969.

Groner, David Michael. "An Analysis of the Professional Aspects of Public Accountancy." Ph.D. diss., University of Illinois, 1977.

Grossman, David Michael. "Professors and Public Service, 1885–1925: A Chapter in the Professionalization of the Social Sciences." Ph.D. diss., Washington University, 1973.

Gurr, Charles Stephen. "Social Leadership and the Medical Profession in Ante-bellum Georgia." Ph.D. diss., University of Georgia, 1973.

Gutenberg, Jeffrey Stephen. "The Meaning of Voluntary Association Memberships of the Professional and His Firm: A Study of Professionals Employed in Certified Public Accounting Firms." Ph.D. diss., University of Southern California, 1978.

Hadley, David Warren. "The Growth of the London Musical Society in the Early Nineteenth Century: Studies in the History of a Profession, 1800–1824." Ph.D. diss., Harvard University, 1972.

Hinsley, Curtis Mathew. "The Development of a Professional Anthropology in Washington, D.C., 1846–1903." Ph.D. diss., University of Wisconsin, 1976.

Hobson, Wayne Karl. "The American Legal Profession and the Organizational Society, 1890–1930." Ph.D. diss., Stanford University, 1977.

Hooper, Hubert Paul, Jr. "A Study of the Evolution of the Legal Liability of Accountants, with Implications for the Future of the Profession." Ph.D. diss., Tulane University, 1976.

Hummer, Patricia Myles. "The Decade of Elusive Promise: Professional Women in the United States, 1920–1930." Ph.D. diss., Duke University, 1976.

Hunthausen, John Mathew. "A History of the CPA Profession in Colorado." Ph.D. diss., University of Missouri, 1974.

Jennings, Robert Martin. "George S. Olive and Company: A History of a Public Accounting Firm." Ph.D. diss., Indiana University, 1959.

Jordan, Kevin Ernest. "Ideology and the Coming of Professionalism: American Urban Police in the 1920s and 1930s." Ph.D. diss., Rutgers University, 1973.

Kaplan, Barry Jerome. "Metropolitization: The Greater New York City Charter of 1897." Ph.D. diss., State University of New York at Buffalo, 1975.

Kaufman, Martin. "Homeopathy and the American Medical Profession, 1820–1960." Ph.D. diss., Tulane University, 1969.

Kwik, Robert Julius. "The Function of Applied Science and the Mechanical Library during the Formation of the Profession of Mechanical Engineering, as Exemplified in the Career of Robert Henry Thurston, 1839–1903." Ph.D. diss., University of Pennsylvania, 1974.

Lavery, Dennis Sherman. "John Gibbon and the Old Army: Portrait of a Professional Soldier, 1827–1896." Ph.D. diss., Pennsylvania State University, 1974.

Lemeron, Everett Gordon. "A Study of the Uniformity of Ethical Standards and Their Enforcement in the Accounting Profession in the U.S." Ph.D. diss., University of Alabama, 1972.

Levine, Jerald Elliot. "Police, Parties, and Polity: The Bureaucratization, Unionization, and Professionalization of the New York City Police, 1870–1917." Ph.D. diss., University of Wisconsin, 1971.

Lewis, Eldon Curtis. "A Study of the Development of the Certified Public Accounting Profession in Kansas." Ph.D. diss., University of Missouri, 1967.

McCarthy, Michael Patrick. "Businessmen and Professionals in Municipal Reform: The Chicago Experience, 1887–1920." Ph.D. diss., Northwestern University, 1970.

McKirdy, Charles Robert. "Lawyers in Crisis: The Massachusetts Legal Profession, 1760–1790." Ph.D. diss., Northwestern University, 1969.

Marchiafava, Louis J. "Institutional and Legal Aspects of the Growth of Professional Urban Police Service: The Houston Experience, 1878–1948." Ph.D. diss., Rice University, 1976.

Mathews, Frederick Hamilton. "Robert E. Park and the Development of American Sociology." Ph.D. diss., Harvard University, 1973.

Mattingly, Paul Harvey. "Professional Strategies and New England Educators, 1825–1960." Ph.D. diss., University of Wisconsin, 1968.

Maxwell, William Joseph. "Francis Kellor in the Progressive Era: A Case Study in the Professionalization of Reform." Ed.D. diss., Columbia University, 1968.

Merino, Barbara D. "The Professionalization of Public Accounting in America: A Comparative Analysis of the Contributions of Selected Practitioners, 1900–1925." Ph.D. diss., University of Alabama, 1975.

Miller, Larry Carl. "Dimensions of Mugwump Thought, 1880–1920: Sons of Massachusetts Abolitionists as Professional Pioneers." Ph.D. diss., Northwestern University, 1969.

Miranti, Paul J., Jr. "From Conflict to Consensus: The American Institute of Accountants and the Professionalization of Public Accountancy, 1886–1940." Ph.D. diss., Johns Hopkins University, 1985.

Mullins, Jack Simpson. "The Sugar Trust: Henry O. Havemeyer and the American Sugar Refining Company." Ph.D. diss., University of South Carolina, 1964.

Napoli, Donald Seymer. "The Architects of Adjustment: The Practice and Professionalization of American Psychology, 1920–1945." Ph.D. diss., University of California, Davis, 1975.

Nenninger, Timothy K. "The Fort Leavenworth Schools: Post-Graduate Military Education and Professionalization in the United States Army (1880–1920)." Ph.D. diss., University of Wisconsin, 1974.

Noble, David Franklin. "Science and Technology in the Corporate Search for Order: American Engineers and Social Reform, 1900–1929." Ph.D. diss., University of Rochester, 1974.

O'Hara, Leo James. "An Emerging Profession: Philadelphia Medicine, 1860–1900." Ph.D. diss., University of Pennsylvania, 1976.

Pitzer, Donald Elden. "Professional Revivalism in Nineteenth-Century Ohio." Ph.D. diss., Ohio State University, 1966.

Previts, Gary John. "A Critical Evaluation of Comparative Financial Accounting Thought in America, 1900 to 1920." Ph.D. diss., University of Florida, 1972.

Ratner, Sidney. "A Political and Social History of Federal Taxation, 1789–1913, with Special Reference to the Income Tax and Inheritance Tax." Ph.D. diss., Columbia University, 1942.

Reid, Robert Louis. "The Professionalization of Public School Teachers: The Chicago Experience, 1895–1920." Ph.D. diss., Northwestern University, 1968.

Riess, Steven Allen. "Professional Baseball and American Culture in the Progressive Era: Myths and Realities, with Special Emphasis on Chicago, Atlanta, and New York." Ph.D. diss., University of Chicago, 1974.

Ritchie, Donald Arthur. "James M. Landis: New Deal, Fair Deal, and New Frontier Administrator." Ph.D. diss., University of Maryland, 1975.

Roberts, Alfred Robert. "Robert H. Montgomery: A Pioneer of American Accounting." Ph.D. diss., University of Alabama, 1971.

Schiesl, Martin John. "The Politics of Efficiency: Municipal Reform in the Progressive Era, 1880–1920." Ph.D. diss., State University of New York at Buffalo, 1972.

Skousen, Clifford Richard. "The Accounting Profession and Public Service Activities." Ph.D. diss., Golden Gate University, 1979.

Smith, Alan McKinley. "Virginia Lawyers, 1680–1776: The Birth of an American Profession." Ph.D. diss., Johns Hopkins University, 1967.

Smykay, Edward Walter. "The National Association of Railroad and Utility Commissioners as the Originators and Promoters of Public Policy for Public Utilities." Ph.D. diss., University of Wisconsin, 1955.

Spiessl, Ronald William. "Professional Associations and State Licensing Laws: The Case of the CPAs and Social Workers." Ph.D. diss., Temple University, 1980.

Sussman, David George. "From Yellow Fever to Cholera: A Study of French Government Policy, Medical Professionalism, and Popular Movements in the Epidemic Crises of the Restoration and July Monarchy." Ph.D. diss., Yale University, 1971.

Van De Wetering, Maxine Schoor. "The New England Clergy and the Development of Scientific Professionalism." Ph.D. diss., University of Washington, 1970.

Walker, Weldon Hobson. "The Development of the CPA Profession in Tennessee." Ph.D. diss., University of Missouri, 1968.

Walsh, Mary Roth. "Sexual Barriers in the Medical Profession: A Case Study of Women Physicians, 1835–1973." Ph.D. diss., Boston University, 1974.

Williams, Sarah Elizabeth. "William Dunlap and the Professionalization of the Arts in the Early Republic." Ph.D. diss., Brown University, 1974.

Woods, Joseph Gerald. "The Progressives and the Police: Urban Reform and the Professionalization of the Los Angeles Police." Ph.D. diss., University of California, Los Angeles, 1973.

Wright, William Eugene. "Comparison of Accountancy with the Legal, Architectural, and Medical Professions." Ph.D. diss., University of Texas at Austin, 1956.

Zimmerman, Vernon Kenneth. "British Backgrounds of American Accountancy." Ph.D. diss., University of Illinois, 1954.

Index

Abbott, Andrew, 181
Aberdeen, Scotland: chartered accountants' institute, 30
Accountics, 39
Accounting: standardization of at Interstate Commerce Commission, 26, 32, 71, 89–93, 135, 185–87; differences in outlook about the nature of knowledge in, 27, 35–39; and chartered accountants, 30–31; and state insurance regulation, 71; for federal income tax regulation, 98; Federal Trade Commission proposals, 107–10, 135, 186–87; deficiencies during 1920s, 127–30, 132–36; efforts at reform before Great Crash, 140–42; and Securities and Exchange Commission, 152–53, 174, 186–88; Accounting Series Releases, 174; Committee on Accounting Procedure, 174–75
"Accounting for Investors" (Hoxsey), 142
Accounting Research Bulletins (ARBs), 174–75
Accounting Review, 134–36, 157, 171
Accounting Series Releases (ASRs), 158, 174, 176
Acheson, Dean, 149
Adams, Henry Carter, 32, 83, 89–93, 141, 185
Adams, Thomas S., 118, 131
Advisory Tax Board, 116, 131
Agricultural Assistance Agency (AAA), 161
Albany, New York, 45, 50, 55, 58, 66–67
Albion College, 119

"Algebra of Accounts" (Sprague), 38
Allen, Frank, 34
Allied powers, 113–14
American Academy of Political and Social Sciences, 77
American Accountants' Manual (Broaker), 57
American Accounting Association (AAA), 156–57; competition with American Institute of Accountants in standardizing financial accounting, 171–72
American Association of Public Accountants (AAPA), 13, 26, 129, 170; emulates chartered accountants, 29–33; formation, 29–35; rivalry with New York Institute, 35–36; and professional education, 40–42; competition with New York State Society of Certified Public Accountants, 57–58, 59–60; and Federation of State Societies of Public Accountants in the United States of America, 62–65, 68; benefits of federal structure, 71–72; definition of professional values, 73–74; and *Journal of Accountancy*, 74–79; and annual meeting, 82–85; in Armstrong life insurance investigation, 88; and railroad reform, 89–94; and Keep Commission, 94–96; and corporate income tax, 96–98; and progressive reform, 98–99; and American Institute of Accountants, 104; and Federal Reserve Board's zone expert plan, 108–9; and Federal Trade Commission's uniform accounting, 108–10; elite

members' dissatisfaction with direction of professionalization program, 110–13; role in preparedness movement, 113; identification of elite members with Allied cause, 113–14; reorganization into American Institute of Accountants, 115–16

American Bankers Association, 133

American Bar Association (ABA), 13, 18, 118, 133, 183

American Engineering Council, 18

American Institute of Accountants (AIA), 3, 104–5, 145–46, 166–67, 173; fiftieth anniversary, 1–6; leaders' backgrounds, 2; relationship to American Institute of Certified Public Accountants, 7; relationship to American Association of Public Accountants, 26, 103; program of professionalization, 105; formation, 115–16; emulates example of chartered accountants, 115–16, 123; leaders' service in World War I, 116; extension of code of professional ethics, 117–19; competition with American Society of Certified Public Accountants, 120; introduces national certification examination, 120–24; seeks congressional charter, 121; challenges National Association of Certified Public Accountants, 122; builds contacts with educators, 124–27; problems in financial accounting, 128–30, 132–33; and tax accounting, 130–32; educators' criticisms of financial accounting, 134–37; and auditor's reports, 137–40; and efforts to reform financial market governance prior to Great Crash, 140–42; and emergence of Securities Acts, 147–55; pressure for professional reunification, 155–56; image as source of authority in financial accounting challenged, 156–59, 171–72; details basis of merger with American Society of Certified Public Accountants, 168–70; merger with American Society of Certified Public Accountants, 172–73; begins to standardize financial accounting, 173–75; begins to standardize auditing, 175–76; amends code of ethics to address auditor independence, 176–77; assessment of strategies and structures for ordering professional affairs, 179–84

American Institute of Biology, 122

American Institute of Certified Public Accountants (AICPA), 7

American Medical Association (AMA), 13, 18, 62

American Society of Certified Public Accountants (ASCPA), 1–2, 124, 135, 145, 156–58, 166, 171; unifies local practitioners during 1920s, 106, 120; committed to defending state licensing, 120–22; merger with American Institute of Accountants, 168–71, 172–73; potential accounting research alliance with American Association of Accountants, 171

American Society of Civil Engineers, 13

American Society of Mechanical Engineers, 13, 29

American Sugar Refining Company, 36

American University of Commerce, 124

America's Founders and Defenders, 43

Anarchism, 144

Andersen, Arthur, 124

Andersen, Arthur, and Company, 174

Andrews, Frank B., 174

Angevine, Fred G., 118

Apprenticeships, 31–32, 41–42

"Approved Methods of Preparing Balance Sheet Statements" (Scobie), 110
Arbuckle Brothers Company, 44
Armistead, George A., 170
Armstrong Committee investigation (New York), 66–67, 87–89, 97
Ashman, Lewis, 171
Ashman, Reedy and Company, 171
Associationalism, 11–21, 183–84; autonomous, 16–19, 103–27; federative, 14–17; countervailing, 19–21, 143–77 passim, 184–91 passim
Association of Certified Public Accountant Examiners (ACPAE), 121
Association of Governmental Accountants, 96
AT&T, 167
Atlantic City, New Jersey, 92–93
Atlantic Monthly, 137
Auditing: of municipal governments, 37; and merger boom, 49; railroads and English style, 92–93; under Federal Reserve Board plan, 108–9; and deficiencies in reports during 1920s, 137–40; reports under Securities Acts, 153–55; and McKesson Robbins case, 175–77; standardization by American Institute of Accountants, 176–77
Augusta, Georgia, 158
Australia, 3
Autocracy, 44
Awakening of American Business (Hurley), 109

Bacteriologists, 16
Bacteriology, 83
Bailey, George D., 174
Bankers' Trust Company, 138
Bank of England, 113
Bankruptcy Act (1831), 30
Barrow, Wade, and Guthrie, 57
Baruch, Bernard, 148, 163; and New Deal, 160–62; opposes undistributed earnings tax, 164–65; conception of associationalism, 167
Bauer, John, 134
Baum, L. Frank, 178
Bay Colony (Massachusetts), 44
Berle, Adolf A., 4, 140–41, 148
Berlin, University of, 32
Biochemists, 9
Biology, 9
Birdseye, Clarence F., 57, 64
Birmingham, University of, 80
Blough, Carman G., 153, 158, 171, 174
Blyth, Lester W., 119
Board of Tax Appeals, 98
Board of Trade, 30
Bonbright, James C., 141
"Boobocracy," 13
Boston, Massachusetts, 123, 172
Boston University, 124
Broad Street Club, 154
Bradley, Daniel, 53–54
Brandeis, Louis D., 77, 107; and Federal Trade Commission, 108–9
Britain, 44–45, 64, 115, 123, 164; status of accounting in, 74–75; accounting education in, 78; investment in United States, 113; professional forms in accounting contrasted with those in United States, 179–84. *See also* Chartered accountants
British Ministry of Information, 114
Broad, Samuel J., 176
Broads, Patterson (firm), 33
Broaker, Frank, 34, 40–41, 46, 50, 55, 57–58, 64, 122
Brooklyn, New York, 37, 54
Brooklyn Polytechnic Institute, 36
Bryan, William Jennings, 55
Bureau of Corporations, 71, 95, 107
Bureau of Economic Research. *See* Harvard University
Bureau of Public Affairs, 120
Butler, Nicholas Murray, 55
Butterfield and Company, 36

California, University of, 81; at
Berkeley, 157
California Society of Certified Public
Accountants, 115
Calvert, Monte A., 12
Cambridge University, 61; Kings
College, 74
Campbell, William B., 138
Canada, 3, 116, 163
Cardozo, Benjamin, 140
Carey, John Lansing, 3, 125
Carleton College, 126
Carnegie Foundation, 122
Carter, Arthur H., 147, 149, 170
Castenholz, William B., 119, 123, 125
Catchings, Waddill, 141
Celtic faction, 64
Census Bureau, 71
Central Bureau of Planning and Sta-
tistics, 157
Central Georgia Railroad Company,
36
Central powers, 114
Certifying examinations, 13, 15, 18;
by New York Institute of Ac-
counts, 45–46; pioneered by New
York State for public accountants,
56–58; criticisms of state-devel-
oped examinations prior to World
War I, 111–12; American Institute
of Accountants uniform national
certified public accounting examination, 120–24
Chapman, Richard M., 34, 46, 50
Chartered accountants, 46, 64; acceptance in America, 13, 27; early
history in Britain, 28–32; services
of, 30–31; social backgrounds, 31–
32; beliefs about nature of accounting knowledge, 39; and apprenticeship training, 42; as model
for licensing in New York State,
53; and licensing in Illinois, 61–62;
influence on American professional values, 73–75, 77–79, 83–85;
as model for American Institute of

Accountants' program, 106, 122,
179–80
Chase, Harvey S., 97
Chase, Stuart, 97
Chemical engineers, 9
Chemistry, 9, 83, 126
Chesapeake and Western Railroad
Company, 36
Chicago, Illinois, 29, 33, 49, 171, 174
Chicago, University of, 9, 81, 124,
126, 171
Chiropractic medicine, 15
Choate, Joseph H., 54
Church, George H., 40
Cincinnati, Ohio, 29
Circular Thirteen, 108–9
City College of New York, 40, 126
Civil engineering, 18
Civil War, 44
Clader, Will A., 169, 173
Cleveland, Grover A., administra-
tion, 36
Cleveland, Ohio, 117–18, 123
Cleveland Democrats, 51–52
Clients: of chartered accountants,
30–31; accountants and protection
of, 90–91, 93–94; affect recruit-
ment patterns, 125; intermediation
on behalf of, 128; and problem of
accounting standardization, 135–
36, 161; and influence in promot-
ing professional reunification,
165–66
Cohen, Benjamin V., 150
College of Accounts, 50–52
Collins, Clem W., 174
Columbia University, 40, 42, 82, 141,
171; Graduate School of Business
Administration, 2, 124; Law
School, 140
Commerce, Accounts, and Finance, 39,
75
Committee of Fourteen, 53
Committee on Accounting Procedure, 174
Committee on Accounting Research

and Education, 135
Committee on Auditing Procedure, 176–77
Committee on Cooperation with the Stock Exchange, 170, 173
Committee on Corporate Relations, 140
Committee on Cost Accounting, 132
Committee on Department Methods of Government, 94–96. *See also* Keep Commission
Committee on Education, 80, 124–25
Committee on Enrollment and Disbarment, 118
Committee on Federal Legislation, 82, 97, 110
Committee on Federal Recognition, 97
Committee on Federal Regulation, 97
Committee on Interstate Commerce Commission, 97
Committee on Legislation, 97
Committee on Procedure, 133
Committee on Professional Ethics, 118
Committee on Relations with Credit Men, 110
Committee on Relations with Outside Organizations, 168
Committee on Standard Schedules for Uniform Reports of Municipal Industries and Public Service Corporations, 97
Committee on Terminology, 129
Committee on the Revenue Act, 163
Committee on the Stock List, 142
Commodore Hotel (New York), 156
Communism, 4, 21
Companies Act of 1900, 30
"Comparative Value of Personal Reputation and Conferred Degrees" (Nau), 121
Conant, Leonard H., 59–60, 63
Conant and Grant, 59–60
Concordia discors, 20

Confederacy, 45
Congress, United States, 130, 147–55, 161
Congress of Accountants, 65, 82
Consensus formation, 27; and professionalization, 10–15 passim; through creation of federal structures in accountancy, 62–68; by shaping accountants' self-image, 73–85; during New Deal, 166–77, 180–84
Constructive fraud, 140
Controllers' Institute, 134
Cook, H. R. M., 41
Cook, Nathan, and Lehman, 154, 170
Cooley, Thomas M., 32
Corcoran, Thomas G., 150
Corporate-liberal historical interpretation. *See* Professions: schools of historical interpretation
Corporate Profits as Shown by Audit Reports (Paton), 125
Coster, Donald F., 176
Cost of service, 90
Council of American Institute of Accountants, 117, 125, 133, 166; and American Society of Certified Public Accountants merger debate, 168–69
Covington, J. Harry, 122, 149
Covington and Rublee, 122
CPA movement, 48–68 passim
Craig v. Anyon, 139
Cravath, de Gersdorff, Swaine, and Wood, 154, 163
Cravath, Henderson, and de Gersdorff, 113, 118, 131
"Crime Tendency, The," 120

Dalhousie University, 163
Dallas, Texas, 173
Dalton, Henry G., 141
Davies, Joseph E., 108–9
Davies, W. Sanders, 57, 115–16
Dawes Reparation Committee, 118

Dean, Arthur H., 170
Delano, Frederic, 108
Deloitte, Dever, Griffiths, and Company, 33
Deloitte, Plender, and Griffiths, 67, 88, 95
Democratic party, 44, 52, 54, 107, 149
Denver, Colorado, 174
Department of Commerce, 17, 71, 107; Advisory and Planning Council, 166–67
Depew, Chauncey M., 43, 51, 66
Dewey, Mevil, 46; and College of Accounts, 50–52; nativism of, 51; and CPA licensing, 54–56; resignation from office, 66–67
Dewey decimal system, 50
Dickinson, Arthur Lowes, 57–58, 112, 179; and Illinois Society of Public Accountants, 60; and Federation of State Societies of Public Accountants in the United States of America, 67–68; as promoter of professional values, 73–77, 82–83; in insurance reform, 88; in railroad reform, 91–92; and Keep Commission, 95
Dickinson, Lowes, 74
District of Columbia, 122. See also Washington, D.C.
Doane, William Croswell, 51, 66
Dockery, Alexander M., 36
Dockery Commission, 36, 95
Draper, Andrew Sloan, 66
Due diligence requirement: under British companies acts, 150; under Securities Act of 1933, 151. See also Companies Act of 1900; Securities Act of 1933

"Earned surplus" study, 132–33
Eclectic medicine, 15
Economic concentration, 27–28
Economic regulation: accountants and associational governance, 26, 46–47; Interstate Commerce Commission as prototype of state regulation, 26, 32, 47, 89–94, 184–86; accountants and state life insurance industry regulation, 87–89; accountants and railroad regulation, 89–94; accountants and tax regulation, 96–97; accountants and integrated plan of Federal Reserve Board and Federal Trade Commission, 106–10, 187; weaknesses in associational governance during 1920s, 128–40 passim; proposed revision of structure of associational governance for financial markets, 140–42; impacts of Securities Acts, 147–55; revival of role for associational governance in conjunction with Securities and Exchange Commission, 173–77; accountants and national executive state, 184–89
Economics, 9, 126, 136
Economics Club of New York, 77
Economists, 15
Edgeworth, Francis Y., 39
Edinburgh, Scotland: chartered accountants' institute, 30
Education, 14, 27, 183; professionalization and university, 9, 12, 18; early patterns of collegiate accounting, 40–43; British apprenticeship model of, 41; failure of College of Accounts, 50–52; British collegiate accounting, 80; relative status in American universities of accounting, 80; Harvard and Wharton models of business, 80–82; and American Institute of Accountants during 1920s, 123–27; and recruitment into national public accounting firms, 125–27; formation of American Association of University Instructors of Accounting, 134–35; and problem of standardizing financial accounting, 134–37, 156–57, 174; formation of

American Accounting Association, 156–57

Edwards, Jackson, and Browning, 74

Electrical engineering, 18

Elkins, Stephen B., 91

Elwell, Fayette H., 134

Emerald City, 178

Emerson, Ralph Waldo, 36–37, 51

Encroachment: problem of professional, 4–5, 11, 19–20; government and threat to accountancy in 1916, 103, 108–10; educators threaten to intervene in financial accounting standardization, 134–37, 171–72; and government threat to accountancy during New Deal, 146–53; 173–77

Engel, Ernst, 32

Engineering profession, 6; changing educational patterns, 12; role in progressive reform, 15; affects of World War I and 1920s, 16–17; and New Deal, 19; in competition with accountants, 32

Equitable Life Assurance Society, 67, 83, 88

Ernst, A. C., 114, 118–19, 123

Ernst, T. C., 118

Ernst and Ernst, 118, 147, 174

Ethics: professional control and codes of, 16, 18; guidance to accountants in *Journal of Accountancy*, 77–79; practitioner independence in auditing and, 93, 137–40, 153; American Institute of Accountants' extension of code of, 117–19; negative reaction to market control implications of ethics extension, 119–20; McKesson Robbins case and new requirements for auditor independence, 176–77

Europe, 3, 27, 34, 36, 49, 113

Everybody's Magazine, 67

"Examinations of Financial Statements by Independent Public Accountants," 175

"Examinations of Financial Statements by Public Accountants," 155

Executive Committee of American Association of Public Accountants, 112

Executive Committee of American Institute of Accountants, 119, 124, 172–73; and American Society of Certified Public Accountants merger debate, 168–70

"Extensions of Auditing Procedures," 176

Fackler, David P., 40

Factionalism: between New York Institute of Accounts and American Association of Public Accountants, 29–47, 50–56; between New York State Society of Certified Public Accountants and American Association of Public Accountants, 56–68; between American Institute of Accountants and American Society of Certified Public Accountants, 111–20, 123–24, 155–57, 159, 166–77; between American Institute of Accountants and National Association of Certified Public Accountants, 122; between American Institute of Accountants and American Accounting Association and American Association of University Instuctors in Accounting, 134–36, 156–57, 159, 171–72, 174

Fairfield, Connecticut, 1

Fascism, 4, 21

Fedde, A. S., 174

Federal excise tax, 77

Federal income tax, 77, 87; and role of American Association of Public Accountants, 96–98

Federal Reserve Board (FRB), 103, 129, 153–54, 175; and New Freedom, 106–7; and zone expert plan, 108

"Federal Tax Simplification," 120

Federal Trade Commission (FTC), 17, 82, 103, 129, 132, 137; and New Freedom, 107–8; and uniform accounting, 107–10; and Securities Acts, 152–53
Federation of State Societies of Public Accountants in the United States of America, 49; early unity efforts, 62–64; plans stalemated, 64–65; merger into American Association of Public Accountants, 68
Fenian Brotherhood, 45
Fernald, Henry B., 133
Financial Executives' Institute, 134
Financial markets, governance of, 140–42, 146–53, 173–77, 184–89
Fire Insurance Association, 34
Fischer, Emil S., 3
Fitzgerald, E. L., 45
Fitzgerald, F. Scott, 126
Forbes, John F., 79, 156, 169–70
Ford, Henry, 114
Forest Service, 95
France, 83, 163
Francis, John, 41
Frankfurter, Felix, 150
Franklin and Marshall College, 126

Gage, Lyman J., 77
Galambos, Louis, 17
Garfield, James R., 95
Gay, Edmund F., 125, 140, 156–57, 163; and Harvard Business School curriculum, 81; and Committee on Federal Legislation, 82; and Harvard Bureau of Economic Research, 82
Geological Survey, 95
George Washington University, 141
German-Americans, 114, 123
Germany, 40, 83, 163
Gerry, Peter G., 165
Gethsemane, 6
Gettysburg, Battle of, 44
Gifford, Walter P., 167
Gilbert, Seymour Parker, 118, 131

Glasgow, Scotland: chartered accountants' institute, 30
Goldman, Sachs and Company, 141, 163
Gore, Edward E., 119, 133
Gottesberger, Francis, 58
Great Depression, 19–21, 142, 173, 177
Greek language, 126
Greer, Howard C., 171
Grey, David L., 132
Gross negligence, 140
Gulf Oil Company, 162
Guthrie, Edwin, 33

Hall, James, 168
Halle, University of, 40–41
Hamilton College, 126
Harding, Warren G., 131
Harney, Henry, 45, 58
Harriman, Edward H., 94, 107, 136
Harvard Business School. See Harvard University
Harvard University, 9, 124, 126, 141, 150, 171, 174; Business School, 80–82, 153, 156; Bureau of Economic Research, 82
Haskins, Charles Waldo, 73, 75, 79, 116, 178–79; background of, 36–37; and science of accounts, 37–39; and formation of School of Commerce, Accounts, and Finance at New York University, 42–43; involvement in patriotic associations, 43–44; and College of Accounts, 50–51; and CPA licensing in New York, 54–56; as CPA examiner, 57; at New York University, 58; founder of New York State Society of Certified Public Accountants, 58; draws closer to American Association of Public Accountants, 59–60; role in Federation of State Societies of Public Accountants in the United States of America, 62
Haskins and Sells, 63, 67, 79, 88, 95,

116, 147, 149, 170
Haskins and Sells Foundation, 157
Hatfield, Henry Rand, 157, 172
Havemeyer, Albert, 36
Havemeyer, Henrietta, 36
Havemeyer, Henry O., 44
Havemeyer, James F., 42
Havemeyer, William F., 36
Havemeyer family, 44, 51
Hawaiian Islands, 45
Healy, Robert M., 153–54
Hecht, Charles, 119, 123
Heins, John, 2, 29, 41
Henderson, Alexander I., 170
Hepburn Act (1906), 87, 89
Hill, David B., 52
Historians, 16
History, 9
Hitchcock, Frank H., 95
Hobart College, 126
Hoboken, New Jersey, 34
Home economics, 56
Homeopathy, 15
Hoover, Herbert, 116; administration, 132
Hopkins, Selden R., 44–45
Horne, Henry A., 174
Hosmer, W. Arnold, 174
Hourigan, John E., 45
House Committee on Interstate Commerce, 148
House Ways and Means Subcommittee, 130
Hoxsey, J. M. B., 142
Hughes, Charles Evans, 67, 87
Hughes, Charles L., 124
Hughes, Rupert S., 57
Hull, Cordell, 130
Humanities, 9
Hundred Days, 146
Hunt, Bishop Carlton, 163
Huntington, Charles C., 134
Hurdman, Frederick H., 168–70
Hurley, Edwin H., 108–9

Illinois, 119, 123; licensing legislation in, 49, 61–62, 111

Illinois, University of, 66, 81, 174
Illinois Society of Certified Public Accountants (ISCPA), 75, 171
Illinois Society of Public Accountants (ISPA), 61–62
Images of professionalism, 71–85
Immigration: and professionalization, 9, 13; and professionalization of accounting, 27, 34–35, 84–85, 112, 126–27, 136, 179–80
Industrialization: and professionalization, 9; and rise of public accountancy, 25, 30–31, 83–84, 136
Institute of Accountants in the United States of America, 116
Institute of Chartered Accountants in America, 122
Institute of Chartered Accountants in England and Wales, 30–31, 50, 53
Insull Companies, 176
Inter-Allied Purchasing Commission, 113
Inter-Allied Transactions Committee, 116
Intermediation and accountancy, 129–30, 153; responsibilities more sharply defined during New Deal, 147–55
Internal Revenue Service (IRS), 98, 118, 122, 129; and standardization of tax accounting, 130–32
International-comparative historical interpretation. See Professions: schools of historical interpretation
International Congress of Arts and Sciences, 65. See also Congress of Accountants
Interstate Commerce Act (1887), 33
Interstate Commerce Commission (ICC), 17, 26, 32, 47, 76, 98, 137, 141, 152; and self-executory regulation, 89–91; and public accountants, 91–94
Investment Bankers Association of America, 158
Ireland, 45

Irish Catholics, 51
Iron Age, 39
Isthmian Canal Commission, 95
Italian government, 38

Jackson, Andrew, 106
Jackson, J. Hugh, 124
James, Edmund J., 40–41, 80–81
Jersey City, New Jersey, 124
Jews: in business and professions, 51, 112; and anti-Semitism, 67, 126–27, 169–70. *See also* Immigration; Nativism
Johns Hopkins University, 9, 32
Johnson, Hugh L., 3, 167
Johnson, Joseph French, 42, 75, 77, 112; on status of accounting educators, 80
Jones and Caesar, 64. *See also* Price Waterhouse and Company
Joplin, J. Porter, 97
Journal of Accountancy, 112, 114; and technical guidance, 75–77; and ethical guidance, 77–79; and professional certification, 79–82; and national tax policies, 131; and standardization of financial accounting, 133

Kansas, University of, 81
Keep, Charles H., 95
Keep Commission, 85, 95–96. *See also* Committee on Department Methods of Government
Kelley, Nicholas, 141
Kelly, James M., 45
Kennedy, Joseph P., 153–54, 164
Kester, Roy B., 172, 174
Keynes, John Maynard, 162
Keynes, John Neville, 74
Kings College. *See* Cambridge University
Kittredge, Anson O., 39, 42, 58, 73
Knapp, Martin A., 91
Kohler, Eric L., 124, 134–36, 157, 171–72, 174

Krueger and Toll, 147, 176
Kuhn Loeb and Company, 34, 83

Lafrentz, Ferdinand W., 60, 66
Lamont, Thomas C., 114
Landell v. Lybrand, 139
Landis, James M., 150, 158, 174
Languages, modern, 126
LaSalle Extension Institute, 125
Last Tycoon, The, 126
Latin America, 45
Latin language, 126
Law: profession of, 6, 31, 47, 93, 98, 113, 125; basis for elite status, 12; changing educational patterns, 12; select federal structures for ordering professional affairs, 14; role in progressive reform, 15; affects of World War I and 1920s, 16–17; licensing in New York State, 53; nature of specialized knowledge, 129; concerned about accountants' function, 130; experience in professionalization compared to accounting and medicine, 179–84
Leffingwell, Russell C., 131
Legal liabilities of accountants, during 1920s, 139–40; under Securities Act of 1933, 148–51; under Securites Act of 1934, 151–53
Lexow bill, 54
Licensing, 6, 13; as part of program of professionalization, 11, 27–28, 183–84; model professional laws, 14, 111, 183–84; during 1920s, 18, 111; for accountancy in New York State, 47–48, 52–56; spread of requirements in accounting to other states, 48–49; in law and medicine in New York State, 47–48, 53; in Illinois and beginnings of interstate reciprocity, 61–62; Federation of State Societies of Public Accountants in the United States of America as a promoter of state licensing for accounting, 62–63; re-

gional differences in, 111; American Institute of Accountants and uniform examination for, 120–25; failure of National Association of Certified Public Accountants' program, 122; commitment of American Society of Certified Public Accountants to state licensing, 123–24

Literature, 126

Little Round Top, Battle of. *See* Gettysburg, Battle of

Littleton, A. C., 174

Liverpool, England: charter accountants' institute, 29

Local practitioners: concern about proposed use of ethics code to order professional affairs, 77–79; alienated by aspects of American Association of Public Accountants' program, 105–6, 111–12, 117–20; support American Society of Certified Public Accountants, 123–24; drawn back to American Institute of Accountants during Great Depression, 166–73, 180–83

Lodge, Henry Cabot, 107

London, England, 62, 67; chartered accountants' institute, 29

London, University of, 80

London Stock Exchange, 30, 34, 59

Loomis, John R., 59, 66, 95

Loomis, Suffern, and Fernald, 133

Los Angeles, California, 145

Louisiana Purchase Exposition, 65. *See also* Congress of Accountants

Lovelock, Whittin, and Dickinson, 74

Low, Seth, 34

Ludlam, Charles S., 65, 116

Lybrand, Ross Brothers, and Montgomery, 2, 63, 110

MacAdoo, William G., 131

MacCracken, John H., 42

McKesson Robbins Company, 175–77

McKinley, William B., 55

McKinsey, James O., 124

MacRae, Farquhar, 46

Madden, John T., 124

Mahoneytown, Pennsylvania, 2

Main, Charles W., 119

Main Street and Wall Street (Ripley), 137

Managerial innovation and professionalization, 9, 128

Manchester, England, 33, 62; chartered accountants' institute, 29

Manchester, University of, 80

Manhattan, New York, 36–38, 54

Manhattan Trust Company, 36

Manning, Horace, 119

Manual of Theoretical Training in the Science of Accounts (Packard), 38

Marshall, Henry, 55

Marwick, Mitchell, and Company, 64. *See also* Peat, Marwick, Mitchell, and Company

Maryland: licensing legislation in, 49

Maryland Society of Certified Public Accountants, 62, 64

Massachusetts, 71, 115, 119, 121; licensing legislation in, 49

Massachusetts Institute of Technology (MIT), 134, 136

Massachusetts Society of Certified Public Accountants, 62, 64

Mathematics, higher, 126

Mathews, George, 149, 157

May, George O., 120, 123, 125, 131, 138–39, 157–58, 160, 170, 174, 179, 182, 187; contributor to *Journal of Accountancy*, 77; and Committee on Federal Legislation, 97; at Treasury during World War I, 116; and American Institute of Accountants code of ethics, 117–18; joins American Institute of Accountants after retirement, 133; concerns over educators' roles in standard-

izing financial accounting, 135–36, 157, 171–72; responds to William Z. Ripley's criticisms, 137; and Social Science Research Council, 140–42; and Senate securities legislation hearings, 147–48; reaction to Securities Act of 1933, 151; and Securities Act of 1934, 152, 154; draws closer to conservative business advisors to New Deal, 162–64; role in undistributed earnings tax debate, 164–66; accepts need for practitioner unity, 166–68
May, Lawrence O., 95
Mayflower, 36
Mead, Edward S., 75, 112
Mead, Margaret, 75
Means, Gardiner C., 4, 140–41, 148
Mechanical engineering, 18
Medicine, profession of, 6, 30, 47; basis of elite status, 12; changing educational patterns, 12; select federal structures for ordering professional affairs, 14; role in progressive reform, 15; affects of World War I and 1920s, 15–17; and New Deal, 19; and professional laws, 49; and licensing in New York State, 53; as model for public accountants, 62, 68; nature of specialized knowledge, 129; experience in professionalization compared to accounting and law, 179–84
Mellon, Andrew W., 162
Mellon family, 163
Mencken, H. L., 13
Michigan, 119
Michigan, University of, 9, 81, 174
Michigan Board of Accountancy, 114–15
Michigan Society of Certified Public Accountants, 62
Michigan State Board of Certified Public Accountants, 119
MIT, 134, 136
Mixter, Charles W., 77

Mining engineering, 18
Minnesota, University of, 171
Missouri, 36
Model state licensing laws, 14; in accounting, 71, 111
Model state society bylaws, 71, 111
Modern Corporation and Private Property (Berle and Means), 141, 148
Modern Language Association, 50
Moley, Raymond, 1, 150
Money trust investigation, 107
Monroe Doctrine, 45
Montgomery, Robert H., 29, 41, 124, 130, 160, 174, 182, 187; career of, 1–3; at American Institute of Accountants' golden anniversary, 3–6; concerns about New Deal, 4–5; and accounting laboratory, 82, and Committee on Federal Legislation, 97; and Federal Trade Commission's uniform accounting plan, 110; at War Industries Board, 116; on Securities Act of 1933, 149; views on government-associational relations, 166–68; elected president of unified American Institute of Accountants, 173
Moore, Underwood, 157, 172
Moral philosophy, 9
Morgan, House of, 74, 163
Morgan, J. P., 107
Morgan, J. P., Jr., 114
Morgan, J. P., and Company, 34, 74, 131, 163
Morgenthau, Henry M., Jr., 161, 165
Morris, Robert, Associates, 138, 154
Morse, Perley, 66, 97
Morton, Levi P., 55
Morton, Paul S., 83, 88
Mucklow, Walter, 129
Muller, Jean Paul, 123
Musica, Philip, 176
Mussolini, Benito, 4
Mutual Insurance Company, 67

National Association of Certified Public Accountants (NACPA), 122

National Bureau of Economic Research (NBER), 125
National City Bank, 167
National Civic Federation, 15
National firm practitioners, 48–49; desire autonomous associationalism, 26, 46, 47, 193; desire access to national markets, 48–49, 61–68 passim, 71–72; identify with British professional forms, 73–74, 75–79, 82–85, 113–15; disappointed in CPA movement on eve of World War I, 104–6, 111–13; form American Institute of Accountants, 115–16, 120–24, 124–27; drawn into conflict with local practitioners, 117–20; propose revision of structure of financial market governance, 140–42; vulnerability to encroachment by federal government during New Deal, 147–58; reunite with local practitioners to preserve professional autonomy, 166–77
National Municipal League, 15, 36
National Recovery Administration (NRA), 149, 161, 167, 187–88
National Securities Commission, 153
National Society of Certified Public Accountants (NSCPA), 59
Nativism: reactions to immigration from eastern and southern Europe, 9, 13, 43–44; professionalism as a palliative for nativistic concerns, 27, 34–35, 83–85, 179–80; reactions to British accountants, 44–45, 119, 123–24; in CPA licensing in New York State, 51, 53, 56; and Melvil Dewey, 67; in accounting recruitment, 125–27; and William Z. Ripley, 136
Natural philosophy, 9
Nau, Carl H., 115, 117–18, 121
Naval Consulting Board, 110, 113
Nazism, 4, 21
Newark, New Jersey, 34
New Deal, 7; relationship with public accountants, 4–6; and professionalization, 19–21; securities legislation of, 147–55; end of first, 160–62; new policies of second, 162–64; affects of securities and tax legislation, 173–77
New Freedom, 105, 109
New Jersey, 59; licensing legislation in, 49
New Jersey Society of Certified Public Accountants (NJSCPA), 64
New Jersey Society of Public Accountants, 59
New Jerusalem, 6, 104
Newsweek, 1
New Willard Hotel (Washington, D.C.), 62
New York, State University of, at Albany, 50
New York Central Railroad Company, 43
New York Cheap Transportation Association, 33
New York City, 29, 33, 37, 54, 56, 67, 123, 141, 147, 154, 163, 174
New York Court of Appeals, 140
New York Institute of Accounts (NYIA): program of professionalization, 35–40; rivalry with American Association of Public Accountants, 36; and professional education, 40–42; competition with American Association of Public Accountants over professional designations, 45–46; role in licensing drive in New York State, 48, 52–55; opposes formation of College of Accounts, 50–52
New York Life Insurance Company, 67
New York State, 29, 47, 88, 99, 112, 115, 118, 121, 158, 165; early professional developments, 28–29; model structure for state professional governance, 71
New York State Assembly, 53
New York State Attorney General, 175

New York State Board of Certified
Public Accountant Examiners, 56–
60, 66–67
New York State Board of Regents,
46, 48, 66
New York State Department of Public Instruction, 52
New York State Insurance Department, 87–88
New York State Library, 54
New York State Senate, 53–54
New York State Society of Certified
Public Accountants (NYSSCPA),
2, 27, 122, 149, 158; founding of,
58–59; and Federation of State So-
cieties of Public Accountants in
the United States of America, 62–
65; and loss of influence in Al-
bany, 66; joins federated American
Association of Public Accountants,
67–68; size and nature of member-
ship, 112
New York Times, 137
New York Tribune, 43, 46, 51, 175
New York University (NYU), 81, 124,
126; School of Commerce, Ac-
counts, and Finance, 2, 42–43, 57–
60, 80–82, 132
Nicaragua, 45
Niles, Henry A., 95
Niles and Niles, 95
Nissley, F. W., 125–27
Niven, John B., 77, 115
Normalcy, 17
North Dakota, University of, 153
Northwestern University, 81, 124,
134
NYU. See New York University

Ocean Steamship Company, 36
Office of Placements, 126
Ohio, 115, 117–18, 131, 158
Ohio State University, 134
Oliphant, Herman M., 161, 165
Ophthalmology, 18
Organizational historical interpreta-
tion. See Professions: schools of

historical interpretation
Osteopathy, 15
Other Peoples' Money and How the
Bankers Use It (Brandeis), 107
Oxford University, 39

Pacific Ocean, 45
Packard, Silas S., 38–39, 50, 55–56
Packard Institute, 124
Palisades, 5
Papen, Franz von, 114
Paradigmatic historical interpreta-
tion. See Professions: schools of
historical interpretation
Paris Exposition of 1900, 65
Parker, Gilbert, 114
Parliament, 53
Parsons, James Russell, Jr., 66
Paton, William A., 125, 174
Patterson, Teele, and Dennis, 168
Peat, Marwick, Mitchell, and Com-
pany, 168. See also Marwick,
Mitchell, and Company
Pecora, Ferdinand, 153
Pecora Commission, 4
Peekskill Military Academy, 44
Pennsylvania, 59, 131, 169; licensing
legislation in, 49
Pennsylvania, University of, 9;
Wharton School of Finance and
Economy, 2, 40–41, 50, 75, 80–81,
126
Pennsylvania Institute of Public Ac-
countants, 59, 62, 64
Penrose, Boies, 131
Phi Beta Kappa, 38
Philadelphia, Pennsylvania, 29
Philadelphia Light Artillery, 3
Philosophy, 126
Philosophy of Accounts (Sprague), 38
Physics, 9
Pinchot, Gifford, 95
Pittsburgh, Pennsylvania, 44, 119
Placid Club, 55–56, 67
"Plan for International Peace"
(Sells), 114. See also Sells, Elijah
Watt

Platt, Thomas C., 53–55, 66
Political economy, 126
Political science, 9
Political scientists, 15
Post Office Department, 94–95
Preparedness movement, 113
Price, Overton W., 95
Price Waterhouse and Company, 33,
    61, 63–64, 67, 73–74, 88, 112–13,
    118, 131, 133, 138–39, 148, 152,
    154, 162–63, 175–76
Pride, Edwin Ober, 123
Princeton University, 125–26
Privity of contract, 139
Professions: characteristics of, 194
    (n. 11); schools of historical inter-
    pretation, 6–8, 95, 105, 189–91;
    general historical model explain-
    ing rise of, 8–21
—governance of. See Strategies and
    structures for professional order-
    ing
Pro forma financial statements, 138
Progressive historical interpretation.
    See Professions: schools of histori-
    cal interpretation
Proprietary accounting schools, 38–
    40, 106, 124
Prussian State Statistical Bureau, 32
Psychologists, 16
Psychology, 9
"Public Accountants and the Inter-
    state Commerce Commission,
    The," 93
Pujo Commission, 107

Quetelet, Lambert-Adolphe-Jacques,
    37
Quigley, Andrew J., 124

Races of Europe: A Sociological Study,
    The (Ripley), 136
Railroads: Finance and Organization
    (Ripley), 137
Railroads: Rates and Regulation (Rip-
    ley), 137
Rand, Waldron H., 113, 115, 124

Rayburn, Sam, 148–50
Reckitt and Williams, 63
Reclamation Service, 95
Regionalism, 178; and professional-
    ization, 9, 11, 15–16; and profes-
    sional elitism, 13, 27; and federal
    structures in accounting, 61–63,
    178–81; and elitism in accounting,
    84–85; and polarization within ac-
    counting, 111–13, 123–24; among
    accounting educators, 172
Registrar of Companies, 30, 88
Reid, Whitelaw, 43, 51
Republican party, 66–67, 107
Revenue Regulations, 131
Richardson, Alphyon P., 77, 112
Ripley, William Z., 4; concerns about
    financial accounting, 136–37; and
    Social Science Research Council,
    140–41; and Securities Acts, 147–
    48. See also Races of Europe: A So-
    ciological Study, The; Railroads: Fi-
    nance and Organization; Railroads,
    Rates and Regulation; Trusts, Pools,
    and Corporations
Robert, Thomas Cullen, 112
Rockefeller family, 163
Rockefeller Foundation, 140
Roles, definition of professional, 86–
    99
Roosevelt, Franklin D., 19, 148, 150,
    164–65; administration, 145, 161
Roosevelt, Theodore, 15, 94–95, 107,
    136; administration, 94–96
Roper, Daniel C., 148, 163
Rousseau, Jean Jacques, 9
Rublee, George, 149
Ryan, James Fortune, 88
Ryan, Thomas P., 65

St. Louis, Missouri, 29, 83
Sanders, Thomas H., 153, 156, 171–
    72, 174
San Francisco, California, 79, 115
Schiff, Jacob H., 82, 107, 114
School of Accounts, 52. See also Col-
    lege of Accounts

School of Commerce, Accounts, and Finance. *See* New York University

Science of accounts, 35–40, 44, 73

Scobie, John C., 110

Scovell, Clinton H., 119

Second National Bank of the United States, 106

Securities Act of 1933, 3–4, 146–47; legislative progress of, 148–50; provisions of, 150–51; reactions of accountants to sanctions, 151

Securities Act of 1934, 146–47, 151–55

Securities and Exchange Commission (SEC), 3, 4, 146, 155; accountants' uncertainties concerning policies of, 4–5; encourages research in financial accounting, 157; clashes with practitioners on accounting matters, 157–58; initiates Accounting Series Releases, 158; accepts American Institute of Accountants' standardization of financial accounting, auditing, and professional ethics, 174–77; comparison of mode of regulation with other federal regulatory agencies, 186–88

Securities Exchange Act (1934), 151. *See also* Securities Act of 1934

Seligman, Isaac N., 77

Seligman, J. and W., Company, 34

Sells, Elijah Watt, 36, 64–65, 73, 83, 88, 91, 95, 114, 149

Senate, United States, 121

Senate Banking Committee, 147

Senate Committee on Commerce and Banking, 149

Senate Finance Committee, 165

Senate Interstate Commerce Committee, 91

Sharfman, Isaiah L., 141

Shaw, Albert D., 33

Sheffield, England: chartered accountants' institute, 29

Shipping Board, 17

Shugrue, Martin J., 134

Silk Importers' Association, 34

Simplified spelling, 50

Smart and Gore, 122

Social contract, 9

Socialism, 44

Socialization: and professionalizaton, 10–11; of chartered accountants, 31; of American accountants, 178–84

Social Science Research Council, 140, 147

Society of Incorporated Accountants and Auditors, 41

Sociologists, 9,

Sociology, 9, 136

Sons of Colonial Wars, 43

Sons of the American Revolution, 43, 51

South, University of the, 40

Southern Pacific Railroad Company, 94

Spanish American War, 3

Sparrow, John, 59, 66

Special Committee on Earned Surplus, 133

Special Committee on Ethical Publicity, 117

Special Committee on Form of Organization of Association, 110, 115–16

Special Committee on Relations with Outside Organizations, 155

Special Committee on the Development of Accounting Principles, 171, 173

Specialization: and professional elitism, 12, 18, 181–82; patterns in accountancy, 181–82

Sprague, Charles E., 38–39, 42, 50, 55–58

Springer, Durand, 114, 119, 123, 171

Stahr, Monroe, 126

Standard Oil Company, 118

Stanton, Lucius M., 33, 57

Starkey, Rodney F., 154

State Department, 33

Statement of Accounting Principles, A (Hatfield, Moore, and Sanders), 157, 172

"Statements on Auditing Procedures," 176

Statisticians, 9, 16

Statistics: and connections to accounting, 37–38

Staub, Walter A., 155–56

Stempf, Victor H., 165

Stern, Fred, and Company, 140

Sterrett, Joseph E., 41, 59, 73, 76, 110, 112, 131; and reorganization of American Association of Public Accountants, 115–16; and American Institute of Accountants' code of ethics, 117–18

Stevens, Richard F., 34, 40–41, 50, 59

Stevens Institute of Technology, 34

Stevenson, Russell H., 171

Stock market crash of 1929, 104, 125, 142, 146

Strategies and structures for professional ordering, 179–84; promoted by American Association of Public Accountants, 29–35, 45–47, 48–49, 52–60, 73–85, 86–99; promoted by New York Institute of Accounts, 35–40, 45–47, 48; promoted by Federation of State Societies of Public Accountants in the United States of America, 49, 62–68; promoted by Illinois Society of Certified Public Accountants, 61–62; promoted by New York State Society of Certified Public Accountants, 56–60; promoted by American Institute of Accountants, 105–6, 111–13, 115–27, 128–42, 166–77; promoted by American Society of Certified Public Accountants, 117–20, 123–24

Strong, William L., administration, 37, 54

Students' Department, 81

Suffern, E. L., 113

Sugar Trust, 44

Sullivan and Cromwell, 154

Supreme Court, 89, 108, 161

Surgery, 18

Swearingen family, 117

Swearingen, Nau, and Rusk, 117

Syracuse University, 126

Tammany Hall, 51–52

Tax accounting, 96–98

"Tax Corner, The" (Niven), 77. *See also* Niven, John B.

Taylor, Frederick W., 77

Technological innovation and professionalization, 7, 30–31, 128

Teele, Arthur W., 95, 97, 168

"Tentative Statement of Accounting Principles, A," 157, 174

Texas, University of, 134

Theology, 9

Thompson, Huston, 148

Thompson bill, 148–49

Thurber, James, 33, 57

Tientsin, China, 3

Tocqueville, Alexis de, 10

Touche, Niven and Company, 77, 115, 140

Treasury Department, 87, 95–96, 116, 118, 161, 163; and standardization of tax accounting, 130–32; and undistributed earnings tax debate, 164–66

Trenholm, William, 40–41

Trevelen, John E., 134

Triocracy, 17, 20, 21

Trusts, Pools, and Corporations (Ripley), 137

Truth in Securities Act (1933), 150. *See also* Securities Act of 1933

Tufts University, 126

Tweed Ring, 36

Twenty-five Years of Accounting Responsibility (May), 135

Ultramares Corporation v. Touche, 140, 142

Undistributed earning tax debate, 164–66
Uniform Commercial Code, 183
Union College, 38, 126
Union Dime Savings Bank, 38
Union Pacific Railroad Company, 94
United States, 5, 62, 74–75, 111, 115, 118, 121, 123
United States Chamber of Commerce, 97, 108, 132–33
United States Civil Service Commission, 116
United States Consular Service, 77
United States Industrial Commission, 137
United States Military Academy at West Point, 44
United States Steel Corporation, 58, 74, 148
United States Tax Court, 98
Untermyer, Samuel, 148
Urbanization: and professionalization, 9; and rise of public accountancy, 25, 35

Vanderlip, Frank A., 107
Veazey, Wheelock G., 89–90
Venezuelan–British Guiana boundary dispute, 45
Vermont, 111
Vermont, University of, 77
Veysey, William H., 41
"Volapük," 38, 50
Volunteerism, 16–17; of accountants during progressive period, 86–99; of accountants during World War I, 116; of accountants in trying to reorder financial markets during 1920s, 140–42; of accountants during New Deal, 149, 173–79

Waddell, William, 46
Waldorf Astoria Hotel (New York), 1
Walton, Seymour, 81
Walton and Joplin, 63
Wanamaker, John, 3
Warburg, Paul M., 107, 114

Warburton, Barclay, 3
War Committee of the United States Chamber of Commerce, 141. See also United States Chamber of Commerce
War Department, 116, 137
War Industries Board, 17, 110, 166; conception of associationalism, 167, 177
Washington, 111, 152
Washington, D.C., 62, 111, 116, 118 121, 123, 145, 165. See also District of Columbia
Weinberg, Sidney J., 163–64, 166, 175
Werntz, Willard W., 174
West Virginia, 91
Wharton School of Finance and Economy. See Pennsylvania, University of
Whitaker, E. G., 53
White, Francis F., 95
Whitney, Harvey E., 138
Wickersham, George S., 97, 99
Wiebe, Robert H., 9–10
Wildman, John R., 81, 124, 134
Wilds, Payson, 53–54
Wilkinson, George, 57; and Federation of State Societies of Public Accountants in the United States of America, 62–63
William and Mary, College of, 126
Wilmot, Henry, M., 57
Wilson, Woodrow: administration, 103, 152; and Louis D. Brandeis, 108–9
Wilson, Mrs. Woodrow (Ellen Axson), 149
Winchester Arms Company, 113
Wisconsin, University of, 9, 81, 134
Wizard of Oz, The (Baum), 178
World War I, 3, 16–17, 79, 86–87, 103, 129, 167, 177, 180
World War II, 121
Wray, Albert A., 55

Yalden, James, 41
Yale University, 40, 118, 125, 131;
   Law School, 174
Young, Arthur, 97

Young, Arthur, and Company, 113,
   125

Zone experts, 108